LEADING IN A NON-LINEAR WORLD

LEADING IN A NON-LINEAR WORLD

BUILDING WELLBEING, STRATEGIC AND INNOVATION MINDSETS FOR THE FUTURE

JEAN GOMES

WILEY

This edition first published 2023.
Copyright © 2023 by Jean Gomes. All rights reserved.

Registered offices

John Wiley & Sons Ltd, The Atrium, Southern Gate, Chichester, West Sussex, PO19 8SQ, UK

John Wiley & Sons, Inc., 111 River Street, Hoboken, NJ 07030, USA

Editorial Office

The Atrium, Southern Gate, Chichester, West Sussex, PO19 8SQ, UK

For details of our global editorial offices, customer services, and more information about Wiley products visit us at www.wiley.com.

Wiley also publishes its books in a variety of electronic formats and by print-on-demand. Some content that appears in standard print versions of this book may not be available in other formats.

Library of Congress Cataloging-in-Publication Data is Available

ISBN 9781119672722 (Hardback)
ISBN 9781119672753 (ePDF)
ISBN 9781119672708 (ePub)

Cover Design and Image and illustrations: Courtesy of Jean Gomes and Michelle Beagley

Set in 11/15pt Sabon LT Std by Straive, Chennai, India
Printed and bound by CPI Group (UK) Ltd, Croydon, CR0 4YY

C672722_211022

CONTENTS

CONTENTS

INTRODUCTION

We are living in a non-linear world, in which more of the problems we face do not have a clear sequence of cause to effect to solution. As the last decade of shocking and unsettling events has shown us, our environment is becoming less stable and predictable. As a result, more of the challenges we encounter in our wellbeing, work, and society cannot be solved using only the linear 'plan and act' approaches, based on assumptions of what's worked in the past.

New and emerging questions require a different way of thinking about our future:

- Can we keep working longer and more continuously?
- How will artificial intelligence (AI) or automation change career paths?
- How will a workforce of four very different generations, skill sets, and values synergise, and what does that mean for the future?
- What if decade-old assumptions about the sustainability of our global economic system no longer hold true?

And today's 'wicked problems',[1] including climate change and the availability and provision of food, energy, and clean water, will continue to play out in unexpected ways as technological innovation and geopolitics unfold.

Linear thinking and action work when problems are well understood, and solutions are conceivable or proven. However, as the complexity and uncertainty of these problems and the solutions we might build (think nanotechnologies or robotics) increase, we need to embrace an additional approach – a non-linear way of thinking and action. This requires us to embrace not knowing what the true nature of a problem is, or how we will solve it. If linear thinking and action is about exploiting past knowledge to achieve a goal, non-linear methods are about action learning: running parallel experiments to rapidly bust our assumptions and find new solutions, as we did in developing Covid vaccines in an astonishingly short time.

Whilst work is undoubtedly more rewarding economically and intellectually than for previous generations, it has also reached a tipping point of burning out more people from top to bottom. For decades, we've gradually adapted to overflowing inboxes, back-to-back meetings, and the relentless expectation of more for less. More people live a negative-normal existence, feeling depleted, defensive, and disconnected from the priorities, people, and passions in their lives that matter outside of work.

Acceptance of the non-linear nature of our world allows us to see better both the complexity of our circumstances and the patterns in our responses. By learning how we make sense of the overwhelming tide of information rolling over us, tuning into our mindset, and drawing on what only the combined forces of thinking, feeling, and seeing can offer, we can start to meet complexity with complexity. I believe hope lies in our inexorable ingenuity as a species to evolve out of a burnout spiral, whilst at the same time recognising that we are always our own worst enemies. In the coming decade, as new technologies automate more routine work, we have an opportunity to ask ourselves: *What should work mean to us in the future, and what do we uniquely bring?*

One part of the answer is to focus on and celebrate how we as humans uniquely create value. Creative problem-solving, nuanced judgement, and decision-making, combined with our ability for sensemaking (our ability to organise chaotic data into a form we can process and understand) in complex and uncertain situations, are vital to surviving a non-linear world. All humans are capable of this – but these qualities are more contingent on mindset than our track record, education, or status.

These qualities are unique to us. AI and other forms of technological automation lack the capacity to perform these 'mystical' acts of intuition, non-linear and counterfactual thinking, and there's no likelihood they will develop the ability to do so in the next 50 or more years.[2]

We are living in an era of *radical uncertainty* according to economists John Kay and Mervyn King,[3] where more of the answers we should be giving as leaders are, 'I don't know'. This provokes feelings and emotions, such as doubt, that have long been seen as signs of weakness and a barrier to rational thinking and problem-solving. As we'll see, nothing could be further from the truth.

Leading in a Non-Linear World aims to give you a deeper understanding of your mindset and the means to grow and strengthen it. It draws on exciting developments in neuroscience, experimental psychology, and physiology, and our team's research and work with over 70,000 people worldwide.

Part 1 begins with a redefinition of the term 'mindset', from being a set of beliefs and attitudes, to widening it to encompass how we make sense of the world through feelings, emotions, thoughts, and perception. This includes recent breakthroughs in the understanding of consciousness, metacognition (our ability to think about thinking), and the influence of our bodies on our sensemaking – including new theories overturning conventional wisdom on how our emotions and perception work. These combine into a model for mindset that enables us to explore ways of building and strengthening it.

In Part 2, we'll explore four mindsets for the future of our life and work, applying the tools and theories discussed in Part 1.

- The *more human* mindset looks at how radical self-awareness increases the flow of information from our mind and bodies, making healthier behaviours and wellbeing a more natural default setting.
- The *future now* mindset tackles the perennial challenge of short termism. How can individuals and organisations simultaneously achieve their short- and long-term goals?
- The *experimental* mindset helps those adopting the 'test and learn' playbook developed by the start-up community to succeed in the many countercultural and counterintuitive ways it asks of us.
- The *open* mindset is about unlocking new ways of seeing the world; how we can pioneer new ways of working and build future organisations.

In Part 3, we'll examine a case study of an enterprise driving change through mindset adoption to improve wellbeing, performance, and growth.

We build our mindsets by intentionally thinking about them. By reading this book, you're taking an important step in building mindsets for your future.

PART 1

THE NEW SCIENCE OF MINDSET AND SELF-AWARENESS

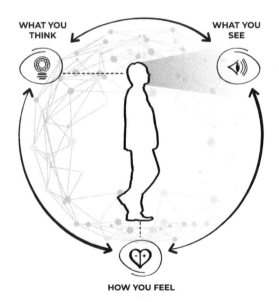

WHAT YOU THINK

WHAT YOU SEE

HOW YOU FEEL

FIGURE P1.1
Source: Jean Gomes

Our mindsets result from the interplay of feeling, thinking, and seeing – creating instances of knowing, doubt, or certainty.

CHAPTER 1

WHAT IS MINDSET?

The term 'mindset' has become laden with significance in recent times. The dictionary definition suggests a fixed set of beliefs and attitudes that shape our actions. But think about this for a moment. Are your actions driven solely by your assumptions and beliefs? I'm sure it won't take you long to recall numerous situations where you acted against your 'beliefs'. Not because of cognitive bias, or social pressure, but for a whole host of urges and feelings that combined to create a sense of certainty in the moment which defied being logical.

And we don't have just one mindset. We have collections of beliefs, many of which occupy contradictory positions, shaped by different contexts, interpretations of risk, uncertainty, and social influences. We may have a playful mindset when working with one group of people and unconsciously adopt a pragmatic one with another. Our mindset can be profoundly different when we're with strangers, travelling, fatigued, overwhelmed, or feeling unfairly treated.

Mindset is now code for everything from the zeitgeist, worldviews, personality, attitudes, beliefs, motivation, political and social affiliation, and identity. Why has the term, relatively little used until a decade ago, become so sticky? Perhaps it helps us to join the dots between the enormous societal change we're experiencing and what's going on inside us.

Most influential in the recent popularity of the term has been Carol Dweck's theory of fixed and growth mindsets in children. According to Dweck, a child with a fixed mindset believes their abilities are permanent traits and can't be changed. The belief, for example, that 'I'm not good at maths', leads to another thought that 'working harder won't pay off'. These beliefs shape behaviours, such as de-prioritising maths revision, and become a self-fulfilling prophecy when they fail or get poor grades – 'see I was right, I'm no good at maths!'. A fixed mindset works the other way too. A child naturally good at maths thinking that their talent and inherent ability is a given may believe they don't need to work any harder. Either way, a fixed mindset becomes a narrowing self-definition of an individual's potential.

A growth mindset is based on the belief that one's talents and abilities can be developed over time through effort and persistence. Dweck observed children with this belief seeing maths problems that they couldn't yet solve as a positive challenge; their belief was 'bring it on!'. In her laboratory, Dweck was able to demonstrate that simple interventions could help children build a growth mindset and positively impact on their performance. Children were taught about the brain's capacity to change and how memory worked. Teachers were encouraged to use specific forms of appreciation to encourage and reinforce when children adopted growth mindset approaches. Evidence showed academic improvements and reduction in aggression and bullying.

The appeal of the growth mindset was such that it was readily adopted as a model in classrooms around the world. However, it soon became clear that it was not as simple as showing children a picture of the fixed and growth mindsets and encouraging them to adopt a new set of beliefs. In a much-cited meta-analysis study[1] of mindset and academic achievement across 400,000 students, classroom training efforts showed a weak effect on improved performance. Another detailed study[2] conducted amongst 600 school children, closely replicating Dweck's studies, failed to show interventions leading to *any* improvement in students overcoming difficult challenges more effectively. There *is* evidence of the positive impact of the training, but generally in settings where the school's culture *already* encourages children to strive beyond their expectations. Where peer norms amongst students discourage challenge-seeking, the impact was unclear. The failure lies not in the theory but in the execution according to Dweck, but she acknowledges[3] that the 'growth mindset is even more complex than we imagined'.

Part of the success of the idea of fixed vs growth mindsets is that it makes intuitive sense. I'm sure we have all seen children, or young adults, perhaps our own, who tell themselves they are incapable of things that we 'know' they could achieve if they just believed in themselves. The immediacy of the idea – its 'rightness' – is a clue as to why teachers may have failed to understand how to create the conditions for building a growth mindset. Dave Paunesku, co-founder of the Project for Education Research in the USA, points to the root of failures being that many 'teachers approach it like quadratic equation. You can't just think of it as a regular thing to teach, because the internalization of it is so important'.[4] The trap lies in thinking that a mindset is simply a cognitive framework or model that you can show people and suddenly they think, 'of course, I could be great at maths if only I believed in myself'.

This is where we depart from Dweck and many other descriptions of mindset. Most of which are, in fact, simply mental models. In other words, they are ways of looking at, or thinking about, situations. As we'll consider later, most smart people have a misplaced belief that once they intellectually understand something, they can master it behaviourally. So, mindset as an idea seems eminently teachable. Of course, the idea part *is* important, but it doesn't reflect fully what's going on inside us to describe how we respond to these models.

CREATING A BIGGER INNER WORLD

What researchers are showing us is that our mindsets result from the interplay of feeling, thinking, and seeing – creating instances of knowing, doubt, or certainty. This opens new possibilities for us taking more control over our lives and gaining greater psychological freedom in the face of uncertainty. This is not just about understanding an idea and adopting positive thinking. Building a mindset modifies and grows the networks and structures in your brain, and the hormones and neurotransmitters you produce. In turn, these impact on your immediate and long-term health, how open you are to new information, the decisions you make, how others see you, and the nature of the relationships you form. Your mindset, for better or worse, defines your life.

The disciplines of neuroscience, psychology, and physiology are showing us a new way of thinking about how our bodies and brain work together to navigate the world. This understanding highlights the central importance of self-awareness, for example how significant it is to be connected to your physical feelings and understand how they are different from emotions and thoughts, which we often confuse.

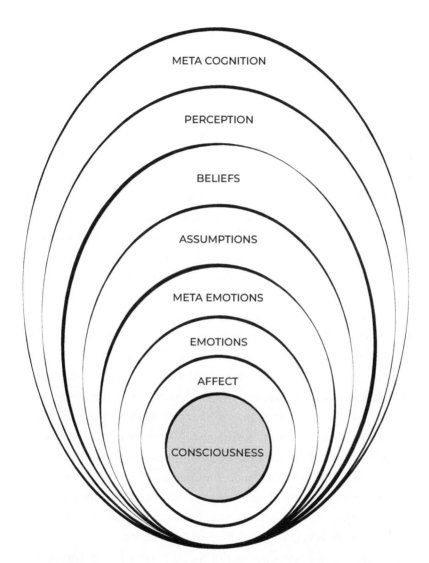

FIGURE 1.1   Layers of self-awareness that comprise mindset
Source: Jean Gomes

At the core of mindset building is a new, deeper form of self-awareness: being able to pay attention to multiple dimensions of your interior world and observe how they influence one another. These 'layers' of self-awareness (Figure 1.1) start with raw **consciousness** – the sense of self. Depending on the metabolic state of your body, you experience positive or negative **affect**, the term psychologists use to describe the sum of your physical feelings. Next in our mindset system come **emotions**, which require a necessary re-evaluation in both their function and potential. As we'll see, your brain runs profoundly on predictions, so the **assumptions** you make and how they inform your **beliefs** are generally inseparable from what you see as reality. **Perception** is part of your prediction system, so we often confuse what we see with what we think. Across each dimension of this system, you have the incredible capacity of **metacognition**, the ability to pull apart and think about how you feel, think, and see. This strategic form of awareness enables you to connect deeply with the signals in your body, to read the invaluable information your emotions are telling you, to challenge and bust unhelpful or limiting assumptions and to see more clearly.

What's truly exciting is that the chief mechanism of mindset building is within the immediate reach of everyone. It's not dependent on intelligence or means. As the metacognition neuroscientist, Stephen Fleming, told me, the most powerful way of building our interior world is *to think about it*. When we do it intentionally, the processes of neuroplasticity, our brain's ability to adapt to experience, enables us to build our mindset. Self-awareness, in its many forms, is key to building mindsets, not conceptually, but architecturally. Our mindset is, at its most fundamental level, the product of the neurochemistry, brain structures, and neural networks we've evolved over the course of our life. As we do so, we gain the power to see and close the knowing–doing gaps in our lives, where we confuse an intellectual understanding of something we should do with actually doing it.

CHAPTER 2

CONSCIOUSNESSES – OUR SENSE OF SELF

Let's start by understanding the importance of connecting deeply with our sense of self and our physical feelings, because when this connection is lost or weakened, it undermines the foundation of our mindset.

Consciousness can be described as the mind's subjective experience, our most profound sense of self. When you wake up in the morning, there are a few moments before you start thinking when you experience it most fully. Our interior world of feelings and thoughts is suffused with this sense of self. Neuroscientist, Anil Seth, borrowing from the philosopher, Thomas Nagel, describes consciousness as what 'it feels like something to be me'.[1] This sensation is *distinct* from the awareness of your thoughts, knowledge, identity, or behaviour.

Consciousness has long been held to have mystic properties and assumed to be beyond our comprehension. In the 17th century René Descartes described the mind–body problem which has continued to challenge us for over four centuries. Whilst consciousness was an undeniable quality of mind, Descartes argued that the structure of the brain and body could not explain its existence. The brain and body exist in space, the mind does not. Therefore, consciousness must be a God-given phenomenon. The belief that it must exist outside the discernible physical universe has exerted a powerful, if sometimes unspoken, influence over science ever since, warning researchers off the territory. Stuart Sutherland's 1989 entry on consciousnesses in no less than the *International Dictionary of Psychology* asserted that 'it is impossible to specify what it is, what it does, or why it evolved. Nothing worth reading has been written on it'.

Until the 1990s, efforts to explain consciousness were still largely the preserve of philosophers. They too regarded it as unfathomable by science. However, in 1994, an unknown 27-year-old philosopher, David Chalmers, threw an intellectual mind bomb that has continued to reverberate ever since. He described the *hard part of consciousness* as 'why and how do neurophysiological activities *produce* the experience of consciousness?'.[2] The easy (not easy, but conceivable) part of consciousness being 'how individual sensory mechanisms such as sight, focus and process information?'. For Chalmers, the hard part of the problem was finding a reason why our mental functions needed to feel like anything in the first place. Memory, or learning, *could* theoretically function, as computers and phones do, without consciousness, without any sense of self.

Chalmers' new framing of consciousness energised the debate with Nobel laureate Francis Crick and Christof Koch kick-starting the current neuroscience-led revolution in understanding.

Using emerging scanning technologies, their work on the *neural correlates* of consciousness gave researchers a practical method of, for example, observing the experience of sensing a specific colour and how that resulted in a consistent and specific pattern of brain activity. Experiments were able to seemingly tease apart sensory responses such as vision and taste from those of consciousness, but they couldn't tell us why. Thirty years on, answers are now starting to emerge as researchers look beyond the brain's cortex, where it was long held to reside.

Mark Solms is part of a new wave of researchers who are taking a different approach which opens up a new way of thinking about mindset. Solms believes that the hard problem arose because we were looking in the wrong place and at the wrong mental functions. Instead of seeking consciousness as a property of higher cortical functions, such as reading or facial recognition, that can run independently of consciousness, he argues we should be looking at functions that are *intrinsically* conscious. This led him to focus on physical feelings that arise from internal sensors in the body. Feelings, he points out, unlike perception and memory, are inherently conscious mental states.

Feelings such as hunger, sleepiness, thirst, rage, and fear that, whilst *registered* in the cortex, are *generated* in the brain stem. Solms believes the cortex is not intrinsically conscious but *borrows* its consciousness from the brain stem. To illustrate this, he points out that even minor damage to certain parts of the brain stem – say the removal of a match head-sized piece – will consistently result in a coma. 'That's how concentrated the consciousness producing power of the brain stem is. Conversely, you can remove large parts of cortex, without obliterating *any* consciousness'. This is evidenced in children born without a cortex, a devastating condition known as hydranencephaly.

Remarkably, these children show a clear sense of self, responding with appropriate emotions to stimuli. They will giggle when tickled, startle when frightened, cry when frustrated. Without *any* cortex, affective consciousness is clearly present.

The earliest forms of consciousness evolved in simple creatures and were no more sophisticated than feeling hot or thirsty. These feelings were rooted in the most basic biological need to survive. Feelings enabled them to discern what was good and bad for them and raised an organism's action beyond automaticity, reflex, and instinct; responses which only work in predictable situations.

The evolutionary advantage of feeling was that it created feedback loops that facilitated voluntary behaviour, allowing organisms to navigate new and uncertain situations by *feeling* their way through them. As Solms puts it, this profound form of decision-making is based on the notion that 'I feel like this about that. Thinking about consciousness from the bottom-up makes the hard problem less hard'.

Just how deeply feeling and the maintenance of our metabolic equilibrium influences our mindset can be seen in the work of researchers looking at the impact of temperature on decision-making.[3] Decision-making under pressure has long been studied as it involves a trade-off between speed and accuracy. Putting people in hot tubs and testing their decision-making confirmed the phenomenon that time appears to speed up when core body temperature increases, reducing the perceived time available and lessening the quality and accuracy of our decisions.

THE PREDICTING BRAIN

Imagine you're picking up your 9.30am cup of coffee from the desk in front of you. Largely unconsciously, your brain is calculating the effects that it will have on your body. But as you start

TOP-DOWN PREDICTIONS

TOP-DOWN
FLOW OF
PREDICTIONS

BOTTOM-UP
FLOW OF
UNPREDICTED
SENSORY
INPUT
(ERRORS)

BOTTOM-UP SENSORY INPUTS

VISUAL   AUDITORY   TACTILE   OLFACTORY   GUSTATORY   VESTIBULAR   PROPRIOCEPTION   INTEROCEPTION
(Sense of head   (Senses from joints   (Senses from
movement in   and muscles)   internal organs)
space)

FIGURE 2.1   A highly conceptualised view of how unpredicted sensory information (prediction errors) flow up to 'course correct' the top-down predictions based on prior experience

Source: Compiled from various sources included: Seth, A., 2021. Being You : A New Science of Consciousness. 1st ed. Penguin Publishing Group; Peter Sterling, Allostasis: A model of predictive regulation, Physiology & Behavior, Volume 106, Issue 1, 2012, Pages 5-15; Clark, A., 2019. Surfing Uncertainty: Prediction, Action, and the Embodied Mind. 1st ed. Oxford University Press; Fleming Stephen M., 2021. Know Thyself, The New Science of Self-Awareness John Murray; Barrett, L., 2017. HOW EMOTIONS ARE MADE. 1st ed. London: Macmillan.

to drink, you realise it's tea not coffee and, despite it being made to your liking, it has created a prediction error which you register as a feeling of surprise, or even mild disgust. You expected coffee, based on prior experiences, and your senses created an error signal registered in your brain stem as a feeling.

This is a key building block in understanding how our mindset operates. Our brain is a prediction-making machine, unremittingly making a series of 'top-down' guesses, based on past experience, which are met with 'bottom-up' sensory information that either confirms or counters those predictions. Karl Friston describes the underlying mechanism of this experience mathematically in his free energy theory.[4] Free energy describes the state resulting from the brain's failure to make a correct prediction. The brain does all it can to avoid free energy. Predictive errors equate to surprise, in other words consciousness. When things do not work as expected, we get consciousness – a state, he believes, the brain tries to limit.

In 1995, a major step towards our current understanding of the predicting brain theory was made by Bharat Biswal.[5] For most of the 20th century, neuroscientists assumed that the brain was mainly a passive system reacting to the environment, reinforcing the computer analogy. In this model, information was processed in one direction, resulting in instructions to make us react. Initially rejected, Biswal's work led to a paradigm shift in how neuroscientists think. Instead of neurons being mostly inactive until aroused, it became clear that they're constantly firing – the phenomenon called intrinsic brain activity. This activity forms part of a system of sensory feedback loops and predictions that are unceasingly, unconsciously, and effortlessly happening, enabling us to *construct* reality and manage precious resources – prediction being more energy efficient than reactivity.

Imagine the doorbell rings late at night. You're not expecting a guest, so your mind starts to formulate inferences of what might be happening. A forgotten Amazon parcel being dropped off by a stressed delivery driver who has fallen behind schedule. A neighbour whose power has failed and is asking for help. Or a more worrying thought; it's the police with bad news. Considering the last possibility causes your body to start mobilising resources for fight or flight. All of this from a late-night press of your doorbell. Turns out it's the Amazon driver after all. This illustrates another key idea in the prediction model; that our brain is continuously running predictions based on a form of Bayesian statistics.

In the 1770s, Revd Thomas Bayes developed a theorem that has become integral to thinking about the brain's modelling of reality. Unlike frequentist statistics, which calculate the *probability* of an event happening, Bayesian statistics describes the degree of *belief* in an event happening, based on prior knowledge, and then updates those probabilities as new information is obtained. Scientists are starting to believe that the brain operates its perception in an approximation to Bayesian statistics. Bayesian thinking is helpful as it points to the brain's goal of reducing uncertainty. A brain running on probability or risk algorithms is going to struggle given the vast number of inverse problems it needs to solve (an inverse problem being where we can see the symptoms but not the causes).

These predictions underpin our social mechanisms. For instance, as you're watching your partner talking, their body language, facial expressions, tone, and your environment fuel hundreds of tiny predictions, guiding you when you should smile, look concerned, or reach out to touch their shoulder to empathise.

CHAPTER 3

WHAT YOUR BODY IS TELLING YOU

The prediction–sensory loops of body and mind explain the fascinating evidence that our body often knows before our mind when good or bad things are about to happen to us. By tuning more intentionally into our physical signals, we strengthen the connection between the body and brain. To achieve this, we need to start by distinguishing between physical feeling and emotion, which we generally lump together in our thoughts. 'I'm feeling tired', or 'I feel blurrghh' are not emotions, but physical feelings. However, many of us are losing connection with these potent signals through overwork and a cocktail of poor diet, insufficient sleep, and exercise, with too much screen time, leaving us numb. At the same time, we feel in some unfathomable way detached from the world and the people and passions that matter most to us.

Affect is the continuous feeling sensation that encapsulates our brain's management of the body's systems – including tracking our heart rate, hormones, immune system, hydration, glucose, oxygen, and salt levels. This tracking coalesces as a general mood, or we might think of it as our body's climate. It can be characterised in two dimensions – pleasant/unpleasant and high/low energy. In our layer model, affect sits between consciousness and emotions. In 1980, James A. Russell created the affective circumplex[1] to help researchers track affect (see Figure 3.1).

The state of our affect profoundly influences the brain's predictions and therefore judgement. If we slept poorly after

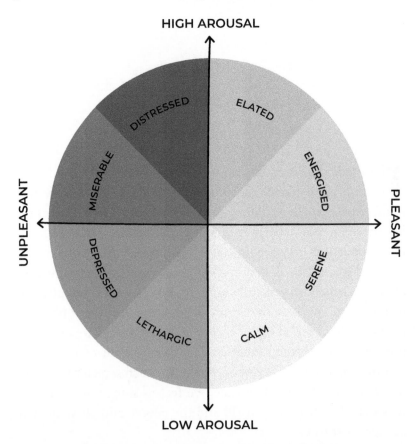

FIGURE 3.1 An example of an affective circumplex
Source: Adapted from James Russel's circumflex model of affect (1980).

a difficult day and went to bed with high levels of stress hormones, it's likely that we won't get much of the deeper levels of
sleep where our metabolism does its heaviest lifting, eliminating
toxins and producing helpful hormones and neurotransmitters.
After a day and night like this, our affect is likely to be negative; we feel tired, toxic, and uncomfortable. But these feelings
are *not* emotions, though they acutely influence them and our
thoughts. Having insufficient fuel in our tank will impact the
predictions our mind makes – 'the day ahead will be hard', 'the
traffic will be hell', 'Liam won't like my proposal', 'I won't have
enough time to work on the new project' and so on.

The critical influence of how resourced we are, whilst perhaps seemingly obvious, has long been under-acknowledged
in mainstream thinking about judgement. In part, it's because
our physical functioning has been seen as private, personal, and
not business relevant. It's your tangible experience, skills, and
expertise that count. But these attributes may count for little if
the bedrock of your mindset is compromised and you haven't
developed the capacity to notice. The psychologist and Nobel
laurate, Daniel Kahneman, in *Thinking, Fast and Slow* cites a
study[2] that brings to life the serious consequences of inattention
to affect and decision-making.

The researchers looked at over a thousand judicial rulings
given by eight Jewish-Israeli judges, presiding over two parole
boards serving four major prisons in Israel. Most of the decisions (78.2%) were parole requests. The analysis is shocking
given the life-altering implications of the decisions. At the start
of the sessions, and after breaks, there's a 65% probability of
being given parole. This reduces to *zero* just before the breaks.
It's safe to say, the same influence of affect is taking place in
every business, school, and institution around the world.

If unacknowledged feelings of hunger or fatigue are the problem, what's the solution? For over 15 years, I worked alongside

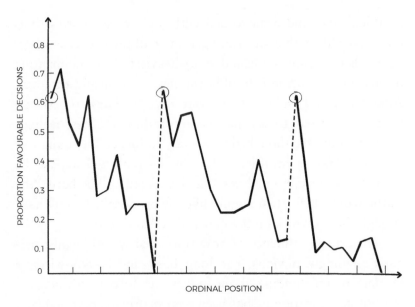

FIGURE 3.2 Proportion of rulings in favour of the prisoners over a day. Circled points indicate the first decision in each of the three decision sessions following food breaks indicated by the dotted line
Source: Danziger, S., Levav, J., & Avnaim-Pesso, L. (2011). Extraneous factors in judicial decisions. Proceedings of the National Academy of Sciences of the United States of America, 108(17), 6889–6892. https://doi.org/10.1073/pnas.1018033108

Tony Schwartz and his pioneering work at The Energy Project. One of our biggest contributions has been to normalise the idea of recovery as an intrinsic part of performance in the organisations we worked with. There is no sustainable peak performance without effective renewal. One of the ways in which we evidenced this, and described in our book, *The Way We're Working Isn't Working*,[3] is the phenomenon of ultradian cycles.

Whilst food plays a role in the judge's decision-making, perhaps even more important is the influence of their deep physiological need for rest throughout the day. In 1953, Eugene Aserinsky and Nathaniel Kleitman uncovered the 90-minute

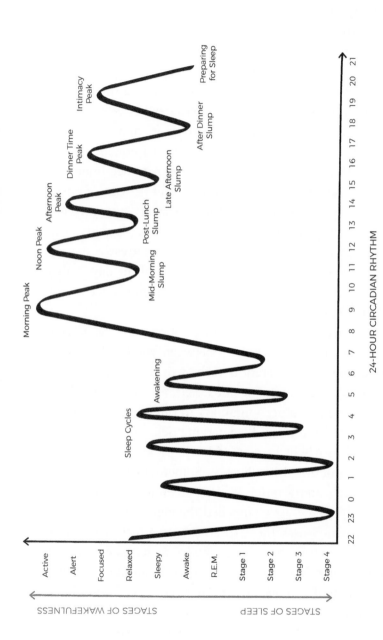

FIGURE 3.3 Ultradian cycles throughout the 24 circadian cycle highlight our need for periodic daytime recovery

Sources: Kleitman, N., Sleep and Wakefulness, 1963; Ultradian Rhythms from Molecules to Mind A New Vision of Life David Lloyd, Ernest Rossi · 2008; Intrinsic Clocks By Timo Partonen, Daniela D. Pollak · 2018.

basic sleep rhythm (BRAC rhythm). Many of us are probably familiar with the left-hand side of Figure 3.3, which shows how brain activity changes as we move through deeper and shallower stages of sleep. Less well known is what's happening on the right-hand side of the picture; that these cycles continue throughout the day as well. Our wakeful brain alternates between higher-frequency, energy-intensive states for around 90 minutes, where we can operate at our peak, followed by lower-frequency activity for about 20 minutes where we might experience brain fog and fatigue. Crucially, flat lining without brief periods of effective renewal encourages the sympathetic nervous system to get aroused, stimulating our fight or flight responses. Not only does pushing through the 90-minute cycle create a progressive energy debt, ensuring that we're exhausted at the end of the day, it also produces a defensive mindset, because fundamentally, we're not getting what we need.

If we're unaware of how physically resourced we are, we risk breaking a link in the causal chain between what only feeling can tell us, and our interpretation of the world. When this happens, we can fall prey to feelings of resentment and powerlessness that undermine our accountability to ourselves and others.

Developments in the rapidly emerging field of interoception suggest that soon it will be seen as having a similar degree of importance as emotional intelligence. Sometimes referred to as the eighth sense, interoception is the perception of sensations *inside* our body. These are channelled through the vagus nerve to the brain, which uses them to construct affect. When this flow is working well it improves our judgement, resilience, and relationships. What we're also coming to understand is a 'feeling first' picture of mindset – that physical feelings precede emotions.

Amongst the first to decode how this operates was the neurobiologist, Antonio Damasio. In the 1990s, he proposed[4] that emotional events begin with physical changes in the body that

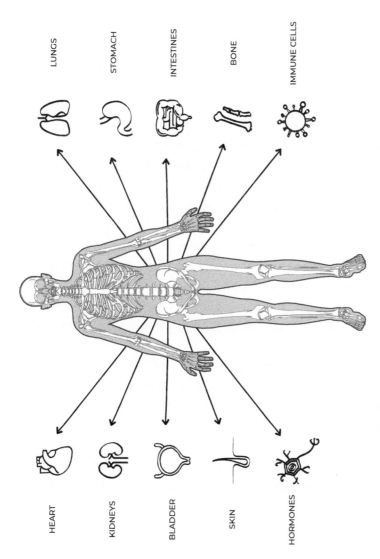

LUNGS

STOMACH

INTESTINES

BONE

IMMUNE CELLS

HEART

KIDNEYS

BLADDER

SKIN

HORMONES

FIGURE 3.4 Interoceptive signals generated within the body
Source: Jean Gomes

we're initially unaware of, called somatic markers. When you see the angry face of a motorist you've inadvertently cut up, your heart pounds, your muscles contract, and your skin sweats *before* you are aware of emotions such as fear, anger, or embarrassment. Neuroscientist Sarah Garfinkel[5] explains, 'If we see a snake, our hearts won't beat faster because we are scared. Seeing the snake will increase our heartbeat and when that's registered in the brain, that's what leads to the feeling of fear'.

The fact that your body knows before your brain what is happening in the world is at the heart of why individuals with better interoceptive sensitivity make superior decisions, can override unconscious bias, and have greater physical resilience. This form of self-awareness gives the brain more information, more quickly. Whilst all of us get intuitive feelings – a sense of right or wrong – those with better interoception can access it faster and seem to be able to rely on it more. As the neurologist Robert Burton puts it, certainty is not a rational process, it's a feeling – the 'brain creates the involuntary sensation of knowing'.[6] Without this feeling of knowing, it's near impossible to decide.

Over the past decade, researchers have been able to show in laboratory studies that individuals with greater *interoceptive sensitivity*, measured by their ability to estimate their heart rate, perform better in risky decision-making.[7,8] In 2004, Hugo Critchley published one of the most influential reports[9] in the field, showing the link between interoceptive sensitivity and activation of grey matter in the insular cortex. He developed a simple method of measurement, asking test subjects to assess their heart rate. The closer their assessment was to their actual heart rate, the higher the activation and grey matter volume of the insular. This measure, called *interoceptive accuracy*, has been applied in hundreds of studies, illuminating its significance across numerous areas of wellbeing and human performance.

In 2016, a study involving Critchley and Garfinkel,[10] conducted on a London trading floor, showed that increases in interoceptive sensitivity amongst traders tracked with a superior ability to generate profit compared to their less-sensitive peers, and they enjoyed longer careers in what is unquestionably a high-stress environment.

Damasio devised a gambling experiment to measure somatic (bodily) responses on unconscious decision-making. Presented with a pot of money and four decks of cards to play with on a computer screen, participants had to click on the decks to win and avoid losses. Their physiological arousal was measured through electrodes that tracked small changes in skin conductance as the body produced momentary sweat in response to perceived threats. Over time, he and his team observed that the participants were detecting that there was a setup at work. Two of the decks were 'bad', producing more losses. Even though they had no conscious awareness of which decks were the bad ones, as their mouse hovered over them, their skin conductance spiked, showing that their bodies knew before their brains.

It appears that the effects of interoceptive training on improving decision-making *and* lowering anxiety can be achieved remarkably rapidly. Research[11] conducted at the National Centre of Neurology and Psychiatry in Tokyo provided four, 40-minute training sessions over the course of a week. Participants were asked to listen to a range of tone sounds, some of which matched their heartbeat, and they were asked to choose which was which. They were also tested for the rationality of their decision-making. After just one week of training, participants' interoceptive accuracy had improved, and their decision-making processes 'shifted in a more rational direction compared with the baseline'.

An athlete with good interoception will draw upon the inner signals generated by their heart rate and the sensory impact of their feet on the track. In contrast, the competitor with poor interoception, lacking these strong feedback loops, becomes over-reliant on external signals from their coach or the crowd for information or affirmation – data which they will likely misinterpret. As a result, a damping of mind–body connection results in moving the locus of their control from within to others, or even the world. In more extreme cases, this diminished sense of self can lead to body dysmorphic disorder, causing an individual to focus more on what their body looks like than how it feels.

A greater awareness of our internal sensations allows us to better regulate when we can push and when we need recovery. Martin Paulus, a professor of psychiatry, has studied interoception's influence on resilience. Assessing individuals on their self-reported sense of resilience, he found a strong connection with their interoceptive accuracy. Those with low interoception were more prone to give up in the face of challenges or suffer burn out. Individuals with greater sensitivity to their internal signals were able to push through discomfort and sustain difficulty for longer.

In one revealing study,[12] Paulus combined testing an individual's cognitive ability while applying an unpleasant stressor (partially restricting their ability to breathe freely) and analysing their brain activity. The participants ranged from elite athletes, highly trained special forces members, and normal healthy individuals. The brain scans revealed that when stressed, those with the best interoception and highest levels of resilience had a significant spike in insular activity *before* the stressor, which quickly subsided during and after the event. Numerous studies[13] in parallel fields, such as pain research, show a similar picture. In low-resilient participants, the insular activity spikes later and lasts longer, provoking a cascade of internal body changes (increased heart rate, vasoconstriction, and sweating) that are interpreted by the brain as stress.

Individuals with good interoception don't have to allocate lots of mental processing resources to interpret these signals. Instead, they can employ resources for the task in hand. In the case of the Paulus study, this was reflected in the fact that stressors *improved* the cognitive ability of those with good interoception on the test. Those with lower interoception were fighting an internal battle, got distracted or confused, and gave up.

Recent studies of autistic patients by Sarah Garfinkel shows just how central interoception is to our relationships. In reviewing a study investigating the empathic reaction of autistic individuals to others' pain, she spotted something that the researchers had missed. The participants in the study had been shown photographs of painful events and asked if they felt the subjects in the pictures were experiencing hurt or not. Their brain activity and skin conductance were monitored. The researchers concentrated their conclusions on the brain scans, which showed a reduced empathy response to a control group. But Garfinkel spotted that the bodily conductance response was dramatically higher amongst the autistic group and wanted to know why.

This led her and Critchley to refine interoceptive testing, introducing a further subjective measure alongside the heartbeat tracking test for interoceptive accuracy, which she called *interoceptive sensibility*. This asked participants questions[14] about the perception of their bodily feelings, ranging from fullness or fatigue, to wanting to urinate or skin itchiness.

By comparing these perspectives, Garfinkel found that whilst autistic adults generally found it difficult to assess their heart rate, they often rated their ability highly. This divergence between interoceptive accuracy and awareness interferes with the normal detection of prediction errors. She explains, 'If you think you have very good interoception, but actually your body is sending signals that you're not able to correctly identify, then that's associated with high anxiety'.[15] This inability to read their bodies results in their ensuing emotions rapidly becoming overwhelming in situations such as social conflict.

As Garfinkel reflected on how to solve this problem, she remembered back to when she initially took the heartbeat accuracy test and got poor results. However, each time she did it again, she improved. So, perhaps instead of interoceptive accuracy being an immutable characteristic as many had thought, could it be trained? If so, might it help those with autism reduce their feelings of anxiety?

In 2017, a team including Lisa Quadt and Garfinkel began the largest randomised clinical trial[16] targeting anxiety in autistic adults. Rapidly, the techniques provided produced improvements in the participants' interoceptive accuracy. Now, being more connected to their physical feelings allowed them to anticipate their ensuing emotional reactions, and to act, through deep-breathing exercises or taking better care of their needs for food or going to the bathroom. In other words, they felt more in control over things most of us take for granted.

EMPATHY AND INTEROCEPTION

Because interoceptive feelings form our sense of self, their role in self-awareness extends beyond just what's happening within us. They form part of the back-and-forth between 'what do I look like through the eyes of others?', 'how do others feel?', and the interoception input of 'how do *I* feel?'.

Poor interoception inhibits our ability to harness the vast processing powers of our intuition, metacognition, and emotional data. It narrows us down to rely on rule-bound analytical thinking that can be draining and unproductive in testing circumstances. Instead of embracing disruption, we may become more inflexible or defensive. As we've seen, interoception allows us to think and act more flexibly and more rationally. Being in

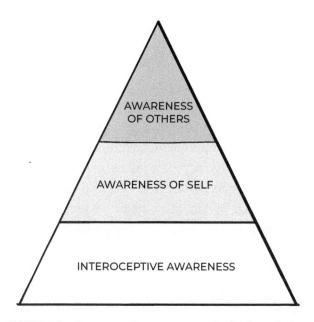

FIGURE 3.5   Interoceptive awareness is the foundation
of self-awareness
Source: Conceptualisation model; Jean Gomes, based on sources including:
Grynberg, D., & Pollatos, O. (2015). Perceiving one's body shapes empathy.
Physiology & Behavior, 140, 54–60. https://doi .org/10.1016/j
.physbeh.2014.12.026; Galvez-Pol, A., Antoine, S., Li, C., & Kilner, J. M.
(2022). People can identify the likely owner of heartbeats by looking at
individu- als' faces. Cortex, 151, 176–187; The Interoceptive Mind - From
Homeostasis to Awareness, Helena De Preester, Manos Tsakiris 2019 Oxford
University Press.

tune with our bodies allows us to 'know' what is expected in a
situation in a more natural and effortless manner. Not only does
it enable us to predict our reactions with greater accuracy, but
also interpret the behaviour of others because it underpins our
powers of empathy. Empathy is being able to experience what
others are feeling. It gives us a visceral, embodied understanding of their mindset. Empathy therefore allows us to appreciate the motivation behind their behaviour more directly. This

helps us to avoid much unnecessary conflict based on flawed assumptions.

In a challenging social situation, say dealing with an angry customer, our heart rate increases, leading us to become more alert. Our brain starts constructing predictions about what's happening. But with poor interoception we may not sense the changes, and then misinterpret what the customer is saying or needs. This suggests that superior interoception allows a greater degree of objectivity to be achieved in social situations, a background script telling us 'yes, this situation is stressful, but it's not about something in my character, appearance, or value that's causing it'.

Better interoception increases our understanding of others as it provides the means to construct a richer emotional experience of relationships, leading to greater empathy.[17] Research[18] led by Alejandro Galvez-Pol suggests that we can read the interoception of others. His team asked 120 participants to watch videos of people's faces side by side and listen to a heartbeat, deciding who was its owner. They found that we 'can judge the most likely owner significantly above chance levels'. When we are numb to what our bodies are telling us, we are left with a less human form of thinking.

Rational thought stripped away from feeling makes us less likely to distinguish logic from being judgemental. Not only does this cut us off from the most valuable sources of information that enable us to see what's happening and make good decisions, but it also separates us from the people we rely upon to work and live successfully.

CHAPTER 4

RETHINKING EMOTIONS

In the past 30 years, a quiet revolution has been taking place in our understanding of the nature of human emotions. The prevailing classical view is that they are 'hardwired' responses, located in specific regions of the brain, and are triggered by external stimuli. This gives rise to the appraisal of emotions as irrational and being associated with a loss of control, particularly in the workplace. Of course, fear, anger, or defensiveness can trip us into self-sabotaging responses, and feelings of optimism can blind us to uncomfortable truths. But a new understanding of emotions will help us to see them as an invaluable source of precious information, often more rational than what we believe our 'logical' arguments to be. One of the most significant pioneers in this revolution is the psychologist and neuroscientist, Lisa Feldman Barrett, whose work has confronted longstanding scientific beliefs and conventional wisdom about the nature of our emotions.

When Barrett and her colleagues built their laboratory over 30 years ago, now one of the largest affective neuroscience laboratories in the world, they assumed their work would focus on helping people to get better at understanding what they were feeling through identifying objective markers of emotion. What they soon discovered was that there were no objective markers – there were no regions of the brain dedicated to anger, happiness, or shame. Instead, they developed a new theory in which emotions are *built* from our brain–body predictive loops that seek

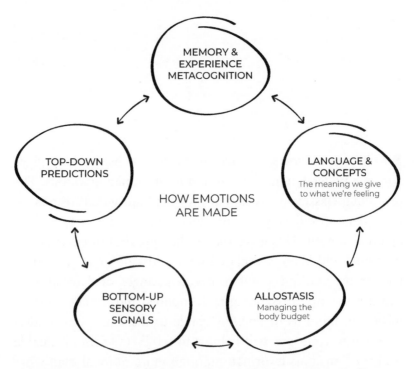

FIGURE 4.1   A simplified picture of Lisa Feldman Barrett's theory of constructed emotion

Source: Conceptualisation by Jean Gomes: Barrett, L., 2017. HOW EMOTIONS ARE MADE. 1st ed. London: Macmillan.

to keep our body budget operating efficiently. This loop draws on memories, and the concepts and language we've created to describe categories of emotional experiences.

When your brain anticipates a conflict, say with a previously unfriendly colleague, it constructs sensemaking emotions of anxiety, vulnerability, or fear. These emotions are also registered in a high, negative state of affective feelings – tenseness, stress, overwhelm, or fatigue – mobilising stress hormones readying you for conflict. The language we use to describe emotions is also integral to what we experience.

CLASSICAL VIEW OF EMOTIONS	CONSTRUCTED VIEW OF EMOTIONS
Feeling and emotion are the same thing.	Feeling and emotion influence one another but are created by different systems.
Different emotions are hard-wired in discrete brain regions.	Emotions are produced across many different neural networks which change dependent on situation.
Our emotional responses are reflexes.	Our predicting brain is constructing emotions to make sense of our body budget, drawing on context, past experiences, and the language we use to interpret the meaning of emotions.
Emotions are irreducible.	We seldom, if ever, experience one emotion – they are generally a mix of conflicting goals and interpretations.
We all experience the same emotions.	Emotions are specific to people and cultures.
Emotions, particularly negative ones, undermine logic and rational thinking.	All emotions are part of your brain's sense-making system – they are an invaluable part of your logic.
We can detect emotions in others.	We can only infer and explore what others are feeling.

FIGURE 4.2 Differences between classical and constructed views of emotion
Source: Conceptualisation by Jean Gomes: Barrett, L., 2017. HOW EMOTIONS ARE MADE. 1st ed. London: Macmillan.

CLASSICAL VS CONSTRUCTED VIEWS OF EMOTIONS

In her influential book, *How Emotions are Made*,[1] Barrett describes just how deeply ingrained the idea is that our emotions are primitive attributes. The classical view of emotions is grounded in a cherished narrative that has existed in Western civilisation since Plato. 'You have an inner beast, and a rational self that constantly battle for dominance', Barrett told me. 'The assumption is that if your inner beast wins the battle, you're either immoral or sick'.

Barrett's team analysed every brain-imaging study conducted over a 20-year period. They separated the human brain into minuscule virtual cubes like three-dimensional pixels (which they called voxels) and computed the probability of increased brain activation within each cube, while patients experienced anger, fear, sadness, or happiness. What they found was that 60% of the studies *did not* link areas of the brain with specific emotions. For example, the amygdala, often labelled *fear central*, didn't consistently become aroused in fearful experiences. From a statistical perspective, this is far below what would be expected if there was a 'neural fingerprint'. Barrett and four colleagues recently surveyed over 1,000 studies[2] on the evidence for emotional fingerprints. 'What we found was that for the Western stereotype of anger – which might be scowling – people only scowl when they're angry 30% of the time. That's more than chance, so yes, scowling is *an* expression of anger, but people do many things with their faces when they're angry. Most of the time, it's not scowling, so we'd call that low reliability. People also scowl when they're *not* angry, when they're concentrating hard, when something isn't very funny, or when they are in discomfort'.

So, if an emotion is not a hardwired response, what is it?

Barrett believes an emotion, such as fear, is best described as the *population of instances of fear* that we've constructed and experienced in our lives to make sense of our affect in relation to the world. Initially, this may seem very difficult to grasp, but it's worth persevering, because it unlocks a new realm of possibilities for how we understand what our emotions can tell us.

Let's remind ourselves that the brain's principal mission is to regulate your body budget. The prediction function of the brain is there to maintain the budget. Sensory cues generate positive physical feelings to let the brain know its predictions are correct and negative ones if they're wrong. Emotions are the means of making sense of *why* things are happening.

As the brain receives this constant flow of sensory data, it has no explanation for it. But it has one other source of comparative data to draw upon – our past experiences. Our brain unconsciously conjures up past experiences to make a guess on what the sense data means *before* it arrives. Part of this will be a prediction of the emotion we will feel. In other words, we construct emotions to make sense of our sensory input.

If affective feeling is the first level of low-resolution sense-making, then emotions are a more complex and nuanced interpretation of what's happening. When your brain has to make sense of sensory data, it isn't asking 'what is this?', it's asking 'what is this like?'.

The ability to pull apart instances of high physical arousal and emotion is incredibly helpful. In a conversation with Barrett, I recalled a recent situation where this happened to me. I was talking with a group of senior leaders, including the CEO, of a longstanding client which we have an excellent relationship with. I made a punchy statement about something, and the CEO responded 'I don't agree with that'. In that moment,

I felt the world tilt. In fact, writing this now, my affect is getting unpleasant! In the past, I might have leapt to my defence – either doubling down on my reasoning or some form of intellectual backtracking. But I didn't, I just focused on lowering my *physical* reactivity.

Within moments, I was listening again and hearing something unexpected. Another member of the team was arguing my point and the CEO was reconsidering their position. By focusing on my affect and not allowing myself to start interpreting the situation emotionally, I'd opened the space for consideration. My reflexive reaction would have exerted an even greater toll on my, and others', body budget.

'Here's what you did', says Barrett, 'you forestalled the meaning making. The negative affect was a cue that something was wrong, that there's a metabolic cost here and I need to do something. If your brain constructs an emotion out of that, that's a solution to the problem. Anger, fear, embarrassment, or shame *could* all be solutions to the problem. Instead, what you did in this moment was stopped and became curious, looking for more information *before* you came up with a solution'. Working through this experience helped me to understand Barrett's belief that emotions are your brain's way of making sense of your affect in relation to the world and the increased agency that this way of thinking can give us.

THE VALUE OF EMOTIONAL GRANULARITY

Just as there's a wide variation in people's interoceptive sensitivity, so is there in their ability to interpret their emotions accurately. We may easily merge feelings of hunger with frustration, or lump together irritation, shame, rejection, fear, and embarrassment under one all-purpose emotion of anger. *Emotional granularity* is the ability to make fine distinctions between our emotions by increasing our emotional vocabulary.

Research by neuroscientists such as Marc Bracket has shown that the process of describing our emotions more precisely creates positive changes in our brains associated with increased learning, receptiveness to new ideas, and improved resilience in the face of setbacks and conflict. In the research studies, these benefits started to happen in days. Barrett believes language is an important wellbeing tool, 'the more precise a tool you have, the more specifically you can construct instances of emotion to suit the needs of the situation. This creates less drag on your body budget. Research shows that you're less likely to get sick, it's much easier for you to cope with change and you're less likely to turn to alcohol and drugs to numb emotions that you're not able to comprehend. There's also evidence that people with greater emotional granularity get better faster when they are sick. The inference is that granularity allows you to regulate your brain more precisely, exerting less tax on your body and that you can communicate to other people more accurately what you're feeling and need. Only having one concept, is like only having one type of screwdriver for all screws'.

One way of achieving this is to ask, 'what problem is this feeling or emotion solving?'. It breaks the assumption that negative emotions are there to be overcome because they stand in the way of clear-sightedness and reason. Strong negative feelings, and the emotions constructed in their wake, do of course overwhelm us at times, primarily because they drain our physical energy, which diminishes our ability to think. As Barrett says: 'The most expensive tasks that brains do are moving your body and learning something new. They both have a metabolic cost that may feel unpleasant. But feeling bad doesn't always mean that something bad happened. You might just be doing something hard'.

As we learnt from Mark Solms, a negative feeling or emotion can be seen as an error signal, telling us we need to act to rebalance our metabolic equilibrium. He describes negative feelings as *an indication that a core human need has not been met*. If we're feeling panicky, for example, what does that mean? For our predicting brains, which strive to reduce uncertainty, panic is signalling action to prevent *separation or a loss*. The feeling of prolonged panic means whatever we're doing isn't working and amplifies the error signal and the resulting suffering. Tuning into the feeling allows us to identify ways in which we're behaving that aren't meeting our needs. Labelling an emotion accurately is half the answer, asking *what is it telling us?* is the other.

This suggests a way of interpretating our emotions more analytically – in other words, *what are our emotions telling us about how our core needs are being met*? In Figure 4.3, I created a framework of human needs and a few of the feelings and emotions that we feel when those needs are and aren't being met. This version is a summary of a more comprehensive picture we've built, too lengthy to include here. In our research, we've found this picture helps individuals and teams to make more accurate and fundamental interpretations of what they're feeling and why.

When we are experiencing negative *physical* feelings it's because we're under-resourced and our basic needs for sleep, nutrition, and movement are not being met. Without being attuned to our physical feelings, it's easy to mistake them as *emotions* rather than as *an input* to emotions. This simple error undermines our sense of control and accountability.

Our emotions are sensemaking loops, so when we feel negative emotions, they might simply be telling us that we're unclear about what's happening and why. Becoming defensive, judgemental, or cynical in these situations blocks this insight. Similarly, certainty is an emotion rather than a rational thought, so

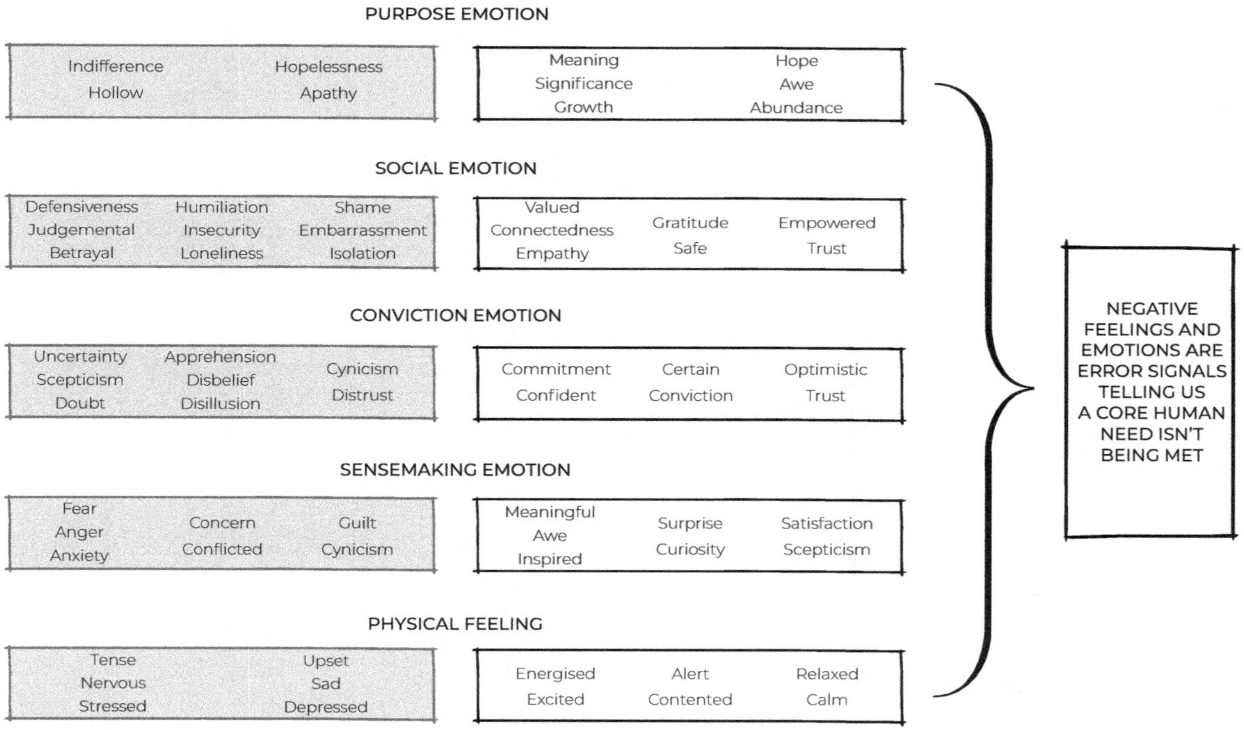

FIGURE 4.3 Feelings, emotions, and core human needs
Source: Jean Gomes

The figure shows a diagram. At the top is a box reading: "NEGATIVE FEELINGS AND EMOTIONS ARE ERROR SIGNALS TELLING US A CORE HUMAN NEED ISN'T BEING MET"

PURPOSE EMOTION
- Meaning, Significance, Growth / Hope, Awe, Abundance
- Indifference, Hollow / Hopelessness, Apathy

SOCIAL EMOTION
- Valued, Connectedness, Empathy / Gratitude, Safe / Empowered, Trust
- Defensiveness, Judgemental, Betrayal / Humiliation, Insecurity, Loneliness / Shame, Embarrassment, Isolation

CONVICTION EMOTION
- Commitment, Confident / Certain, Conviction / Optimistic, Trust
- Uncertainty, Scepticism, Doubt / Apprehension, Disbelief, Disillusion / Cynicism, Distrust

SENSEMAKING EMOTION
- Meaningful, Awe, Inspired / Surprise, Curiosity / Satisfaction, Scepticism
- Fear, Anger, Anxiety / Concern, Conflicted / Guilt, Cynicism

PHYSICAL FEELING
- Energised, Excited / Alert, Contented / Relaxed, Calm
- Tense, Nervous, Stressed / Upset, Sad, Depressed

when we feel significant doubt in information or distrust in others, it might signal that we're unclear or unprepared rather than others being the source of our disquiet.

Social emotions such as vulnerability tell us our needs of feeling valued and connected to others aren't being fully met. Finally, feelings of indifference or unrest signal that our needs to be allied to something meaningful and bigger than ourselves aren't being fulfilled. It results in us feeling lost.

WHAT ARE POSITIVE EMOTIONS FOR?

Surprisingly, little research has been conducted on the purpose of positive emotions. Negative feelings grab the limelight because, as Brackett's research[3] shows, we experience some form of negative emotion up to 70% of the time. If negative feelings are there to help us avoid risk, positive ones may be the counterbalance, creating the mental conditions to encourage us to imagine and play in uncertain situations, to try new experiences, trust strangers, and commit our futures to a partner or outcome with few guarantees.

Positive emotions restore our metabolism, increasing our wellbeing and future resilience. They offset the costs of energy expenditure. They help us reduce stress hormones, feel resourced, safe, and assured, to seek new experiences, gain mastery over difficult-to-acquire skills, feel connection to others, and find meaning in the world. Barbara Fredrickson's 'Broaden and Build' theory[4] suggests that positive emotions balance the survival function of negative emotions, in that they enable us to build skills, relationships, and imaginings of our future. Curiosity, for example, frees us to question 'why?' things are as they are, moving us out of a blind acceptance of the status quo. Curiosity sparks creativity, which turns into new knowledge. The joy associated with play turns into friendships that enable collective action.

THINKING MORE CLEARLY WITH META EMOTION

The final feeling layer to consider is meta emotion; how we think and feel about our emotions. Understanding meta emotions allows us to *feel strategically*, to see more clearly the layers of feeling and emotion and their influence on our assumptions. Studies[5] have shown that low meta-emotional awareness impacts moral decision-making. For example, the inability of heavy drinkers to distinguish between meta emotions and their core emotions might be a root cause of their alcohol misuse.[6] Low meta-emotional awareness means we can confuse and be conflicted about what we're feeling. For example, a core emotion is getting angry with your child for interrupting you when you were lost in concentration on an email. The meta emotion might be guilt at feeling angry with them.

Since the 1990s, when the field started, most meta-emotion research has been about exploring parent–child relationships.[7] If a child is told to suppress feelings of sadness by a parent or caregiver, they may grow up to feel meta emotions of shame or resentment when they feel sad. The child adapts to avoid sadness by becoming the social joker or ever-optimistic friend. Masking what they're feeling creates a dissonance between the core emotion of sadness and how they act out – outwardly happy. The meta emotion then becomes anxiety or depression at the self-deception.

So, when we think about how we feel, we have three mindset-building levels of self-awareness: *pulling apart our physical feelings*, which signal the state of our metabolism; *our emotions*, which enable us to make sense of what's happening; and *meta emotions*, which give us perspective on how we interpret our feelings.

CHAPTER 5

THINK – THE ASSUMPTIONS THAT DEFINE US

Negotiating a non-linear world means staying open. Listening to our feelings and interpretating them as core needs, provides us with a shrewd internal coach. Staying open in a non-linear situation, such as a rapidly changing market, or confronting a complex topic we know nothing about, also means holding our expertise and experience at arm's length and simultaneously exploring our ignorance, uncertainty, and doubt. Intellectual humility allows us to free our self-worth from the problems we face. By 'think', I'm not referring to the logic processes we can learn, such as deductive, abductive, or inductive reasoning,[1] or creative problem-solving. Instead, the focus here is on how you surface and challenge the assumptions that define what you 'know'. The consequence of our brain's predictive nature is that it produces a powerful sense of what we 'know' in any given moment fuelled by assumptions. It can be hard, therefore, to distinguish between an assumption and an objective truth. Our inner world of unspoken beliefs *is* our reality.

This often leads us to set our frame of reference for what we believe we can control, or do, far too tightly. The executives of struggling firms with outdated technologies in a diminishing sector cling to beliefs that they just need to gain more market share by working their assets harder, because they can't see beyond their mental box; or an executive at 50 loses her job and thinks she will never work again because younger people are 'cheaper, better, faster'.

So, we could substitute think for *believe*. This is important because our mindset isn't driven by rationality as we might like to sometimes believe. This enables us to grasp why assumptions are so hard to even accept, let alone see and break down. We assume our assumptions are true because they *feel* true. If our sensory data doesn't provide us with sufficient error signals, our assumptions coalesce into a sense of rightness or certainty.

WHAT WE BELIEVE INFLUENCES OBJECTIVE REALITY

The relationship between beliefs and the body's autonomous processes has long been the preserve of ancient practices such as meditation, remaining at the margins of science. Now though studies on 'belief effects' are explicitly showing that our core beliefs, or assumptions, *do* indeed change our bodies and dramatically influence the outcomes we seek. One of the most studied of these is the placebo effect, because every drug trial requires control groups being administered inert sugar pills, or other benign interventions. These control groups often report experiencing the beneficial outcomes of the real drug, *even* when they're told they are taking the placebo. The effects aren't just psychological either, their bodies often produce hormones and neurotransmitters that the drug would elicit. The work of Alia Crum at the Stanford Mind and Body Lab provides a fascinating insight into how our assumptions can, as she puts it, 'alter objective reality' through physiological, psychological, and behavioural changes. Crum wanted to know, 'do our beliefs about what we're eating, change our body's physiological response to that food?'.

In one of her earliest experiments,[2] she demonstrated the remarkable influence our assumptions have over physiological responses in our body. Participants were offered an indulgent milkshake full of ice-cream and sugar which was labelled with suitably enticing descriptions and rated as having over 600 calories. A few weeks later, the same people were invited back to try a sensible fat- and sugar-free milkshake with only 140 calories.

What the participants didn't realise was that both milkshakes were the same, somewhere at the midpoint of healthy and indulgent, with around 380 calories. On both occasions blood samples were taken before the test, after they had read the descriptions of the milkshakes, which were designed to prime their beliefs, and after consuming them. What Crum's team were looking for was how the different expectations of consuming an indulgent vs worthy drink influenced the production of the hormone ghrelin. Ghrelin, together with other hormones such as leptin, performs several functions in regulating our appetite, satiation, and energy. When the stomach is empty it is secreted, increasing appetite, and lowering our metabolism and promoting fat storage.

What Crum's team found was deeply counterintuitive. When the group consumed the 'indulgent' shake their ghrelin levels dropped at a threefold rate in comparison to the sensible shake.

The *expectation* of high calorific intake meant their bodies responded as if they had eaten more food than they had. This was one of the first experiments to demonstrate that belief in what you're eating has a metabolic effect.

Up to this point, Crum had believed that adopting a mindset about eating healthy food was the obvious goal. But that was too one-dimensional. Participants who *believed* they were eating the healthy option, were left physiologically hungry, less satiated and satisfied, and potentially with a lower metabolism and energy levels. Crum now believes if you want to maintain or lose weight, you must cultivate a mindset that you're getting enough, that whatever you eat *is* indulgent and rewarding. Thinking of the salad as delicious rather than healthy, for example, is key to changing the body's response to it.

Our beliefs about stress have a similarly striking impact on us. Instead of seeing stress as either good or bad, we should think of it as a paradox. Too little stress and we become weak and atrophy physically, emotionally, mentally, and intellectually. Too much and we become overwhelmed, or eventually things break down. Stress mobilises the resources that help us face adversity, overcome challenges, and achieve meaningful goals. It can usefully narrow our focus and increase our information processing. It can trigger hormones to help us grow and build new neural pathways necessary for learning.

Richard Tedeschi and Lawrence Calhoun coined the term *post-traumatic growth* in which even terrible life events such as abuse, injury, or illness can lead to the exact opposite of destruction – to one of several forms of growth:

- Enhanced appreciation of life
- Greater gratitude for and strengthening of close relationships
- Compassion and altruism
- Seeing new options or finding more purpose in life

- Greater awareness and use of personal strengths
- Creative expression

The key insight to how individuals gain this remarkable response can be seen in the work of psychologist Todd Kashdan. In a study[3] conducted with Jennifer Kane, they tested the notion that when trauma sufferers *avoid* fearful thoughts, feelings, and emotions, they cut off the ability to accept what's happened to them and reduce their ability to move forward in pursuing their long-term goals. They found that the greater the trauma, the greater potential for post-traumatic growth, but only in those who had the lowest levels of experiential avoidance.

The aging researcher Becca Levy believes that society's messages about age and the stereotypes we internalise not only influence our self-esteem and behaviour, but also how we biologically age. In her laboratory at Yale University, Levy shows that when participants are subliminally primed to adopt positive frames about age, for example by using words such as 'wise', their motivation, memory, balance, and walking speed can be improved in minutes. Levy found that amongst the 15% of the US population genetically more susceptible to Alzheimer's, those with positive age beliefs are nearly 50% *less likely* to develop dementia than those with negative age beliefs.

Although individuals who have a positive outlook in older age are more likely to engage in exercise and social activity, their biological markers are younger as well. For example, they have lower blood pressure.[4] Or take their cortisol levels, the stress hormone, which tends to increase as we age and is associated with impaired cognitive and physical health. Levy asked 439 participants to provide cortisol measurements. In those aged 50 or above, the cortisol of the more negative age-stereotype group increased by 44%, whereas the more positive age-stereotype group showed no increase.

ASSUMPTION BUSTING – DEEP DISRUPTIVE THINKING

If our lives are, in part, propelled by hidden assumptions, the ability to see and question them is one of the greatest levers of our growth potential. It can open new possibilities for your work, health, and relationships. In the process what typically happens is that we discover we're solving the wrong problems to achieve our aims, or that we don't really understand their nature in the first place.

Interrogating the beliefs that shape our mindsets is tough, because we mostly don't see beliefs as assumptions but as an objective reality. And it's frequently painful because we unconsciously know that we're avoiding acknowledging them because to do so means questioning past actions and the possibility that we'll need to give up privilege or comfort.

One way to start is simply writing them down. I'm guessing you're unlikely to have made a list of the core beliefs you hold about food, fitness, climate change, marriage, parenting, and so on. Bill, an executive I coached, took on the challenge of keeping an assumption journal for a month. He listed the assumptions in several areas we'd been working on together, without trying to interrogate them – about his colleagues, family, choices around exercise, food, alcohol, and anything he wanted, needed, or craved. In the first week, he almost gave up. 'I thought it felt pointless, like I was talking into my 10-year-old diary. But then I realised, it felt frightening, and I decided I needed to find out why'.

One of the conclusions Bill came to was that the 'mental box' in which he operated, and many of the unspoken goals that were shaping his life, were based on values and beliefs he had when he was 20. Now, he's 46. After a month, Bill had identified five assumptions about his family life and work that were making him unhappy and unproductive, including:

- *Constantly buying things would result in happier downtime* – when in fact these purchases largely went unused and caused tension and arguments. Online shopping, he came to see, was more about avoiding boredom.
- *Alcohol consumption helped him relax and unwind* – instead, it closed him off from his family, leaving him feeling tired and cantankerous at the weekends, with little motivation to exercise or do things his family might want to try.

'It was undoubtedly painful, but it was also like having a thorn taken out of your finger – the relief was immense. I now had real options going forward', he told me.

Listing your assumptions is far from easy because they sit within layers of models (assumptions in themselves) that define the 'box' in which we operate. Bill stepped back to see his box, erased its borders, and drew a new, larger territory in which to operate. He developed what he called a 'family-first' mindset that also incorporated time and priorities for his recovery and hobbies. The same holds true for many teams and organisations, who define themselves tightly by beliefs about what they're not and cannot do.

Most advice on assumption busting, however, starts with an assumption – that you know what they are in the first place. 'Reverse the assumptions, list the opposites, and use them to generate creative alternatives' is one common piece of advice given in creativity books. But many of our assumptions are core beliefs that seem like objective truths. To supermarket executives not so long ago, stating 'We are a supermarket' may have seemed pointless, until supermarkets became banks, insurance providers, petrol stations, and mobile phone operators.

The philosopher Karim Benammar describes a process[5] that might help us to go deeper. It starts by determining a core belief where we feel something is impossible, or incredibly hard for us to change. Then we make a search for supporting beliefs that we don't necessarily realise provide the mental scaffolding that hold the core belief in place unchallenged. Next, we create extreme opposites of those supporting beliefs before going back to the original core belief to rethink it.

An individual's core belief might be 'I'm too old to exercise'. The supporting beliefs are 'I never saw my parents exercise and they were fine', 'I'm able to do whatever I need to physically, so I don't need to exercise', 'what I can do today, I will be able to do tomorrow', 'exercise is unpleasant, and I don't have the time for it'.

The next step is to flip the supporting beliefs (remember we're not talking about facts or how we might go about acting on these new beliefs in reality). For the individual these might include 'you can exercise into your 90s', 'my parents could have lived a healthier 10–15 years longer if they had exercised', 'I would feel better if I exercised', 'exercise gives me more energy so I can get more done in less time'.

Finally, we use these as inputs to flip the core belief into something like, 'exercise is unlocking more of who I want to be'. Having used this technique many times with senior teams, once individuals let go of thinking of this as a decision-making process, but instead giving them the mental freedom to explore new possibilities and redraw their 'box', assumption busting becomes emancipating, leading to new possibilities.

HOW TO BUILD AN ASSUMPTION-BUSTING LOG

Project managers have long used assumption logs to track progress. In a typical log, there are columns for assumptions, a risk rating, a suggestion to take if the assumption proves to be false, dates to validate, and the owner. These tend to work fine as a project management tool in situations where the assumptions being made by a team are largely low risk and easy to test. When activity is 'plan and act', an assumption log is mostly about ensuring mutual understanding to maximise speed and efficiency.

But, in situations of greater risk and uncertainty, like an innovation project, where the team needs to continually 'test, learn, pivot, and adapt', the *blind* and *informed* assumptions that need to be verified are of a different order of magnitude of difficulty and potential impact on the success of the team's output. In this situation, I've modified the assumption log to help move it beyond just listing assumptions and to categorise them on an *informed to blind spectrum*.

The team starts with its overall hypothesis, for example:

We believe that by providing _ solution, we will solve _ problem and the customer will be willing to pay _ price. We will take _% market worth £_ billion in four years maintaining a _% gross margin.

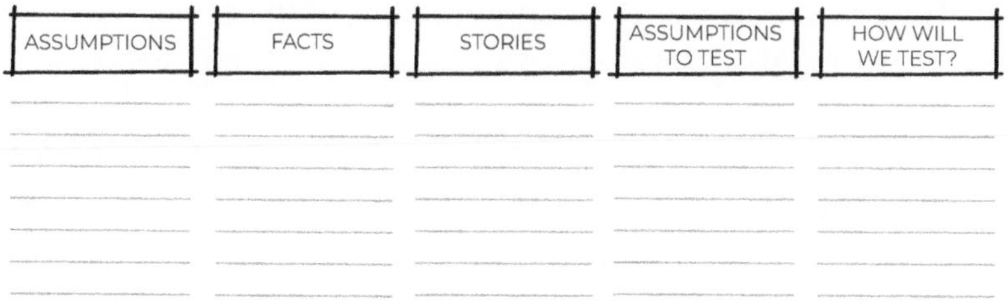

ASSUMPTIONS	FACTS	STORIES	ASSUMPTIONS TO TEST	HOW WILL WE TEST?

FIGURE 5.1   Experimental assumption log
Source: Jean Gomes

The team then starts to make a long list of assumptions, including:

The customer is. . .

Their pains regarding this problem are. . .

The gains from our solution will be. . .

Their willingness to pay for this solution is. . .

The customer experience required to win is. . .

They will accept us as a credible supplier because. . .

The total addressable market is worth. . .

This market will grow £. . . in five years

We can gain X% of this market in four years because. . .

Our route to market will be. . .

Our competitors will be. . .

We will beat them because. . .

Our barriers to entry will be. . .

We have what we need to design and make the product because. . .

Our supply chain will provide what we need, which is. . .

We will evolve the product by. . .

The greatest risks to success are. . .

Having itemised core assumptions about the project, we ask that they rank them on one of four levels of risk and uncertainty:

1. *Informed Assumptions* – we're confident that we understand the risks in this assumption (evidenced by. . .). These are informed assumptions where the risk is, we believe, reasonably low.

2. *Partially Informed Assumptions* – we're confident that we can learn about risks that we don't understand right now from

the market, others who are doing what we're attempting to, or experts (we will achieve this by. . .). These are informed assumptions where the risk is, we believe, reasonably high.

3. *Partially Blind Assumptions* – we know little about the assumptions we're making and currently don't have access to those who do (we need to gain access to this knowledge by. . .). These are partially blind assumptions where the uncertainty is, we believe, reasonably low.

4. *Blind Assumptions* – we don't know anything about the assumptions we're making or if there is any knowledge about them available (our discovery mode will be. . .). These are blind assumptions where the uncertainty is, we believe, reasonably or very high.

Next, the assumption-busting log helps the team to pull apart the facts from the stories that shape their assumptions. As much as anything, this step interrupts our natural tendency to default into motivated reasoning where we unconsciously seek to fit facts to our existing beliefs and goals. In the face of uncertainty, it also empowers us to think more freely by shrinking defensive emotions which otherwise propels our thinking into self-justification.

The next column asks the team to list the *facts*, which can be objectively verified, that it currently has about each assumption. Tellingly, this column is often quite sparse at the beginning, which hopefully creates an incentive to populate it with data.

However, the next column, the *stories* we tell about this assumption, is often overflowing. That's because, as the philosopher and historian Yuval Noah Harari[6] points out, humans think in stories, not in facts, numbers, or equations. And the simpler the story, the better. The evolutionary advantage of stories is profound, allowing humans to gain power over one another, maintain knowledge over generations, and build vast collective endeavours. As he puts it, 'you could never convince a monkey to give you a banana by promising him limitless bananas after death in monkey heaven'.

The point of pulling out stories in the assumption log is two-fold. Firstly, to make an explicit distinction between what's fact and what's interpretation. Secondly, to prevent our stories from betraying us. Researchers have shown that the evolutionary advantage of arguing, of which the story is a key component, is to win, not to be right. We must remember that we don't want to win the argument and lose the truth.

When we hear stories, we construct images and emotions to accompany them. That's why they help us to build emotional conviction to take on uncertain and unknown challenges. But equally, stories can narrow our thinking and reduce our moti-vation. We prefer simple, whole stories with a start, middle, and end, which often place us into the trap of filling in missing pieces of information. One of the most common gaps we plug as we endlessly build stories is to automatically ascribe motiva-tion to people's actions – good/bad person thinking – rather than considering the context in which those behaviours might make sense. This cognitive bias is known as fundamental attri-bution error, one of the numerous ways in which the brain is trying to reduce uncertainty and lower the energy required to operate in the world. Try for yourself the simple experiment of questioning your judgemental stories in the moment and see how difficult it often is to overcome the feeling of rightness in them, and the effort it takes to reconsider and leave them incomplete. It seems to inevitably provoke a degree of stress and confusion in us.

Let's take an unrelated example that many of us will have experienced as a manager. Imagine it's the start of your day at the office. You're walking past the desk of Chris, one of your team members, who, to be honest, you consider to be a little casual in their attitudes to discipline and they're not there. The rest of the team is working hard on an urgent deadline. Your core need for feeling supported isn't met in this moment and you feel both a physical reaction of stress and an emotionally driven mistrust that Chris is malingering at home.

'Anybody know where Chris is?', you ask in a flat tone, expecting someone to tell you he's called in sick. 'Yeah', someone replies, 'he got here three hours ago to set up the customer demo room, he's in there now and I think he's closed a big order from the texts I've seen'. In that moment, the physical reaction shifts again into a mix of relief that you didn't say anything cutting about Chris to the team, and hopefully a degree of shame for thinking the worst of someone who's going the extra mile to support your success.

The point of this scenario, which could have turned out worse if you'd acted on your assumptions, is that you formed a distorting story based on one very slender piece of information. Chris wasn't at his desk.

THE ART OF ASKING AND BEING ASKED DISRUPTIVE QUESTIONS

Our natural meaning-making system, the construction of instantly convincing stories based on partial knowledge, means we need to train ourselves to be able to ask positively disruptive questions of ourselves, of others, and be more open to being asked them. The academic Marilee Adams provides a helpful lens for leaders to recognise the power of the questions they ask by making the distinction[7] between *judger questions* and *learner questions*. Judger questions often aren't questions at all but thinly veiled instructions or put downs. They originate from negative emotions such as frustration, scepticism, and anger.

JUDGER QUESTIONS	LEARNER QUESTIONS
How am I right?	How am I wrong?
Who is to blame?	What am I not seeing?
Why didn't you get this right?	What are my goals?
Why aren't you motivated by this?	How do we make this better?
Why is this person so clueless?	What have you learnt through this?
How can I prove I'm right?	How can I help this person/team get this done more effectively?
How can I prove they are wrong?	What am I responsible for here?
How can I keep control over the outcome?	How can I learn and grow in this situation?
What are we going to lose by doing this?	What do our customers want and need?
	What's our most important next step?

FIGURE 5.2   Examples of judger and learner questions
Source: Jean Gomes inspired by Marilee Adams

Judger questions are shaped by assumptions and beliefs, such as 'I'm an expert in this already', 'I'm right', or 'why are we wasting time when we already know the answer?'. You wouldn't necessarily say these things out loud, but everyone knows you're thinking them by your body language, and the tone and intent in what you do say. Judger questions generally produce unproductive binary, defensive responses or just frozen silence.

Learner questions, on the other hand, are neutral or positive in their emotional intent. The goal is to understand and make progress. *'What are we trying to achieve?'*, *'how can I make this better?'*, *'what assumptions am I making here?'*. Asking learner questions means quietening the expert voice in our head.

There are three useful starting points in being able to build the muscle of self-questioning. They help us find new, difficult, naïve, and constructively disruptive questions to gain better insight. The first is to ask *why* questions: '*Do I understand what's really happening or am I responding to a partial understanding?*', '*Is that the reason why I'm zoning in too narrowly to gain what feels like some control here?*', '*Do I understand the underlying causes of why this is happening?*'. Sakichi Toyoda's Five Why's methodology[8] is a useful means of pushing ourselves to find root causes.

The second category can be described as '*What am I, or we, not seeing?*', '*How do others see this differently and why?*', '*What information am I excluding as unimportant or irrelevant?*', '*What information gets us into trouble if we raise it?*', '*What might this situation look like in 10, 20, 30 years' time?*'.

The third set of base questions are: '*How might I, or we, be wrong?*', '*What do I, or we, believe to be true where we have no real objective evidence just conviction, or limited experience?*', '*How might our "expertise" stand in the way of seeing what's happening?*', '*Am I asking people who I know will disagree with me or us?*'.

Innovation thinker Rita McGrath suggests that, 'like it or not, we're in a space now where our ratio of assumptions to knowledge is terribly high. Human beings are dreadful about handling assumptions – either we forget them altogether or we turn them into facts in our minds'.[9] Whilst the incredibly sophisticated human system is optimised to run on assumptions, it's our capacity to see and blow-up those assumptions that becomes an indispensable asset in navigating a non-linear world.

CHAPTER 6

SEE – THE FRAMES WE HOLD

Because our brains crave stability, we often see what we want to see when we might need to let in the unforeseen or unwelcome. Building a mindset challenges us to question the reliability of what we see, and therefore what we 'know'. Seeing intentionally means harnessing our metacognition to stand back and consider the frames, or lenses, we hold up to the world and ask what they allow us to discern, disregard, or discount.

We should start by challenging a fundamental assumption about our perception; that what we see is objective reality. Since we have an extraordinarily high-definition visual experience of the world, unsurprisingly we assume that it's an objective, comprehensive, and accurate representation. It's not.

As we survey the world and notice people, mountains, or a can of soup, what we're seeing is a representation of those objects *after* we process the information, not the information itself. It's not reality but a *construction* that our brain pieces together based on our experiences, biases, and assumptions. The information from the light photons hitting our eyes is entirely ambiguous on its own and only 10% of the data that our brains use to construct our experience of vision comes from our eyes. As the perceptual neuroscientist Beau Lotto suggests, 'the brain didn't evolve to create an accurate representation of the world, but one that is useful'. Being able to question what we see – our most tangible and seemingly real experience of the world – allows us to change our *future* perception.

WE SEE WHAT ONCE WAS

The brain's top-down predictive functioning that underpins feeling, emotion, and thought also drives perception. Throughout the day, to track changes in the environment, our eyes perform over 100,000 rapid eye movements called saccades. As soon as our eyes rest for as little as 100 milliseconds, our visual system shifts into prediction mode. When our eyes re-engage, our brain compares previous and current visual data, registering prediction errors. It's like video compression, the benefit is that our brain has considerably less data to process.

One of the most visceral and endlessly surprising ways of experiencing how the predicting brain over-rides reality is a video[1] where the late neuroscientist, Richard Gregory, holds a hollow mask of a man's face. The mask has pronounced concave and convex sides. Regardless of which side he holds up, *both* look as if the features are projecting outwardly. It's thoroughly bizarre, because even though you *know* you're looking at something recessed, you can't see it any other way than protruding outwardly. Your brain's predictions of what a face *should* look like are so strong that they over-ride the error signals, recasting the information about the shadows and lines. Similarly, we often see what we expect to see in data, in people's gestures and body language, or other patterns of human behaviour.

Another fascinating example of how our vision is less reliable than we might imagine can be seen in the research[2] of neuroscientists Mauro Manassi and David Whitney. Go to YouTube[3] and watch their video, *An Illusion of Stability*. It starts with the images of two young identical twins. One of the twin's faces is covered up and over 60 seconds, the other's face gradually ages. At the end, the concealed twin is revealed still as their earlier self, allowing you to compare the aging process. For most people, it's a surprise as the changes appear tiny until the final reveal. We don't seem to notice.

The point of the experiment, however, is to explain how we experience *visual stability*. Imagine attaching your phone to your forehead and using the video camera to record your whole day. The result would be an exceedingly unpleasant, jolting, and disorientating experience to watch. But we don't experience our perception like that. Somehow, it's smoothed out to create a consistent and stable experience. What the brain appears to be doing is averaging out what we've seen in the last 15 seconds, pulling together data that seems more similar and editing out the rest to prevent overload. It's called *serial dependence*. Our perception is built on the past. As Manassi and Whitney point out, 'if our brains were always updating in real time, the world would feel like a chaotic place with constant fluctuations in light, shadow, and movement. We would feel like we were hallucinating all the time'.[4]

In the experiment, the researchers asked hundreds of participants to watch the video and estimate the age of the twin at the end. Invariably, they reported the age of the face that was presented 15 seconds before the end. We're always seeing the past and using it as a predictor of the future because the brain is recycling data to increase efficiency and do less work.

Because our brain sacrifices accuracy for stability, we don't always notice subtle changes that happen over time.

Whilst the positive effect is that we're not overwhelmed by a constant deluge of visual change, the downside is that it may lead us to miss critical changes in our environment that risk perilous outcomes. For example, Manassi looked at the judgement of clinicians assessing X-rays for lesions.[5] The daily error rate is estimated to be 3–5%, potentially leading to critical or fatal outcomes for those patients. The assumption is that the visual radiological screening by highly skilled experts on a current radiograph happens independently of previously seen radiographs. What Manassi's team found was that serial dependence shaped their recognition of simulated lesions on average by 13% *towards* previous images. The takeaway in terms of increasing our self-awareness is that we don't just metaphorically live in the past, our perception and therefore our judgement is grounded in the past even when we believe we're dealing in current reality.

Psychology researcher Anna Antinori looked at the relationship between visual awareness and the personality trait of openness.[6] Individuals with high openness scores tend to be more able to dream up counterfactual scenarios, find new uses for objects, and explore new ideas and experiences. What Antinori found was that they can see differently too.

She used a binocular rivalry test which simultaneously presents each eye with a different-coloured image (green and red). Most people can only see one colour at a time and therefore experience the image flipping between red and green. Some, though, reported a patchwork of green and red. The more highly participants scored for openness on personality tests, the more they reported the dual-coloured image, a phenomenon known as *mixed percept*.

So, why is that interesting? More open people can engage with the incoming information in a less conventional way, not choosing between options but *combining* them. Antinori believes this is the first empirical evidence that creative people have different visual experiences. They can arrive at new ways of thinking about the world because they really do see it differently.

DO WE SEE WHAT WE FEEL?

Recall watching a horror film or a very tense thriller, and it's self-evident that *what* we see can change *how* we feel, but what if the opposite was true? Does *how* you feel change *what* you see? Eric Anderson led a team studying how feeling impacts perception.[7] They too used the binocular rivalry test showing faces smiling, scowling, or resting neutrally to one eye, and a house to the other eye. At the same time, they induced positive, neutral, or negative feelings in the participants. When the participants experienced negative physical feelings, *all* the facial expressions were more dominant in their perception than when they were experiencing the neutral physical experience. Smiling faces became more dominant when they felt positive physical feelings and the scowling ones were more conspicuous when they felt negative affect.

What this tells us is that our perception is *embodied*. We can only understand all our senses, including vision, when we consider the attributes of the body. If you're tired or overweight, distances look further away to you.[8] Listening to happy or sad music affects our ability to recognise happy or sad expressions in others.[9] The 19th-century American psychologist, William James, presciently described our visual attention system as a spotlight that we shine on the world. It is attuned more to threat as a means of survival, so our brain privileges anything that might be a risk over neutral or positive information. That's why being in the dark, or swimming in a deep part of the ocean, is so anxiety provoking; we're awash with uncertainty signals.

THE FRAMES WE HOLD

How can we see the world with fresh eyes, better understand the root causes of today's complex problems, and imagine new possibilities for our future? In part, the answer lies in the frames that we hold up to the world and how they fundamentally determine what we see, feel, and think. A frame is a mental model – a theory, idea, or framework – that allows us to see the world in a particular way. Frames focus our attention and mental resources selectively on certain things and deprioritise or withdraw attention from others. Frames form over the course of our lives from childhood through to maturity. Some of us cling rigidly to seeing the world through one frame in the hope that it will provide continuity. Others are adept at swapping frames to adapt to changing circumstances and opportunities.

As the interconnectedness and interdependencies of our world have deepened, the tensions arising from competing ways of seeing will only amplify. Being able to better understand our and others' ways of perceiving the world offers us the hope of finding new creative paths forward. When we pull apart frames and feelings, there's also the possibility of recognising that we've confused ideas with our sense of value, giving us the freedom to think again and feel differently.

Building a mindset requires us to think about the frames we *currently* deploy and which ones we might be better off using. Which frames dominate our thinking and action? Where do they serve us well or constrain us? Frames range in their complexity and nature. They can be abstract, practical, moral, or theoretical. Free speech, design thinking, liberal democracy, game theory, memes, business models, natural selection, ecosystems, intellectual property, are all frameworks and models that help us to make the complex comprehensible.

A frame isn't an attitude, as we sometimes hear. It is a mental model that we use to make sense of the world. Mostly, though, we are unaware of the frames we're employing. If, for example, you're an adept project manager, and have a well-developed frame of linear problem-solving and attention to detail, without realising this might make you unsuited to a new situation that requires open situational analysis and creative problem-solving. You may have the aptitude or potential for these things, but you haven't changed the frame and so you feel and appear stuck.

Frames can turn one experience into a set of general rules which we can apply to future experiences. But frames can also create an intelligence trap where we believe our established ways of thinking in one domain are equally applicable elsewhere. A fixed frame makes us vulnerable and inflexible to the point that we can confuse purpose or belief with deficit emotions such as rage and anger. Or they can help us to see the world afresh and break free of being limited to what we currently know.

When organisations hold frames too tightly, particularly around a business model, their field of vision narrows and shortens precariously. Blockbuster's business model frame centred on the importance of its retail network. Perhaps by surviving the upheaval that the VHS to DVD transition brought, it believed it continued to be relevant as the internet disrupted the service economies. Even when Netflix offered to partner with the company in 2000, its CEO, John Antioco, ridiculed the idea as absurd. A decade later, Blockbuster filed for bankruptcy because its business model was irrelevant.

Frames have the potential to positively disrupt our thinking if we pay close attention to how they make us feel and think. New frames that challenge our assumptions can create defensive emotions and negative affect.

As we'll see in several examples in Part 2, zooming our perception in and out helps us to disrupt fixed perceptions of the world and get us better at noticing more objectively. By zooming into a scenario, we can get rich data on the emotional territory of situations, subtleties, and incongruities. We can understand the nuances between people's wants and needs, desires and practicalities. Zooming out, we can see how patterns and trends are forming, how different parts of an organisation, community, or market are thinking about or tackling issues. We can see weak signals of future change, enabling us to switch into learning mode and not pre-judge too fast.

Zooming in benefits from the approach of the anthropologist, noticing without judgement 'what is happening?'. As Simon Roberts, one of the world's leading business anthropologists, told me, most of what you learn in unfamiliar environments is from what makes you feel uncomfortable, or where you break unspoken implicit rules or make mistakes.[10] As a young researcher, Roberts first experienced this deeply in a North Indian tea shop. Placing his empty cup on the table prompted barely concealed disgust from his fellow diners. The cultural norm is that you put it on the floor when you've finished because it is dirty. Of course, there's no sign telling you this, everyone knows. You can only discover the hidden layers of social order by deep observation, or inadvertently breaking the unspoken rules.

Executives who are consumed with the internal activities of their organisation starve themselves of this rich data. By contrast, those who spend time on the shop floor observing the reality of how their organisation serves their people, who regularly listen to customers and suppliers, and who hang out with potential disruptors – start-ups, unlikely future competitors, and divergent thinkers – are building new frames for future mindsets to develop.

RECONCILING VS MANAGING PARADOXES

One of the most powerful benefits of switching frames is their ability to move us beyond what can be a false choice between two or more options. 'It's either my health, time with my family, *or* success at work'. The frames we hold can grip us in a binary either/or position that seems to make the status quo the only option. The most fundamental frame switching is the move from what *we* see, think, feel, know, and want, to how *others* are feeling, thinking, and seeing. But it's easy to confuse *judging* others' mindsets from our vantage point with the *empathy of understanding* them from theirs. The precious insight that this simple shift unlocks is as relevant to a marriage, parenting, or understanding customers. Business professors Wendy Smith, Marianne Lewis, and Michael Tushman suggest, however, there's another reason why we might choose upsides in an either/or scenario. That's because there is a deep cultural antipathy towards paradoxes, particularly in Western thought. 'Aristotelian logic treats contradictions and tensions as signals that we need to seek a more accurate, unified truth. If one idea is "right", its opposite must be wrong; if that seems not to be the case, then we must redefine our idea to eliminate the contradiction'.[11]

They point out that either/or thinking results in a deficit mindset. For example, you either direct resources to this project or that one. This fuels conflict and politics amongst managers. Both/and thinking encourages us to move past the zero-sum game of 'I win at your expense', to figuring creative ways of answering 'how can we both grow the pie?'. As Smith and Co. suggest, 'tapping the potential of paradox begins with respecting the distinct needs of groups with different agendas. Doing so requires pulling apart the organisation's goals and valuing each of them individually'.

Just appreciating the paradox is insufficient, if we believe that it can be 'solved'. When we do this, we're still taking an either/or approach as we're making trade-offs that ultimately move the problem elsewhere. If a leader prioritises one challenge over another to create stability, eventually the stability breaks down elsewhere. We see this with organisations perpetually restructuring themselves, swinging power and accountability between localised and centralised structures. The both/and frame encourages leaders to see and manage a dynamic equilibrium that doesn't seek stability but recognises, for example, that disruptive innovation and operational efficiency are conflicting goals. The challenge is to divert creative problem-solving to how to *do both*.

Managing a paradox requires constant curiosity and alertness. It is easy to feel that having 'solved' it for a period, the paradox has revealed its secrets and we have managed to find another form of stability. But managing paradoxes necessitates leaders asking the deeper question of not 'what is' happening but 'why'; being prepared to go deeper. Often the root causes are *temporal*; they play out as symptoms in waves over time – for example, as products move from maturity into decline, resulting in an organisation built for one purpose no longer being fit for the next wave of innovation. They might be *cultural*, where strong sets of identities with conflicting perspectives and motivations are played off against each other with short-term either/or decision-making. This creates a jockeying for positions of safety and status which is unspoken but corrosive. It is often concealed with a shallow veneer of affable conviviality, masking that there's insufficient trust to confront the deeper, more difficult areas of uncertainty in a culture or team. It might be *strategic*, where there is a constant battle between performance and growth, which we explore more fully in Part 2 (Building Mindsets for the Future).

REIMAGINE

New frames can inspire us to imagine things are currently not possible or believed to be even necessary. The innovation literature is littered with quotations about the beliefs of smart and experienced people who supposed we would never need home computers, airplanes, or smartphones. Frames help us to imagine counterfactual realities; things that don't yet exist. As we've seen, creating the conditions that allow imagination to drive value creation in established institutions and organisations is far from straightforward. The symbols, language, and imagery of established enterprises combine into mental models that generally inhibit imagination.

In one exercise, we ask teams to complete a jigsaw puzzle, which gives them a powerful experience of how assumptions and vision work together. The pieces of the puzzle have a single colour on one side. Most participants immediately assume that it's a team-building or mental performance exercise to see how well they cope in solving a puzzle that doesn't have the typical visual cues of a picture to help them match the shapes. Many groups get exasperated after only a few minutes, with some people giving up and leaning out of the group or getting cross that their suggestions aren't being listened to.

The real aim of the puzzle is to see if participants can challenge their assumptions about the 'rules' of jigsaws. These are that all the pieces must have the colour, or normally an image, on the top and that the edges are straight lines or corners. The only way to solve the puzzle is to *break these rules*. What's really fascinating is when somebody in the team first suggests trying these countermoves; one or two people will get upset and dismiss the idea. Even when they do try these counterintuitive approaches, and start finding they work, many in the group *still* feel emotionally uncomfortable about the approach. 'It just doesn't look right' one participant cried out. It's worth pointing out that the puzzle isn't a persistence test as some groups assume, it's solvable. But right up until the final few pieces have fallen into place, it still looks wrong to most people's eyes. Psychologist Karl Duncker describes this inability to see that something with one use can have completely other uses as *functional fixedness*. In this case, our mental model of a jigsaw blocks our ability to see that it might have alternate forms. The error signals create a sense of risk and anxiety that we are failing and that our existing skills and knowledge aren't working.

Many of us have been encouraged to see functional fixedness as a necessity, or even an advantage, both in terms of conforming to the expectations of the organisations we work for, but also because of our training. As the educationist Ken Robinson lamented, the obsession of schools and universities that their students have the right answers has driven curiosity, creativity, and experimentation out of our culture.[12]

Emily Clements is part of a team conducting the world's first study into the neuroscience of entrepreneurs and the disruptive thinking processes they employ to find new opportunities.[13] She explains that one clear pattern is their ability to move *flexibly* between two types of thought, which psychologists refer to as divergent and convergent thinking. Convergent thinking focuses attention intently and is driven by brain regions called the multiple-demand network (MDN). Comprised of networks in our frontoparietal brain, these regions switch on when a task is difficult. We could call this the 'zoom-in' state of the brain, as it narrows in on details and problems to solve.

As Clements puts it, 'The MDN and its engagement is one of our greatest strengths as it underlies much of our fluid intelligence, ability to analyse, stay engaged in tasks and be productive'. An over-reliance on convergent thinking, however, can lead us to become tunnel-focused and lose sight of the big picture.

Zooming out, and engaging divergent thought, is the role of the default-mode network (DMN), which allows our mind to wander and daydream. It was discovered in the early use of magnetic resonance imaging (MRI) scanners, when – between experiments – neuroscientists noticed the same network kept engaging when participants were lying doing nothing and waiting for instruction. But the DMN isn't just the brain idling, it's engaged in conscious metacognition, thinking about past events, beliefs, the future, and musing on our sense of self.

The ability to move dynamically between these networks enables the disruptive thinking associated with creativity and innovation. Defining problems to solve, for example, is more challenging than forming goals. This is because it requires us to confront the assumptions we make in our ability to achieve those goals. Defining a problem, which teams often find difficult and avoid, requires shuttling between zooming in and zooming out. This is where emotions become so important to factor in.

When we become immersed in creative tasks, studies show that we often experience positive emotions and an increased sense of autonomy. But creativity is frustrating too, and so a moderate level of stress and associated emotions of anger, frustration, and uncertainty are often essential, if they don't become overwhelming. This is where interpreting our emotions can help us to avoid getting stuck and encourage us to shuttle between the modes of thinking as necessary.

As we switch from zooming out to zooming in, the sense of freedom from daydreaming must shift to feelings of accountability and determination. You often see members of teams trying to break new ground being in different states and unable to understand why they're arguing – 'just let me think!'. As Clements suggests, 'disruptive thinking is the sweet spot in human decision-making which both evaluates and understands a situation, whilst coming up with creative solutions'.

Consultants Martin Reeves and Jack Fuller propose some interesting techniques to help us see differently. For example, they suggest that you go to meetings on a project that you're *not* expected to attend. I've tried this and realised there's a completely different mental model at work to the ones I'm leading or supposed to be participating in. Not only has it shed new light on the problems I need to solve, but my creativity has also increased significantly because my thinking isn't so governed by an existing frame of 'rules'. Now, I often try to adopt an *imagined* position of being in the wrong meeting, even when I'm not, to gain that fresh perspective.

Because we are so wedded to our mental models, changing frames can be difficult. One effective way of letting go of these attachments is play. Play allows us to explore analogies. 'Our business model is like a factory. . . imagine if it was more like a theme park, or hospital, or farm, what would that look like?' Play allows us to experiment, fail, and be imperfect with these mental models. It allows us to recognise that our existing mental model *isn't* the reality that it seems and that we can create multiple models.

ARE YOU THINKING OR SEEING?

Amy Herman helps specialists, who depend on their ability to see things clearly, improve their visual intelligence. She's worked with crime scene detectives, Navy Seals units, and the intelligence community to increase their ability to notice what others don't by making order out of chaos. It starts by asking them to step out of their visual comfort zone. By taking her clients to art galleries, not their usual or preferred habitat, Herman immediately changes their environment and therefore what they're looking at.

Herman told me, 'These people's experience and talent have combined into a highly attuned sense of pattern recognition. The challenge is to prevent it from becoming *patterns of expectation*. Every sense becomes prone to habitualisation, and the visual success strategies of a forensic detective, for example, are no different. When we're unable to notice fully, performance drops off'.

In one exercise, she asks her clients to study two paintings and compare them. Mostly, their first reaction is 'they have nothing in common', so she leaves, encouraging them to spend time discussing similarities and differences, to look for details and nuances. 'It doesn't matter that it's art, or a battlefield map, you're still looking at visual data. What this exercise does is engage different parts of their brain to make visual assessments. When they encounter something that is analogous to this in their day job, because of neural plasticity, they now have additional mental processing routes to draw upon'.

'We live in a subjective world, where too often we're shutting down debate based on biases and assumptions that are simply not true. What I'm doing is using art to clean our visual slate, by seeing things more clearly'. In another exercise, she uses three paintings of US presidents to make the point. First, she asks them to compare a painting of George Washington and a photograph of Abraham Lincoln. 'People typically tell me what they *know* rather than what they *see* – for example, "Lincoln looks exhausted" because they assume he's just been through the civil war'.

'This has nothing to do with what they're seeing; it is what they're thinking. Incredibly, I rarely get anyone noticing the most obvious difference – that one's an oil painting and the other a photograph'. Then she reveals a painting of Barak Obama and the room transforms – some smile, some look really unhappy, crossing their arms or rolling their eyes. She asks them, what's changed? 'What's changed is that everyone now has skin in the game – they've all lived through two administrations of Obama and their biases have kicked in. They stopped looking because all they can do is think'.

What Herman's exercises achieve is to help people become more aware of confusing what they think with what they see. 'If you consider a situation where a leader recognizes their business has a major problem and calls their team together, the first thing they should do is ask people to discuss *what they see* happening. That rarely happens; they dive straight into *what they think about*. She uses a provocative exercise using two nude female studies to illustrate the point. 'One of the women is morbidly obese but no one ever wants to talk about it. Today we have so many difficult topics that we need to openly discuss, but we fear sharing what we think. If we got into the habit of saying what we see instead, we could move faster forward'.

How are the frames you hold up to the world allowing you to discern, disregard, or discount what's happening?

CHAPTER 7

METACOGNITION – STRATEGIC SELF-AWARENESS

As the human brain evolved and the cortex grew to be able to create memories, learn and interpret information, new forms of self-awareness started to come on stream. One that helps us observe and think diagnostically is called metacognition. It's our truly remarkable ability to think about *how* we think. It sits at the apex of our sensing systems, letting us question ourselves, appreciate how we learn, and observe the world through others' eyes. The most significant benefit it accords us is the ability to compare our first- and third-person perspectives, enabling us to challenge our assumptions and therefore doubt our existing beliefs.

Think of how you continuously switch between these perspectives as you present ideas to colleagues wanting their feedback. At your best, you're able to hold multiple vantage points;

maintaining a belief in your proposal at the same time as seeing how it's being received and understood by your teammates. As you toggle back and forth, you're able to explore how their perspective could make your proposal stronger or more accessible.

Metacognition comes in implicit and explicit forms. Implicit metacognition allows us to process vast amounts of data about the world without overloading our finite attention and conscious memory. For example, without being aware, you're taking in your colleagues' body language and the unspoken communication between them. In doing so, you can effortlessly incorporate the knowledge, motivation, and intent of others to enable co-operative action. Explicit metacognition allows you to reflect on your implicit understanding, and rationalise your interpretations, judgements, and behaviour to yourself and others. In this case, you're able to acknowledge that one of your ideas is lacking concrete detail and is too abstract and needs further clarification. At the same time, you're calculating how these changes will improve the chances of the proposal being signed off by senior management. Implicit and explicit metacognition allow us to track uncertainty and monitor our internal states and actions. Together, they enable us to engage in *recursive thinking*, where we place problems within problems to unlock insights into situations where we can only see symptoms but not root causes.

One of the world's leading metacognition experts is Stephen Fleming. He believes that metacognition evolved to help us solve inverse problems, like the Amazon delivery example earlier – where, despite having incomplete information, we can make educated guesses without being tied down to having to have a rational explanation.

One of the valuable insights of Fleming and others' research is being able to quantify our metacognition accuracy – the extent to which our evaluations of being right or wrong turn out to be correct.

Within this research, the *experience of doubt* is the most significant contribution metacognition adds to our understanding of judgement. Doubt is vital in our ability to challenge our assumptions about ourselves, the environment, and if others see the world the way we do. We also use this information to hold the balance between our needs and the confidence we feel about something. For example, we might know our argument or position is weak, but in a given situation we may need to fake confidence. Think of bluffing a bad hand in poker. This allows us to separate the confidence we're feeling internally and projecting externally.

Together with the neurologist Rimona Weil, Fleming set out to find what makes one person's metacognition better than another's. They took as inspiration the work of Joseph Hart who, at Stanford University in the 1960s, conducted the first rigorous metacognition judgement studies.[1] He devised a set of tasks to investigate the *feeling* of knowing, by tracking participants' confidence and doubt in their performance on various cognitive challenges.

Fleming and Weil conducted similar cognitive tests[2] to quantify metacognition, then, in a second stage, the same people had their brains scanned using MRI. This showed that people who had greater metacognition had more grey matter in the frontal pole of the pre-frontal cortex of the brain and greater white matter integrity in the bundles of fibres surrounding the area. These results[3,4] have subsequently been repeated in other neuroscience laboratories around the world.

Participants with better metacognitive sensitivity tend to have higher confidence when they're right and lower confidence when they're wrong, in other words, they make better predictions in the face of uncertainty. One of the most interesting findings was confirmatory evidence of the independence of intelligence and self-awareness. Whilst the intelligence of the participants was a reliable predictor of their ability to perform the tasks – they got more answers right – it was *unrelated* to their metacognitive sensitivity; knowing when they were wrong.

Increased metacognitive sensitivity means we're more alert to our cognitive biases – our mental shortcuts, the over-reliance on previous experiences, or where we use proxies for knowledge in situations that we can't access or comprehend. Better metacognition can help us challenge ourselves to over-ride illusionary beliefs and the effect psychologists call overclaiming. The Dunning–Kruger[5] effect describes the cognitive error where we believe ourselves to be more knowledgeable than we really are. In one study,[6] participants over-rate their knowledge, at times asserting an understanding of ideas, events, and people that do not exist and cannot be known. In addition to the psychological reasons that individuals overclaim – for example, narcissism is a reliable predictor – scientists are trying to pull apart the cognitive processes at work. For example, overclaiming may be the result of a memory default where people believe that everything they encounter is familiar to them. Metacognitive sensitivity enables us to better doubt ourselves and over-ride these errors.

Like the corneas in our eyes becoming inflexible and unable to accurately refract light in later life, our intelligence can also become rigid as we mature, unless we actively continue to challenge our thinking. In a study[7] of over 3,600 managers across roles and industries, leaders significantly overvalued their skills, including emotional intelligence, trustworthiness, and leadership (compared with others' assessments of them) relative to lower levels of management. The researchers found that most types of self-reflection failed to improve this situation as they led to self-referential rumination – the unproductive churning over negative feelings – and formulating self-justifying arguments to shore up their existing beliefs.

In an age of deep and rapid transformation, mental inflexibility will leave us with beliefs, values, and opinions that are out of step with new realities. Fleming found that low metacognition was one of the best predictors of those holding dogmatic views; people unwilling to re-evaluate their beliefs in the light of new information. Together with Max Rollwage, Fleming[8] conducted simple cognitive tasks amongst participants with radical views on both ends of the political spectrum. The tasks were unrelated to their political, religious, or social views. Compared with the general population, radicals showed reduced insight into the accuracy of their choices and less sensitivity to post-decision evidence that they were wrong, indicating a generic resistance to reflection and revaluation following mistakes. Again, remembering that IQ and metacognition are separate mechanisms helps us to understand that intelligent people holding irrational beliefs is not an oxymoron.

This insight is critical in finding the right leaders to navigate uncertainty. Hiring for raw intelligence alone may result in a plateau being reached, when their IQ becomes insufficient to meet the complexity of the problems they face. For example, asking candidates to reflect and rate their performances on tests and challenges, as the British Civil Service does, finds bright people who also know their own minds better.

IMPROVING METACOGNITION

Can metacognition be improved? Fleming believes so. A growing body of research is showing that meditation rapidly increases participants' metacognitive sensitivity.[9] In simple cognitive tests, Fleming has shown that within two weeks of meditative training for 20 minutes a day, metacognitive sensitivity is heighted, and participants become more open-minded and reflective in their decision-making.

Emilie Thienot is a performance psychologist who has worked in the British, Australian, and French elite sport systems. I got to know her when she was supporting the British Sailing Teams in the run-up to the Rio Olympics in 2016. One of her aims was to understand how she could improve the focus of individuals and teams, particularly when they made mistakes, got distracted, or became emotionally triggered.[10] She found that mindfulness was a highly effective metacognitive strategy for improving cognitive flexibility in the volatile situations that high performance entails. The more the athletes she worked with practiced mindfulness, the more able they were to recognise and observe their emotional responses and when they lost focus. Simple practices such as mindful breathing, body scans, mindful teeth brushing, and stretching were able to be integrated into everyday life without additional time being needed. A key element is the ability to develop 'acceptance' skills, for example, that you've been triggered by a teammate making a mistake, and then build refocusing skills switching from the distractor to the task. Bryony Shaw, who won Britain's first Olympic medal for windsurfing, credits Thienot's approach in helping her to 'develop a high level of adaptability and acceptance, while encouraging a clarity in my decision-making'.

One of the empowering aspects of recognising that metacognition is not IQ is its potential to help students improve their academic accomplishments. Metacognition is fast becoming a popular subject in educational research because it points to the gap students often have between what they know and what they think they know. If a student has good metacognitive judgement, then their prediction of how well they will do in a test and their performance will be a close match – a perfect correlation would have a value of 1. Several studies show[11] that students' accuracy in predicting their performance is, on average, quite poor, closer to 0.27.

Carolina Kuepper-Tetzel, a cognitive psychologist who specialises in learning, looks at ways in which students can improve their metacognition to boost their learning performance. She explains: 'Students will base the decision on what, when, and for how long to study on their metacognition. Students may stop studying when in fact the material has not yet been fully comprehended or may waste time going over material that has already been mastered'.[12]

By asking students to read a passage and then either write a summary of the text immediately, or do the same thing after a break, or write no summary, they found a significant variance in performance.[13] Those writing the immediate summary gave a prediction accuracy of 0.3 of how well they would later recall the information. Those who took the break were on average above 0.6. The control participants were around the same as the immediate note takers – in other words, average. By delaying writing the summary, the researchers believe it increases the students' metacognitive accuracy because they're not relying on the short-term memory effect – 'I know this'. It encourages them to see the information more strategically and identify what they do and don't understand.

CHAPTER 8

HOW TO BUILD A MINDSET

Your mindset is perhaps your most precious mental asset, potentially even more valuable than the knowledge, experience, and wisdom you've acquired over the course of your life. Because, regardless of how smart and experienced you are, if your mindset is unsuited for the goals you're pursuing, you risk being blindsided by new realities. And, your mindsets aren't fixed; they can be built and evolved at every stage of your life.

We developed the process of building and strengthening mindsets through decades of applying scientific research to the real-world challenges facing high performers in many areas, ranging from elite athletes and entrepreneurs in start-ups to leaders and their teams in global organisations.

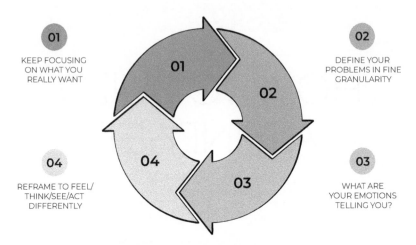

FIGURE 8.1 How to build a mindset
Source: Jean Gomes

1. WHAT DO YOU *REALLY* WANT?

The process of building a mindset starts by exploring perhaps the hardest question we can ask ourselves – 'what do I *really* want from my life?'. The *really* part of this question is key. It's not the expedient, quick-fix answer, but what the *true* self wants. In most situations, our immediate response is far from this; more shaped by our unseen assumptions, the expectations of others, habit, history, or context. To successfully build a mindset, the driving force must be a deep sense of purpose, a why for what we're doing. Answering the question pushes us into uncertainty, which is why we avoid it. When we ask teams what they *really* want to achieve, they often smile and shrug their shoulders as if to say, 'we don't know, we're just doing what we're expected to do'.

One way of getting to the answer is to zoom right out and see what we might gain from embracing our 'endgame' – how will we look back at our life at 80 or 90, from the perspective of having no regrets? Most of us put off thinking about the final stages of life, but it offers us a powerful perspective on the present. It challenges us to shift out of reactivity and think more about who we are and what we really want. By working on this question, we create a 'why' that sets us a commitment to the future. This also enables us to recognise that commitment and motivation are very different things. By pulling them apart, when we commit to a goal, we can accept that our motivation will ebb and flow during its pursuit. This allows us permission to reset when we struggle or fail, rather than give up.

A consequence of how we might have adapted to rising demands – to accept the negative normal – is that we have become numb to the costs of our choices. This prevents us from seeing and owning those costs because we focus on input rather than outcome. If you think of a team that's working incredibly hard but failing to innovate or make a step change in sales performance, the root cause is typically that they are focused on inputs rather than outcomes. Another way of thinking about this is that they have made a set of assumptions that what they're doing is all they can do to achieve their targets. An individual in a similar situation who is over-indexing on work, but neglecting their wellbeing, may similarly be blinded because they are focusing on the input. 'I'm working as hard as I can – there are no more hours in the day'.

In breaking the link between cause and effect, the team or individual has traded away their power to influence the outcome. Defining what we *really* want – staying with the question long enough for it to yield valuable insights and answers – begins our journey, where we can be more honest with ourselves about the gap between what we're currently doing and what we need to do in the future. As we focus with greater intent on this gap, we might start to become more aware of how our value seems to be tied up in preserving the status quo.

Our value, after all, is at its core our sense of safety. When threats to our safety materialise, we default to creating self-justifying stories to preserve our sense of security, which range from denial to aggression. These negative emotions drive a form of thinking that produces an argument to externalise responsibility for how we feel, pushing us into a victim mindset. This often stalls the development of a mindset from the onset of trying.

'Will eating these foods really make me healthier in old age?', 'Will investing time with this team really pay off when I have so much work to do for myself?', 'Will doing this exercise routine now really matter to me in 30 years' time?'. The dismissive answer is no. 'How could you know?'. But if we ask ourselves what we *really* want, what does our future self want, the answer is clearly YES! This is where we need to keep thinking about the arguments we're making to ourselves for maintaining things as they are. I suggest you start writing them down and think about what your 80-year-old self would say about them.

So, as you commit to building any mindset, keep coming back to this first question – what do you *really* want? It will keep you anchored in purpose and honesty.

2. WHAT ARE YOU SOLVING FOR?

Having become clearer about the 'why', the next step is to rethink the 'what' of your mindset; 'what are you solving for?'. One of the most effective ways of breaking down knowing/doing gaps in our lives is to become extremely granular in determining precisely what problems you need to solve to get what you want. The true value in this question is that it exposes how we often simply don't know. The gap between the goals and objectives we have set and what we're actually doing, driven by the comfort zone of habit and reactivity, is exposed when you ask people to convert their plans into a series of problems to solve. The first clue is that they typically find it frustratingly hard to do. But by redefining your goals and objectives as problems to solve in fine granularity, you start to recognise blind spots and under-acknowledged areas of risk and opportunity.

Here are the starter questions that we've found help to define what we're solving for in building a mindset within organisations (See Figure 8.2):

STRATEGIC

What outcomes are we creating and for which stakeholders?

Will this really deliver against our desired strategic outcomes?

How might it fall short?

What resources, systems, and processes are necessary to encourage and enable this?

LEADERSHIP

What changes in leadership focus and activity will signal this is a priority?

Where should accountability and autonomy for solving this sit?

How will leaders need to change their relationship with their teams to make this happen?

BEHAVIOURAL

What behaviours are required to solve this problem?

What current behaviors will prevent or slow us down in solving this problem?

MINDSET

What mindsets will enable this to be solved?

What mindsets currently stand in the way of this being solved?

What action needs to be taken to resolve this?

FIGURE 8.2 Mindset-building starter questions
Source: Jean Gomes

Taking strategic goals and breaking them down into problems to solve helps us to recognise where our focus may be missing. We may be trying to achieve a goal by solving just one part of the challenge. A team trying to innovate, but with just technical experts, will narrow down too quickly on building the product, without asking the right customer, commercial, and operational questions in parallel. Attempting to change our lifestyle, say becoming more focused on our loved ones, isn't simply about finding the time, but also how to be present. The real problem is how to deal with our interior set of competing commitments, so that we're truly there with them, not distracted by the mental and emotional pull of work.

Often the problems that we need to identify and solve are hidden to us in a blind spot created by our strengths overused. Someone who is incredibly determined can slip into becoming overwhelming or uncompromising, so the problem they need to solve might be how to balance their grit with empathy. One of the breakthroughs we helped the Performance Directorate team at UK Sport to achieve was to see how their undeniably incredible talent and success had a shadow. This was a team which, amongst numerous achievements, had done what no one else had ever accomplished – improving the medal haul in the Rio Olympics after the home advantage in London 2012. In reviewing their goals, considering the team's strengths overused, it became apparent that many of the problems they needed to solve involved balancing their expertise, drive, and positivity. These created a shadow that left other parts of their organisation, and their stakeholders, the sports they oversaw, sometimes feeling diminished and judged. This jolted the team, one of the best I've ever encountered, to work on a new set of problems that involved nurturing balancing qualities of listening, humility, and patience, and investing time in new ways to build their stakeholder relationships.

3. WHAT ARE YOUR FEELINGS TELLING YOU?

When we start to move out of a comfort zone and try something new or different, we usually experience a physical or emotional response. Paying attention to these feelings is incredibly useful, because they are an invaluable source of information about what's really going on.

Ask yourself:

What am I feeling trying to solve these problems?

How is what I'm feeling influencing my mindset?

What are my emotions *telling* me about what's going on?

For example, Sam, who is trying to build a mindset around renewal, finds that at night he is drawn to watching TV instead of doing some stretches, having a bath, and reading a book to wind down for a good sleep. As he sits in front of the TV, an old habit, his new commitment to greater self-awareness means that he starts to recognise that he's constantly multi-tasking, looking at his iPad the whole time and frequently switching channels. What is that telling him?

The habit of TV watching is borne out of his assumption that it will provide renewal. Occasionally it does when he's watching something he really enjoys and is not too tired to really engage. But with more awareness, Sam comes to see that much of the time, as evidenced by his multi-tasking, what he's *actually* feeling is low-level boredom and anxiety. Those feelings drive him to search for something to fill the hole – social media and email – but also, the urge to go to the fridge and eat something even though he's not hungry. Some nights this can result in 300–400 calories he doesn't want, need, or even enjoy. By becoming clearer about how he's feeling, Sam becomes more determined to try something different because his current habit is clearly not meeting his renewal needs.

Maya leads the tax planning division of a global accounting firm responsible for over 4,000 people. She wants to build a mindset to lead more innovation and growth as competitive pressures continue to erode profitability. Her initial attempts to learn about how other firms are managing to balance short-term performance and growth seem fruitless as she never has enough time or energy to gain more than a superficial knowledge, so she hands down the responsibility to various individuals and teams to figure out what to do. Like Maya, these teams are also overwhelmed by immediate demands and struggle to find the capacity to take on the challenge. They work long hours and weekends to meet expectations and present a series of recommendations for innovative new services and suggestions for business model innovation.

When they present the proposals, Maya seems initially receptive but progressively becomes more critical and defensive about their proposals. She questions the fit the new services would have with the firm's existing business model. She demands evidence that untested and emerging technologies will deliver revenue. If she paused for a moment to step into the team's shoes and ask how she might be able to answer these questions, things would look different. However, uncertainty and status emotions are running the show – anxiety, defensiveness, and isolation have created a closed and distracted mindset. The teams leave feeling bruised, devalued, and resentful. The cycle repeats itself over several months until Maya convinces herself that these people and the culture make innovation impossible.

One evening, at a networking event, Maya starts talking to Satish, the head of growth at a large law firm. She recounts her experiences and asks how he's managed to succeed. Satish, it seems, has been on a similar journey. Previously, he was a highly successful operations director at a Magic Circle law firm. When he was given the job of setting up innovation teams to automate workflows and case research, he quickly found himself running up against huge resistance from partners reluctant to divert resources or focus onto his work. He was operating in a state of constant fear and defensiveness and within two years, he left to find a safer haven. Perhaps counterintuitively, that experience led him to take on another innovation role. In speaking to others in similar situations he found most were going through the same experiences. That is, until a recruiter suggested he talk to Marco, who set up the growth lab at one of the world's leading management consultancies.

Marco didn't pull any punches and pointed out that the reason why Satish and the people he had talked to were failing was that they had adopted a victim mindset, which meant they weren't exerting maximum control and influence over the things they had the power to change. Satish started to justify his experience and Marco stopped him mid-sentence. 'You're repeating the script that reinforces the mindset. The first mistake leaders make, is that they delegate the incredibly hard task of discovering and validating new problems and solutions and then don't like those ideas when they get presented back to them because they challenge the status quo mindset they have. They need to be on the field alongside their teams understanding from customers, start-ups and others what's going on'. Satish took this advice and made a condition of accepting the new role that the CEO and their team spent three hours a week working with him to stay in the loop. Four years later, he successfully delivered one of the biggest digital transformations witnessed in the legal world.

4. REFRAME TO FEEL/THINK/SEE/ACT DIFFERENTLY

Having become more aware of what our emotions are telling us, the final step is to reframe the situation to give us more options and therefore greater opportunities to take control over the situation.

In the case of Sam, he starts to reframe his evenings differently. His current frame is that TV is a good way to decompress. It doesn't ask anything of him, so he can get renewal passively. Having come to the realisation that this is often not the case, because it leaves him feeling agitated and to his surprise bored and restless, he becomes determined to reframe the last hour before bed as the priming stage for 7.5 hours of great sleep. In this priming hour, he stretches out his back, shoulders, and legs; has a shower, reads for 10 minutes, and then listens to a guided mediation on a timer. He finds that this becomes increasingly successful and over 80% of the time he sleeps well, feeling at least a 7/10 in terms of energy when he gets up. The more he does it, the more he looks forward to it. Having become more attuned to what his emotions are telling him, Sam's able to know when he will enjoy TV and when his wellbeing needs are better met by his sleep-priming approach.

In the case of Maya, the meeting with Satish represents a turning point in how she looks at the world. Satish agrees to mentor her, and their conversations frequently centre on what her feelings and emotions are telling her about what is happening and the frames she is holding up. These conversations unlock motivation and determination to lean into the hard parts of the problems she faces. She starts to break down the problems she needs to solve into different categories of risk and uncertainty, so she can better assess the ideas of her teams and secure support from partners. In a culture where failure is not tolerated or acknowledged, Maya finds the frame of experimental-driven learning lowers the threshold of resistance to failed tests and opens senior people's minds to new possibilities. She recognises that adopting new frames gives her more mental space and helps her to metabolise the negative physical experience of uncertainty emotions more quickly.

TWO KEYS TO STRENGTHENING SELF-AWARENESS

There are two complementary ways to extend and strengthen the multi-dimensional self-awareness that builds our mindsets. The *first* is strengthening our metacognition – the surveillance form of awareness that enables us to *think about* how we see, think, and feel. It directs our attention and *intellectual* processes to assess:

- What is our body telling us about our resourcing needs?
- What are our emotions signalling in terms of our core human needs being met?
- How are we feeling about what we're feeling?
- What assumptions underly our beliefs?
- What are we seeing and how does that information influence our choices?

The *second* form of inner knowing can be gained from meditation and mindfulness practices that train our attention on *perceptual experience* rather than *intellectual interpretation*; in other words, noticing vs thinking. To some this distinction may seem too abstract or even non-rational, but please persevere as it offers one of the most powerful sets of tools in building our mindset. They provide a proven and practical means of exploring our inner space, gathering knowledge from our internal senses, and strengthening the self-awareness regions of our brains. They are as old as humanity and likely to have arisen when our consciousness was deeply immersed with nature, so perhaps that's why they tap into the deepest parts of our minds.

Many people we talk to have had a short-lived attempt at meditation or mindfulness and gained little perceived value, or dismissed it out of hand as 'not being for them' or even 'new age drivel'. Interestingly, for decades, many of the most successful senior executives, some very well known, that we've worked with quietly used these techniques to clear their minds and gain greater psychological freedom. Even today, as firms roll out mindfulness classes to tackle mental health problems, there's still considerable resistance to doing something that feels the opposite of work, or of questionable value.

Evidence that mindfulness promotes objective wellbeing is growing. Studies show that some forms of mindfulness calm our bodies[1] and reduce inflammatory responses. Others can energise the brain's metabolism.[2] Ivana Buric conducted a review[3] of 18 mindfulness studies where gene expression changes were measured. Although this is a small number, overall, they 'indicate that the practices are associated with a downregulation of nuclear factor kappa B pathway; this is the opposite of the effects of chronic stress on gene expression and suggests that practices may lead to a reduced risk of inflammation-related diseases'.

A team led by Justin J. Polcari has been studying[4] the underlying mechanisms that result in the positive effects mindfulness has on the hypertension-related illnesses that affect 1.1 billion around the world. Using brain imaging, participants practicing mindfulness showed increased interoception and decreased depressive symptoms compared to controls.

Since the late 1990s, psychologist Amishi P. Jha has been refining experiments that test participants' ability to sustain their attention on tasks in a range of circumstances including under stress. In her extensive trials, mindfulness significantly increases the ability to lessen mind wandering and stay on task. Additionally, attentional brain structures appear to be strengthened. Whilst there is much work needed to validate the causal mechanisms at work (and there's necessary scepticism at play[5]), it appears that mindfulness practices offer some of the most effective means of strengthening the underlying apparatuses of our mindset.

CHAPTER 9

MINDSET-BUILDING EXPERIMENTS

Here are a few very simple experiments you can start immediately to strengthen your mindset. Rather than seeing these practices as commitments, I'm suggesting you simply become curious and try them to see what happens. Don't look at poor results as failure, but as the means to ask new questions – for example, 'why might it not have worked?', 'what happens if I try in different circumstances?'.

High achievers tend to write off small gains as inconsequential, seeking instead silver bullets to gain big wins fast. That's not how your mindset works. These small gains add up to huge culminative effects over time. For me, the body scan exercise yielded little at first, but over time, the practice gave me tremendous insight and perspective. A 30-minute walking meeting each day results in up to 4,000 calories used every month. Over time, six minutes of focused breathing a day might sustain your energy and help you sleep better.

THE BODY SCAN

The moment you wake up, before thoughts flood into your mind, spend a minute focusing your attention on your body – noticing how you feel. Start at the top of your head and linger for 5–10 seconds on your forehead, throat, heart, stomach, groin, thighs, knees, shins, and feet.

When you start thinking about the day ahead, given how your body feels, how resourced are you? This helps you prevent misreading your feelings and emotions. It places you in greater control.

MEASURE YOUR INTEROCEPTIVE ACCURACY

Use a heart rate measuring app on your phone or use a heart rate monitor (e.g. Fitbit, Garmin, Apple Watch, etc.) to record your heart rate. Simultaneously, close your eyes and for a minute estimate how many times your heart beats. Compare the difference. Do this once a week to see if other techniques such as the body scan or breathing exercises are improving your sensitivity. Measure the percentage gap between estimated and real heart rate, and how it changes over time.

KEEP A PERSONAL ASSUMPTION LOG

Start a personal assumption log to test your assumptions about your beliefs – rate your confidence in your assumptions and why. Experiment with factors in your life that you may have taken for granted, such as your relationships with your family, the course of your career, and the activities that you believe give you comfort and happiness.

WALKING MEETINGS

Walking meetings provide several benefits. Wellbeing – a 30-minute walk equals 3–4,000 steps (100–200 calories). Doing it every day quickly adds up to a significant fitness contribution. Walking meetings increase divergent (creative) thinking. They make difficult conversations easier (less eye contact and more open thinking). After 20 minutes, endorphins are released, reducing stress and making you feel happier. After a walk, your problem-solving ability increases. After 30 minutes, brain-derived neurotrophic factor (BDNF) increases, a protein that improves brain health.[1,2]

Look at where you can have walking meetings virtually. Schedule check-ins and progress meetings where everyone is walking individually. For one-to-one meetings, plan a 20- to 40-minute route – discussing the problem on the way out, exploring and agreeing the solution on the way back. Take a small notepad and pen to capture anything you might need for later.

SWITCHING ON DIVERGENT THINKING

Divergent thinking is the ability to see the big picture and develop creative solutions to complex problems. One way of priming the brain to switch into the divergent thinking mode is to train it using bi-stable images – images that can be seen in two mutually exclusive ways. In this case, a cube facing up to the right or down to the left. By increasing our ability to switch between the different ways of seeing the cube, we activate a region of the brain, the anterior cingulate cortex, that notices conflict and mobilises mental mechanisms to reconcile it.

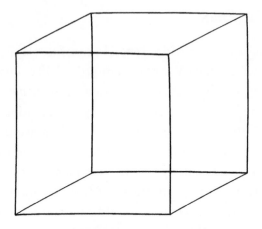

FIGURE 9.1   The cube
Source: Laukkonen, R. and Tangen, J., 2017. Can observing a Necker cube make you more insightful? Consciousness and Cognition, 48, pp.198–211.

Take a few moments to see both and see how easily you switch between them. Researchers found that, on average, people could switch between the two cubes 12 times in a minute. The more times test subjects could do it, the better it turns out they were at divergent thinking and non-linear idea generation.

Practice for one minute, twice a day – most people can double the switches in a week. Don't stop, repeated practice is a useful means of switching on divergent thinking and building the brain structures that support it.

FOCUSED BREATHING

Two minutes of focused breathing three times a day will cumulatively give you significant health benefits and short-term performance gains. Paying singular attention to the breath going in through your nose and out through your mouth switches on the parasympathetic nervous system responsible for reducing stress hormones and quickly putting the body into recovery mode. Closing the eyes switches off cognitive functions, giving you mental recovery.

Find somewhere you won't feel self-conscious about closing your eyes. Spend 10 seconds getting your body into a comfortable position with your feet flat on the floor, your lower back supported, and your neck in a neutral position. Take two or three deep breaths to the base of your stomach. Then spend two minutes focusing on your breathing, in through the nose, out through the mouth. If you lose concentration, let go of what you're thinking about and refocus on the breathing.

HAVE A DOUBTFUL 30 MINUTES

One of the functions of our metacognition (our ability to think about thinking) is to doubt our beliefs and feelings of certainty. The stronger our metacognition, the better we are at eliminating bias and awareness blind spots. A 'doubtful 30 minutes' once a week could help you become more aware of what's holding you back.

Set aside 30 minutes at the end of the week to reflect on decisions where you are doubtful the right choice has been made, where you don't understand important information, or whether the intent between you and someone else isn't clear and healthy. Write down where the doubt lies, specifically what the reason for this is, and what you want to do about it.

SPEND TIME WITH PEOPLE UNLIKE YOU

Spending time with people unlike us (ethnicity, social, worldview, values) helps us to gain new perspectives on ourselves and the world. It's common to feel vulnerable with others we don't understand or share common ground with. Embracing this vulnerability is the first step in building an open mindset.

Identify people in the organisation who are very different from you. Ask them to spend 60 minutes with you in their environment, showing you what their world looks like, what they do, the challenges they face, their motivations and aspirations. Don't solve, just be curious and open. Notice how this makes you feel and what you learn.

EMOTIONAL JUDGEMENT

When we experience negative emotions, it's an error signal that a core emotional need in us isn't being met. This is helpful to understand because it allows us to interpret our emotions differently. Instead of seeing negative emotions as being the result of something or somebody doing things to us and then telling ourselves disempowering stories, we can get to a new, more accurate interpretation. Use the chart on the following page to consider what your emotions are telling you, (See Figure 9.2).

RETHINKING CONFLICT

When we experience setbacks, conflict, and uncertainty, we often over-focus on our emotional reactions, leading to periods of rumination that create negative interpretations of situations and a narrowing of the options available to us. The next time you face a situation that provokes these feelings, focus on your physical reactions first. Stay with feelings of elevated heart rate, fatigue, and jitteriness. Recognise that these just tell you that your body is mobilising resources for uncertainty, not anything more. When we defer judgement until these feelings subside, we

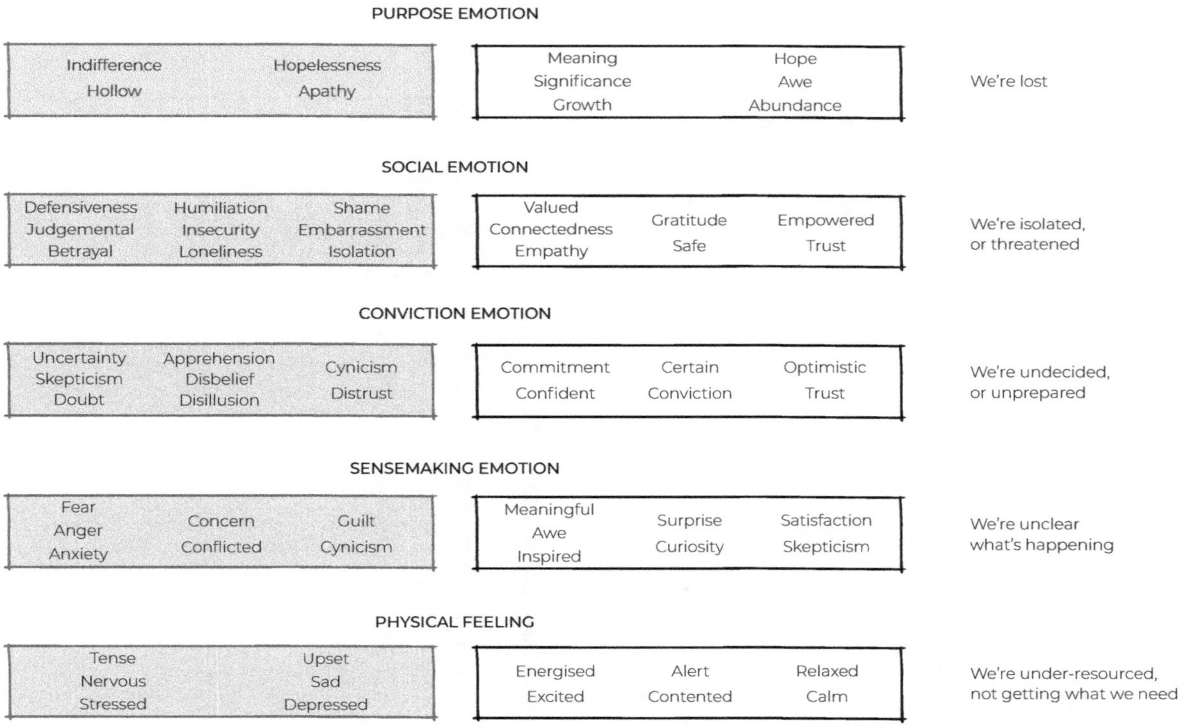

PURPOSE EMOTION

| Indifference, Hollow | Hopelessness, Apathy | | Meaning, Significance, Growth | Hope, Awe, Abundance | We're lost |

SOCIAL EMOTION

| Defensiveness, Judgemental, Betrayal | Humiliation, Insecurity, Loneliness | Shame, Embarrassment, Isolation | Valued, Connectedness, Empathy | Gratitude, Safe | Empowered, Trust | We're isolated, or threatened |

CONVICTION EMOTION

| Uncertainty, Skepticism, Doubt | Apprehension, Disbelief, Disillusion | Cynicism, Distrust | Commitment, Confident | Certain, Conviction | Optimistic, Trust | We're undecided, or unprepared |

SENSEMAKING EMOTION

| Fear, Anger, Anxiety | Guilt, Cynicism | Meaningful, Awe, Inspired | Surprise, Curiosity | Satisfaction, Skepticism | We're unclear what's happening |

PHYSICAL FEELING

| Tense, Nervous, Stressed | Upset, Sad, Depressed | Energised, Excited | Alert, Contented | Relaxed, Calm | We're under-resourced, not getting what we need |

FIGURE 9.2 What are your emotions telling you?
Source: Jean Gomes

101

find that either our fears were unwarranted, or that we are now better resourced to deal with matters.

IMPROVING EMOTIONAL GRANULARITY

We construct emotions to make sense of the world. Most people have a limited emotional vocabulary, which means they are unable to describe what their emotions are signalling to them.

Once a day, look through a magazine or newspaper and focus on images that have an emotional quality – write down two to three words to describe how the image made you feel. Notice if the words truly represent what the images make you feel. I suggest getting a copy of the *Emotional Thesaurus* by Angela Ackerman and Becca Puglisi[3] as a useful tool in expanding your emotional expression.

MEET YOUR 80-YEAR-OLD SELF

Close your eyes and imagine meeting your 80-year-old self – what advice do they have for you about how you're currently living your life? Write down, 'what must change?'.

PART 2

BUILDING MINDSETS FOR THE FUTURE OF WORK AND LIFE

CHAPTER 10

A MORE HUMAN MINDSET – ALIVE, OPEN, AND CONNECTED

The foundational mindset on which we build all others we call *more human*. It connects us to our mind and body, unlocking the interior resources that fuel our wellbeing. Building this mindset starts by deepening our self-awareness so we can see more clearly the gap between what we know, what we need, and what we do. The critical assumption we're continuously testing is that we're getting what we need to feel alive, open, and connected.

By strengthening the feedback loops that attune us to our needs, healthier behaviours become our choices more naturally, rather than attempting to rely on willpower or habit-building

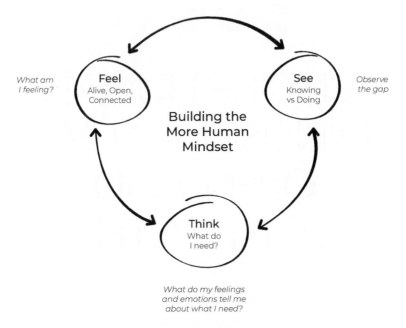

FIGURE 10.1 Building the 'more human' mindset
Source: Jean Gomes

techniques – both of which we have found to be ineffective sustainable strategies.

We have an extraordinary capacity to dissociate ourselves from our most fundamental needs. We often describe and treat our bodies as if they were machines that we own and that will function regardless of what we do to them. At the point of his imminent death from cancer, the public intellectual, Christopher Hitchens, reflected that 'I don't have a body, I am a body'.

We live in an era of abundant information and resources to support our wellbeing. At the same time, lifestyle diseases, mental health, and social problems are soaring. We are wealthier, more informed, *and* unhappier and unhealthier. Many of the people we talk to feel their wellbeing is *competing with*, rather than fuelling, work, parenting, friendship, and other important aspects of their lives. I believe that in our efforts to adopt, and our struggle to maintain, healthier behaviours, we're starting from the wrong place.

In employing numerous habit-building techniques with thousands of people over a decade, we found that fewer than 15% adopted lasting behaviours. When the behaviour is singular, easily defined, and manageable in a known situation, habit formation stands a reasonable chance of success. For example, in giving up coffee in the afternoon, designing a habit is reasonably straightforward. You become more aware of things that *cue* the existing habit, for example, associating coffee with a certain time or situation, or other people offering you a coffee, and you try to either eliminate the cues or find new ways to respond to them by replacing with a non-caffeinated alternative. You become attuned to the craving that *not* having the coffee creates, and how having the alternative easily to hand reduces that feeling. Over time, the alternative becomes the habit.

The reality, however, is that most wellbeing behaviours are generally complex and multi-dimensional. Going to the gym, for example, is not one behaviour but dozens. And success is far from just about automating behaviours. How you feel emotionally, mentally, or socially can motivate you going, give you a get-out clause, or mean you give up mid-point. Planning, contingencies for travel, packing kit, getting there, what to do in the session, eating around the session, what's going on in your mind as you train – these are just some of the many components that a simple habit routine quickly becomes overwhelmed by. Attempting to design and implement a habit for such a diversity of mental, emotional, and physical activities may work if you have the focus and support of an elite athlete, but it's totally unrealistic for the rest of us. We need a more fundamental approach that creates the general conditions for success.

THE NEGATIVE NORMAL

Creating a more human mindset means confronting how we've negatively adapted to a changing world where it feels natural to *not* get what you need – what we term living a *negative normal* existence.

The periods in my life when this has happened – overworking, not looking after my body, relationships, or passions – have not generally been because of crisis, but instead originated from a good place. From a state of being healthy, balanced, and fulfilled, I traded on whatever forms of capacity I had to get things done, particularly through intense periods of travel, without refuelling myself effectively.

Over time I became numb to the feedback loops that were telling me I was tired all the time, full, frustrated, or shutting others out. I'm not talking about a breakdown or catastrophe, just that I wasn't fully enjoying my whole life, I was just getting through parts of it. Somewhere in the back of my mind, I sensed the mounting health and relational debt I was accruing. Ironically, operating in the performance world for decades, I knew the answers about what I should be doing – about what to eat, how to exercise, how to practice appreciation, meditation, and the dozens of other ways in which I could feel fully fuelled.

After perhaps three or four weeks of feeling overweight, fatigued, apathetic, or guilty, I would double down and get back into the practices that I knew would restore me, but eventually slip back into another negative normal trough as demand intensified at work or home. My fitness tracker stalked the wellbeing rollercoaster, nagging me about my sleep. My electronic scales similarly made it unavoidable to see the consequences of too much comfort eating. I noticed the energy and resolve I'd get from understanding something new about how to sleep, exercise, eat, or perform better. But still the pattern seemed to be unbreakable.

THE AGE OF AUTOPILOT

One of the most challenging aspects of responding positively to a fast-changing situation is that most of our adaptation happens unconsciously. This is particularly the case when we're trying to multi-task and have little time for reflection. We simply don't have enough reserves of energy to pay attention to what's happening inside us. When I started work, success seemed to reward managers with more freedom to think. Today, the prize is more work. Less time to think, reflect and be self-aware.

Think back to a period in your life when things changed quickly. It might have been a positive occasion – a new relationship, job, or the birth of a child. It might have been a period of uncertainty, poor health, or suffering a loss. When you look back, you may come to see that the beliefs, behaviours, and priorities you held then may look very different now. But, like most of us, I'm guessing you weren't so aware that those events would come to change your future.

We let the autopilot take over and although we may not notice things moving, our mind and body adapt rapidly to unconsciously automate new responses. Soon, those responses become normal. For example, when you overwork it becomes 'natural' to feel weary all the time, react in frustration with people you care about, or continuously be distracted instead of focused.

A consequence of this is that we feel we're not in control of our lives; things just happen to us and we are reacting in the only possible way we can. If we allow that feeling to become too dominant, it ultimately means we retain even less control; thinking 'what's the point?'. It can produce such negative feelings that, over time for some people, it triggers symptoms of anxiety and depression.

So, what's the answer? It starts by coming to terms with our new realities – seeing and accepting things we can and can't influence; and consciously recognising where we may be negatively adapting to a changing world. Once we can gain clearer sight of this picture, we can start taking back control by asking 'what do I *really* want?'.

Technology has blurred, or even eliminated, the lines that were once in place between work and the rest of our lives. If we're honest, the idea of work–life balance is based on a world that no longer exists for most people. In the past, natural boundaries and transitions between work and home enabled renewal and refocus. You left your computer at work. Mobile phones weren't a mobile office. A train journey to work was mostly about reading the paper, daydreaming, or having a doze. Life was more sequential as a result and that created a sense of predictability and, therefore, control.

The increased adoption of remote working, accelerated by the pandemic, has further challenged our boundaries and transitions, colliding together work and home in ways we've never experienced before. Of course, technology has also provided tremendous new benefits for individuals, communities, and businesses. But it has also created a new blended environment – a new reality that is non-linear. This has a profound impact on our brains, designed to help us survive, by reducing uncertainty and conserving energy. Today's non-linear world is, instead, constantly challenging our brain with new stimuli, which can quickly flip it into overload and overwhelm.

DEPLETED, DEFENSIVE, DISCONNECTED

In our research, unchecked, this hyperstimulation results in three reactive cycles dominating our lives that leave us depleted, defensive, and disconnected from the things that matter most to us. The first reactive cycle that forms the negative normal is *depletion*. When we eat poorly, move infrequently, take no recovery during the day, and deprioritise sleep, we drain the most foundational aspect of our wellbeing – our physical capacity. Over time, this has immediate and long-term consequences – we feel frequently fatigued, it adversely affects our emotions and relationships, and in the long term it undermines our health.

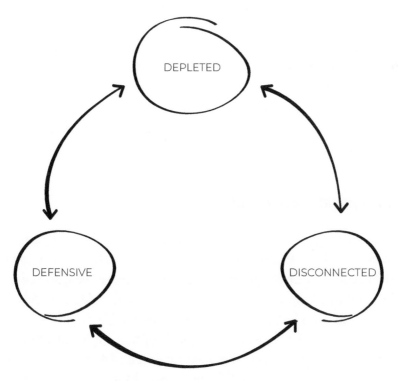

FIGURE 10.2   The reactive cycles
Source: Jean Gomes

Being physically depleted increases the likelihood that under demand, our mindset becomes defensive. When we feel under-resourced to rise to the challenges we face in any part of our lives, we tend to feel some form of fear, anger, and defensiveness – 'this is not my fault', or judgement – 'this is your fault'. Or powerlessness, 'this is not fair or reasonable'.

The more we feel these emotions, the more closed, rigid, and irrational our thinking becomes, making us blinkered and short-sighted; we are likely to adopt fight or flight behaviours to cope. In other words, we accept a *defensive* mindset. At the core of this is a sense of resentfulness that we're not getting what we need. This is corrosive over time.

When we're depleted and defensive, it undermines our personal and professional relationships, and we risk becoming disconnected from the people, priorities, and passions that matter most to us. An important means of positively breaking these cycles is increased self-awareness and taking the time to consciously reflect on who you are and what you want. Every time we achieve this, we disrupt survival patterns and connect with our most fundamental wellbeing needs.

THE KNOWING–DOING GAP

We asked a group of 300 middle managers[1] to assess their familiarity with 30 wellbeing strategies, ranging from how to get good sleep, eat healthily, regulate their emotions, listen well, and combat multi-tasking at work. On average, they assessed themselves as having a high degree of practical knowledge about 76% of the strategies. When asked how much of that knowledge translated into habits or regular behaviour, it fell to 43%. When they were asked to get feedback from others observing those behaviours (from their line reports and family), it plummeted to 22%.

The knowing–doing gap is where we confuse having an intellectual understanding of a subject – for example, knowing that good-quality sleep increases our ability to learn, problem solve, or metabolise sugar efficiently – with what we're doing to act on that knowledge. Closing the distance between what we know and what we're doing relies on being more honest about the gaps. When we do this and start to focus on action, we're taking a big step towards building a mindset of deep accountability.

However, observing and accepting a knowing–doing gap can often be painful, particularly when we recognise that it's the cause of unhappiness, frustration, or a sense of unfulfilled potential. We've identified five ways in which we can fall into the knowing–doing gap and what we can do to eliminate it.

NUMBNESS

One effect of our ability to adapt is that we quickly become numb to the consequences of the negative normal and our natural feedback loops stop influencing healthy behaviour. We don't go to bed when we feel tired. We don't stop eating when we're full. We don't take a break when we can't concentrate. Think back to Part 1 and the importance of the information our body is giving us and how it shapes our judgement. It's not surprising then that when we numb out this information we feel somewhat detached from reality. This is where focusing attention on our affect – our physical feeling – can offer so much value.

As we've reviewed in earlier chapters, affect is produced by the signals from within our body that gauge our total use of energy. By increasing our attention and therefore increasing our sensitivity to what we're feeling physically, we strengthen the feedback that encourages wellbeing behaviours more naturally.

INSUFFICIENT PURPOSE

The best way to start operationalising new behaviours, or restart ones that have languished, is to establish or strengthen their purpose by defining clearly *why* they matter to us. Plainly articulating why a specific behaviour *feels* important sustains action in the uncomfortable phase of adoption until our life starts to mould around new ways of being and working. In time, the natural process of habit formation kicks in, reducing the amount of willpower we need to perform these behaviours. They then become innately part of us.

Creating the *why* means moving our attention past the short term – 'I need to lose weight for my holiday'. Or, 'I need to sleep tonight to be on good form for tomorrow's important meeting'. There's nothing wrong in trying to optimise for the immediate, but it's unlikely to tackle the knowing–doing gap. This means spending time asking:

Why is this behaviour important to fulfilling my long-term goals?

Why is the adoption of this behaviour important to the people who matter most to me?

What's the cost of *not* putting this behaviour into practice in the long term?

BREAKING THE INTELLIGENCE TRAP

A third approach to seeing the knowing–doing gap involves letting go of being right or smart, or even being the expert. When our sense of value is tied up in knowing something, it's easy to fall prey to feeling defensive about how we're living that knowledge. Knowledge can therefore be part of the problem.

Psychology researchers have shown a consistent phenomenon, called the intelligence trap, where greater expertise and knowledge, ironically, often leads to a tendency to believe we're acting upon something we know. A repeated pattern in the thousands of coaching conversations we've had on this topic suggests that talking and learning about, or even teaching others, can easily *seem* like doing. Perhaps a greater fluency or familiarity with a topic creates a sense that we've got it covered. You can risk shirking accountability by saying to yourself – 'yeah. . . I know that!'.

The antidote to the intelligence trap is humility. If we shift our mindset from knowing to discovery, we can acknowledge the limits of our knowledge and expertise and embrace what we *don't* know. For example, we can say to ourselves, 'I know why sleep is important, but I haven't yet figured out how to get more of it'.

RECOGNISING RUMINATION

Our fourth path to closing the knowing–doing gap is to accept that thinking about a behaviour we've failed to adopt may make us feel bad about ourselves, causing feelings of defensiveness, shame, guilt, powerlessness, or anger. When this happens, negative emotions can sometimes roll around in our heads for what can feel like an eternity – what's called rumination. Not only is this draining, it's not a state where rational solutions form. So, how we can use rumination productively?

Start by recognising that what we're experiencing is mostly feelings rather than thoughts. Our goal is to shift our brain's attention to thinking. We can do this by asking ourselves some accountability questions.

- *What am I feeling?* Always start with how the body is feeling. As we've reviewed, our emotional interpretation isn't always accurate when we're feeling in a negative mindset. However, when we're not deep in rumination, naming emotions becomes a way of interpreting them more clearly. If we see that rather than being angry, we're in fact fearful, or wronged when we're really feeling indignant at being caught out, our way of thinking about what to do will be very different.

- *Why am I feeling this?* Here, start with our responsibility in this situation rather than going immediately to finding fault and blame in others. Where have we let go of our accountability to ourselves or others?
- *What can I do right now?* What first step can we take to put ourselves in control? Is it understanding more about what's happening, is it planning, learning, or doing?

HOW CAN YOU FIND THE BLIND SPOT?

Our last positively disruptive self-awareness practice is to ask ourselves, 'what's the blind spot that enables the gap to exist?'. These gaps are built on untested assumptions and beliefs that form a narrative we tell ourselves, and perhaps others, to justify them.

It often helps to write down, in a short paragraph, what's the story we tell ourselves about why we can't, for example, spend enough time with our children, prioritise coaching our team, or learning about new ideas? The first thing we're looking for are the statements that describe ourselves as a victim in the situation – 'it's been done to me' – 'I don't have enough time' or 'it's simply not possible'. Anything that makes us feel defensive, or powerless when we imagine explaining it to someone we care about, is more than likely to be a cluster of untested assumptions rather than facts.

Next, think about 'what are the facts?'. For example, *when I think about exercising, it's always at the end of the day when*

I'm tired and hungry. Finally, ask yourself, what's a new story you could tell yourself, without negating those facts – one that places you in greater control and gives you what you need. For example, *I'm not prioritising exercise because I'm trying to do it at a time of day that isn't practical for me.*

What we're doing here is testing, and hopefully busting, the assumptions of what's possible in our life by telling ourselves a better story. *I'll exercise first thing in the morning, when I have fewer competing commitments.* By identifying knowing–doing gaps, we can see the blind spots that stand in the way of the life we want.

AN EXPERIMENT IN BUILDING RADICAL SELF-AWARENESS

The negative normal takes hold when we lose sight of, and connection to, the foundational importance of our physical capacity. When we become numb, we sense a deep feeling of resentment that we're not resourced adequately to face the world. As we undermine accountability to ourselves, we break the link between our purpose and goals and the means to achieve them.

What the new science of self-awareness and mindset was suggesting to me was that there might be a different way to tackle the negative reactive cycles that we fall into in the face of rising demands. Instead of focusing on a series of behavioural habits, what if I grounded myself in a deeper form of awareness about what my body was telling me? The pandemic seemed to offer the opportunity to run a personal experiment that I'd been meaning to do for a few years. Based on what I'd been learning about how interoceptive sensitivity could strengthen mindset, I was fascinated to see what would happen if I sustained my focus on it.

My hypothesis was that by focusing my attention first thing in the morning on my physical feelings using a body scan, I would be able to increase my motivation towards healthier behaviour over time.

I committed to a daily practice of a body scan in the first 30–60 seconds of waking up. This simply involved running my mind's eye from the top of my head to my toes, lingering for a few seconds on my forehead, eyes, throat, chest, stomach, groin, thighs, knees, shins, feet, and toes, and asking myself, 'what do I feel?'. Anyone familiar with meditation will see the parallel with the practice of focusing on the chakras, but I was less interested in unblocking energy, and more in seeing if sustained awareness on the state of my body budget might help me be healthier.

It may seem obvious in hindsight, but intensively tracking cause and effect over time is a powerful motivator for change. In me, it broke past intellectual understanding and created an *embodied* sense of what was happening to me.

On those mornings when I'd had poor sleep, or one glass of wine too many the night before, sampling how my body was doing started to create a very powerful shift in me. When I spoke about this with Lisa Feldman Barrett, she pointed out how easy it is to confuse physical feelings with emotions, and therefore predictions and interpretations about the day ahead.

'If you wake up feeling physically crappy and step into the shower, the emotions you construct about the day ahead will all be based on deficient', she told me. Simply the act of separating physical feeling and emotion gives you the ability to reframe in that instant. It's not that the day ahead looks that bad, it's that you're under-resourced. This enables you to consider several important things. First, it places responsibility back on you. It allows you to think differently about that meeting, that task or relationship. It also allows you to monitor, and come to terms with, patterns in your behaviour that have contributed to being in this state in the first place. I found that it gave me a profound sense of being more in control, regardless of my physical state being positive or not. I started to experience my inner world increasing.

Let me take you through what I did, measured, and learnt through 16 months of experimentation. Apart from a three-week period around my father's death, I managed to capture data every day (bar one) and measure my interoceptive accuracy once a week. Over 441 days, I captured readings across 11 aspects of my behaviour and mindset (see Figure 10.3).

I'm not claiming scientific validity in either the experiment or the results. The goal was to subjectively explore what would happen when I concentrated awareness on how my physical state was influencing other aspects of my wellbeing. The first data point was to capture what my state of affect was each morning. I used the affective circumplex to describe: 1, unpleasant high arousal; 2, unpleasant low arousal; 3, neutrality; 4, pleasant low positive arousal; and 5, pleasant high positive arousal. I'd describe state 5 as buzzing with energy at the prospect of the day ahead.

Using the body-scan technique, I found I was able to quickly tune into how my body budget was doing. Did I feel relaxed? Was I refreshed or drained? Calm or tense? Energised or distressed? Was anything hurting or inflamed? In under a minute, it became possible to gather a lot of insight into what was happening within my body and gain a reading on how resourced I was to face the day.

Over time, on days when the reading was negative, instead of feeling victim, my thoughts turned to 'what do I need now and in the longer term?'. Perhaps I needed to be less hard on myself that day and catch myself becoming demanding of others because I was feeling tense, not because the situation required it. It also taught me to be watchful of the emotion of irrational certainty that feelings of depletion can heighten.

FACTORS	PRACTICE	MEASUREMENT
AFFECT	Body scan (awareness)	Which zone on the affective circumplex? 5 – pleasant/high/low arousal 1 – unpleasant/high/low arousal
INTEROCEPTION	Heart rate assessment	Weekly measure using pulse meter
DIET	Tracking consumption	1 (processed foods, overeating, high carbs, etc.), 3 (neutral), 5 (optimal)
ALCOHOL	Reflecting on relationships at work, home, and friendships	How many units? 1 (above limit), 3 (recommended limit), 5 (under limit or none)
SOCIAL	2 Breathing exercises, 3 times a day	1 – conflict 3 – neutral 5 – positive
RECOVERY	Bedtime wind down – stretching, no electronics, reading, meditation	1 – no 5 – yes
EXERCISE	6am exercise sessions and general levels of activity (including Fitbit data)	1 – <5K steps 3 – >5-10K steps or 10K+ steps including 10 minutes of threshold exercise 5 – 10K+ steps including 20 mins of exercise session or 10K+ steps including 45 mins+ exercise session
SLEEP	Capturing Fitbit data	1 – <6 hours 3 – 7.15 hours 5 – >1.5 hours of deep sleep
FEELING	Defensive vs open	1 – defensive 5 – open
THINKING	Churn vs creative problem-solving	1 – churn 3 – neutral 5 – assumption busting and creative problem-solving
SEEING	Inside out vs outside in	1 – living in my head 5 – seeing how others see things

FIGURE 10.3 An experiment in radical self-awareness
Source: Jean Gomes

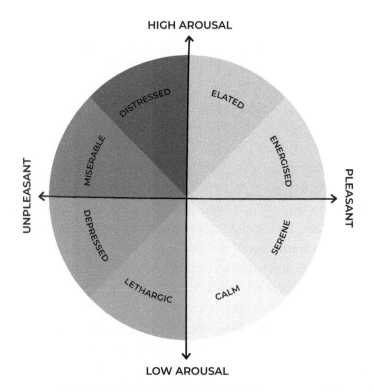

FIGURE 10.4 The affective circumplex
Source: Adapted from James Russel's circumflex model of affect (1980).

Once a week, I measured my interoception by using a pulse meter. I set a one-minute timer on my phone and estimated how many beats my heart made. At the end, I looked at the reading on the pulse meter to see the difference between my estimate and the actual heart rate. I plugged the data into the ratio[2] used by Hugo Critchley to calculate interoceptive accuracy. I soon recognised that this might not be very accurate as the end reading might not reflect variations over the minute, so I got my wife to read my pulse to get a better real score. I saw this as the baseline data to compare all other readings against. How would my mindset and these physical and social factors track alongside my ability to tune in accurately with my body?

I also kept a simple spreadsheet at the end of each day to record a high-level qualitative assessment of my diet, alcohol consumption, social interactions, recovery practices during the day – such as taking a short walk or mindful breathing, the amount of exercise and movement, and quality and quantity of sleep. I spent a couple of minutes to summarise where my mindset netted out in the day. Emotionally, had the day largely been dominated by open-minded feelings or defensive ones? For thinking, had I been able to bust assumptions and engage in creative problem-solving (which is of paramount importance to my work), or was I experiencing distraction, churn, or rumination? What frame was I holding up? Had I been living in my head, inside-out, or managed to flex my perception, outside-in, and see how others were seeing and feeling about things?

On average, this took me around 5–10 minutes each evening and afforded me the additional benefits[3,4] that mindful journaling brings in helping the brain reconcile memory, reduce stress, and boost the immune system. On my spreadsheet, I also kept a brief note of any events that might – for better or worse – influence the tracking data, such as achievements, holidays, intensive activity, conflict, or setbacks.

So, what happened? The data can't fully describe the experience. In the first few weeks, between March and April 2020, I started to feel a greater sense of mental space and the capacity to think more openly. This was while Covid was creating huge uncertainty both for our family's personal safety and that of our team, business, and clients. The biggest impact was that I could feel a growing level of sensitivity to my physical, emotional, and mental needs developing. As time progressed, I felt more drawn towards the behaviours that I knew would improve my mood, rather than having to employ willpower and discipline to do them. This was a very different feeling from when one fails to maintain a habit, like not brushing your teeth. There, you feel the absence of something and feel compelled to complete the action. This was a deeper sensation of need. Regardless of how well or poorly I was resourced, it guided me more instinctively to what I knew would help me.

My average interoception accuracy scores consistently improved (Figure 10.5), except for the period around my father's

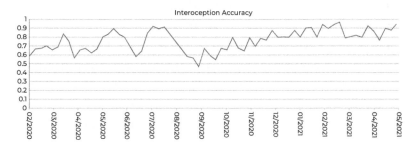

FIGURE 10.5   Weekly interoception accuracy readings

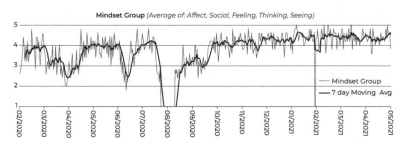

FIGURE 10.6   Daily mindset readings (affect, social, emotion, thinking, seeing)

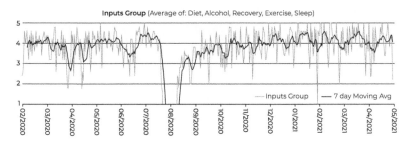

FIGURE 10.7   Daily input scores (diet, alcohol, recovery, exercise, sleep)
Source: Jean Gomes experimental data (Feb 2020–May 2021).

death and a few short-lived blips where exceptional periods of workload or conflict happened. From a low start of 0.585, by December 2020 my scores were consistently above 0.7, which is regarded as high accuracy.[5]

In practical terms, my awareness meant I was able to see the difference between negative affect and emotions and instinctively reframe my day. This strengthened feedback loop encouraged me to take better care of myself, particularly when I knew demand would be high, such as the week when I was running a global online conference with early starts and late finishes.

As the data built a more comprehensive picture over time, I could see the cause and effect of how not taking care of myself damped interoception, cutting off the vital feedback my mindset needed to course-correct in challenging situations. It's not that I don't still get overwhelmed by conflict, uncertainty, and demand, but I now have a stronger interior compass navigating me back faster and more effortlessly to an optimal balance.

CHAPTER 11

FUTURE NOW – THE ULTIMATE STRATEGIC MINDSET

For individuals, communities, and organisations, the biggest risk we take in an uncertain and non-linear world is to walk backwards into the future, extrapolating from the past, assuming that what was true yesterday will be true tomorrow. The *future now* mindset helps us to achieve that trickiest of all balancing acts; to hold the tension between the needs of today *and* tomorrow. It inspires us to feel open and curious and to bust the assumptions that short termism is our only option.

The frame we typically hold up to think about our future, however, is the *past present*, where historical assumptions and beliefs define what we see as possible or desirable. In most

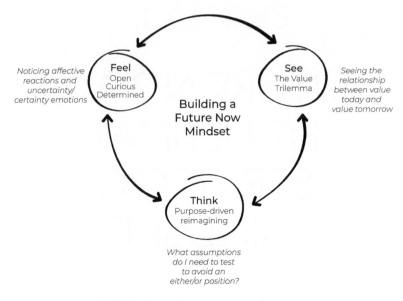

FIGURE 11.1 The 'future now' mindset
Source: Jean Gomes

mature organisations, the 'past present' mindset is deeply rooted in its goals, measures, values, processes, systems, structures, and habits.

For the individual, the future now mindset helps us see who we might become by embracing a non-linear path. For some, this is achieved with a side-hustle run in parallel with their career giving them future options, but also a wider perspective on the problems they currently face. A friend of mine, who runs a data science business and who studied mathematics and computer science, took up learning philosophy as he finds the questions have 'expanded my situational awareness and creativity. I wish I had done this decade ago'. Others build wider networks and diverse friendships, allowing them to tune into changes that are coming, preparing their mindset for adaptation.

For the organisation, it's the ultimate strategic mindset because it helps leaders to consider the question *how are we different?* in a new way. In the past, an organisation might have been able to hold onto the competitive advantage that a brilliant idea accorded it for 5–10 years, or even more. Today, the half-life of that advantage has reduced to 12 months as the world deconstructs, recreates, and improves ideas at lightning speed. Patents, money, and pace only go so far in extending the edge. Being able to balance creativity and pragmatism, today and tomorrow, *is* the new strategy.

For leaders, a future now mindset helps them to manage the balance between short- and long-term value creation and reduce the entropy that marks the decline of their organisation's vitality by:

Seeing a productive symbiosis between value today and value tomorrow rather than being competing commitments

Thinking constructively about the baseline assumptions that block future growth

Feeling open, curious, and determined to confront uncertainty and embrace disruption

THE ENTROPY PROBLEM

As the Nobel laureate, Ilya Prigogine, a specialist in thermodynamics, reflected, 'entropy is the price of systems' and so it seems enviable that most organisations pay the price, running out of energy as they mature. The management thinker, Ichak Adizes, neatly described the arc that organisations move through from birth to death in his description of the 'corporate

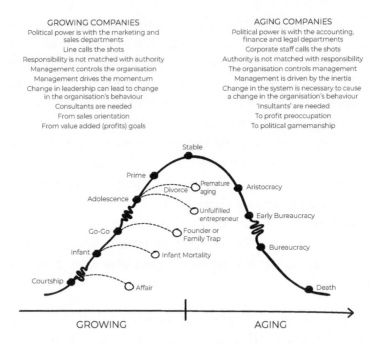

GROWING COMPANIES
Political power is with the marketing and sales departments
Line calls the shots
Responsibility is not matched with authority
Management controls the organisation
Management drives the momentum
Change in leadership can lead to change in the organisation's behaviour
Consultants are needed
From sales orientation
From value added (profits) goals

AGING COMPANIES
Political power is with the accounting, finance and legal departments
Corporate staff calls the shots
Authority is not matched with responsibility
The organisation controls management
Management is driven by the inertia
Change in the system is necessary to cause a change in the organisation's behaviour
'Insultants' are needed
To profit preoccupation
To political gamemanship

FIGURE 11.2 The corporate lifecycle, Adizes Institute 2022®[1]

lifecycle'[2] (see Figure 11.2). Avoiding this fate and maintaining organisational health, requires leaders to be acutely aware of building a future now mindset and culture, which maintains a constant balance between the needs of today and tomorrow.

Entropy, of course, isn't the only reason organisations wither and perish. They also fail to notice the market changes taking place, having become preoccupied with their own interests. In the 1940s, the economist Joseph Schumpeter coined the term 'creative destruction' to describe the process of new innovations rendering existing technologies, business models, and skills obsolete. Disruptors typically attack on three fronts – radically lowering established price expectations through new cost structures, delivering significant innovation in products and experiences for consumers, and breaking down incumbent defences and barriers to entry.

Since 2000, 52% of Fortune 500 companies have disappeared.[3] We are witnessing what Silicon Valley entrepreneur, Thomas Siebel,[4] describes as an 'era of mass extinction' for the conventional, analogue company. In the 1990s, Clayton Christensen built on Schumpeter's idea with 'disruptive innovation'. In essence, he described how the logic of established firms in overdrive (which is directed almost entirely towards incrementally perfecting existing offerings) becomes a liability as they ignore and dismiss the threats that start-ups and players in emerging markets pose to them until it's too late.

The power that digital technologies confer on start-ups and well-funded scale-ups means that incumbents are often shocked by their emergence. Peter Diamandis, founder of the X-Prize, which revitalised the private space sector – inspiring SpaceX, Blue Origin, and Virgin Galactic – points out that enterprises powered by digital technologies have a 'deceptive phase' where even exponential growth is largely invisible to their mature competitors because it comes from such a low base.

Finbarr Joy, who has led the digital transformation of dozens of global firms, told me that 'most Chief Financial Officers see technology simply as the means to continually reduce the cost of transactions with customers and increase the organisation's ability to sweat its assets. Everything is about return on investment and the short term. What they're missing is what's happening in the world. Disruptive adopters of digital technology are thinking about uncertainty differently. They are using it to forge new business models that can continuously adapt to market forces. In trying to de-risk technology adoption by assessing it as a quantifiable efficiency enabler, it only makes the traditional organisation more prone to future disruption'.

THE FATAL (BASELINE) ASSUMPTION

Corporate longevity is about fighting entropy, the natural tendency of any system to move to an increasing state of disorder. On average, our metabolisms fight entropy for around 80 years. Corporations' average ability to achieve this trick is much less and on the decline. Industries where the dominant player has held the top spot for more than five years have nearly halved in the last 20 years.[5] At the root of this decline is a deadly assumption buried deep in the mindset, culture, and systems of an organisation. Fighting organisational entropy means profoundly challenging the *baseline assumption* that what was relevant yesterday will be equally relevant and valuable tomorrow. . . plus 10%.

Many of today's corporations were built on the belief that one idea could be perfected, scaled, and extended over the course of many decades, and consequently provide a predictable career for its leaders. Growth came from incremental improvements to that idea, the refinement of the underpinning business model, and finding new adjacent market opportunities. The command and control, machine-like hierarchy matched the needs of that assumption.

Today, companies like Apple, Amazon, and Tencent are fighting entropy based on a very different assumption – that their value creation system is about producing a constant stream of new ideas and requires an organisation where more people are engaged in market foresight, imagination, and innovation. Much of their execution work is farmed out to a global set of specialist partners.

The machine model struggles to fight entropy in a fast-changing world, because focus, energy, and resources are directed predominantly at exploiting and preserving the model, rather than growing and evolving it. In the process, the most important human qualities that enable innovation and adaptation are dialled out of the system.

Few organisations retain the founding entrepreneurs and culture of their start-up phase. They are replaced with system builders and process managers, and the organisation progressively becomes more introverted and less sensitive to its environment, becoming engrossed in efficiency and financialisation. It then relies increasingly upon proxies for what's happening in its market rather than through direct experience with customers, new entrants, and even employees. The assumption is that more data leads to greater actionable insight. Christian Madsbjerg[6] points to the gap in understanding that this belief creates; 'our fixation with STEM-based knowledge erodes our sensitivity to the non-linear shifts that occur in all human behaviour and dulls our natural ability to extract qualitative information'.

Machine learning and the abstraction of big data goes wide, but it can't go deep. In the process, leaders create a thin, one-dimensional picture of the world. Understanding, imagination, and innovation go hand-in-hand. As these qualities become less valued, entropy increases. The research of Martin Reeves, a strategy consultant, shows that for every doubling in the size of an organisation, its growth potential, or vitality, reduces by 3%. A major reason for this, he suggests, is that as leaders build the efficient, predictable machine, imagination is lost from the cognitive repertoire of managers' problem-solving.

In the machine model, metrics, for example about customer needs, are often little to do with *real* customer problems (particularly future ones) and more about internally driven goals such as sales and production capacity. Another clue that the baseline assumption prevails is that metrics are mostly, if not all, lagging indicators of performance, only telling leaders what happened in the past. This blinds the organisation to what's *about* to happen, creating a rollercoaster of complacency when things are going well and panic when they're not. The reason is that these metrics have no predictive value.

Having seen this so many times, it made us wonder why leaders avoid leading indicators of performance and future competitiveness, which would seem an obvious way of building and maintaining a future now mindset. In hundreds of conversations with senior leaders to dig deep into their mindset, it became clear that a collective fatal assumption breeds a culture that values certainty over unknown and untested opportunities. At the same time, the capacity to reimagine what the organisation could become is so depleted at the expense of an over-reliance on operational excellence, leaders *don't want to know* about things that challenge their ignorance.

Even those who are solely tasked with innovation and growth frequently feel exposed and unsupported, believing that they are carrying a disproportionate risk on behalf of the organisation. The life of these roles is unsurprisingly short, often ending in mutual disappointment or worse. There's an undertone that the organisation is somehow doing these people a favour in allowing them to *play* with new stuff. Anyone who has seriously been in this position can tell you that nothing could be further from the truth. It highlights the parent–child relationship that's often at work between senior managers and innovation teams in a top-down hierarchy, highlighting the lack of transparent mutual accountabilities.

Leaders who don't have 'skin in the game' for value tomorrow, but expect others lower down the organisation to bear the risks, are again blinding themselves. If leaders aren't involved and accountable, they won't get into the detail or understand the differences between risk and uncertainty that an opportunity presents. Instead, they'll demand slick pitches that don't require too much of their precious attention and offer magical risk-free opportunities. This is the best culture to kill innovation and value for tomorrow. In fact, it goes further by reinforcing the complacency that the fatal assumption is valid.

THE VALUE TRILEMMA

The root of why organisations *really* become enfeebled and die lies in the fact that leaders have failed to see and take hold of their most fundamental responsibility for the organisation's value creation system. That duty is summed up in the 'value trilemma'.

Leaders must deliver *value today*, harnessing and optimising the organisation's existing opportunities, capabilities, and advantages. They also must create *value for tomorrow*, which requires market foresight, new ideas, technology and business model innovation, new skills, partnerships, and resources. Increasingly, it also means having a strong, compelling purpose – a *why* to

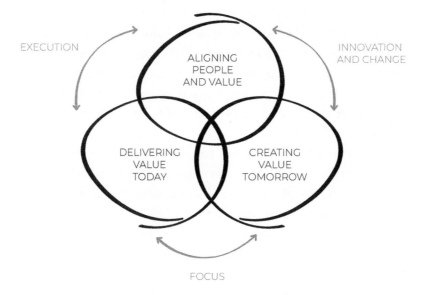

FIGURE 11.3 The value trilemma
Source: Jean Gomes

exist – that extends past defending value today. A sense of purpose to improve the world in some way pulls the organisation towards the future, attracting the best talent. It also gives stakeholders greater confidence in supporting leaders in long-term decisions around their vision. And leaders must *align people and value.*

Each of these value creation domains needs different mindset approaches. Trying to create value tomorrow with the execution mindset of value today is unlikely to achieve little more than spitting out variants of the past, or deprioritising innovation and growth so much that it becomes a trail of half-hearted failures.

The ability to stand back and see the relationship between the value domains is essential for the leader who wants to ensure their organisation's long-term viability isn't being compromised by over-focus on the immediate. The interplay between the domains represents the primary paradoxes and tensions in any enterprise. Between today and tomorrow is *strategic tension*, knowing where to calibrate the focus of time and resources between the two. The tension between value today and aligning people and value is the *execution challenge* – getting the most out of existing products, revenue streams, and people, but in the service of the big picture. The tension between value tomorrow and aligning people and value is the *reimagination, innovation, and change challenge.*

Creating organisations that can encompass short- and long-term performance is described as *organisational health* by McKinsey Partner, Brook Weddle.[7] In extensive research into the success factors of transformation, they acknowledge that mindset is perhaps the *most* important factor. 'The companies that did no work on diagnosing mindsets also never rated their change programmes as "extremely successful", whereas companies that took the time to identify deep-seated mindsets were *four times* more likely to rate their change programmes as successful'.[8]

Numerous studies highlight the positive impact on performance of adopting a long-term focus. For example, a study of over 600 US companies' investment, growth, and earnings management from 2001 to 2015[9] identified those with a long-term focus and compared their relative performance, after factoring in industry dynamics and company size. The results are compelling. The revenues of long-term focused companies grew cumulatively on average 47% more than the revenue of other firms, and with less volatility.

Cumulatively, the earnings of long-term firms grew 36% more on average over this period than those of other firms, and their economic profit grew 81% more than average. Interestingly, they spent almost 50% more on R&D than other companies and this continued throughout the financial crisis. Their market capitalisation also grew on average $7 billion more than that of other firms in the 14-year period. Their total return to shareholders was superior as well, with a 50% greater likelihood that they would be in the top decile or top quartile by 2014. Although long-term firms took bigger hits to their market capitalisation during the financial crisis than other firms, their share prices recovered more quickly afterwards.

Long-term firms added nearly 12,000 more jobs on average than other firms. Had all firms created as many jobs as the long-term ones, the US economy would have added more than five million additional jobs over this period. The researchers concluded that the potential value unlocked by companies taking a longer-term approach was worth more than $1 trillion in forgone US GDP over the previous decade.

We have huge pressing value trilemmas facing humanity, not least of which is the tension between maintaining today's fossil fuel-dependent socio-economic world vs tomorrow's carbon-free future. The key challenge is to move fast enough without incurring an unpalatable level of disruption.

The components of accelerating the shift are vision, innovation, and mindset-building.

THE PAST PRESENT ORGANISATION: 95/5 FOCUS

The most significant consequence of an organisation being defined by the *baseline assumption* – that value today will continue to be the foundation of future success – is of collective and unconscious short termism. In the last 20 years, a series of factors have driven the mindset of many senior leaders to ever shorter-term judgement. In a broad analysis of the economic impact of short termism, McKinsey developed the Corporate Horizon Index to analyse the investment, growth, and earnings quality of companies. It found that since it started tracking firms in 1999, there has been a steady rise in the number of S&P 500 companies adopting short-term strategies.

In an analysis[10] of Europe's largest 1,000 companies, the firms whose CEOs had the longest tenure, had the highest

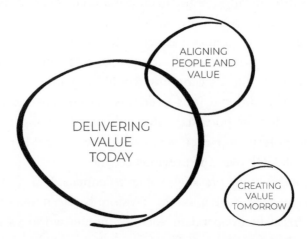

FIGURE 11.4   The *95/5* focus of the past organisation
Source: Jean Gomes

long-term performance. This was attributed to their ability to find the balance between strategic investments in growth and short-term performance. The leaders on the *Harvard Business Review*'s 2019 list of the world's best-performing CEOs held their jobs for an average of 15 years, more than twice the average tenure of an S&P 500 CEO.

For over 15 years, we've analysed the focus of hundreds of leadership teams using the value trilemma framework. In three-quarters of organisations we surveyed, the focus of the most senior leaders was *95% on value today and 5% on the future*. One executive joked with us, 'value tomorrow is a quarterly offsite for the leadership team to discuss things we never end up doing'. The analysis of Rajesh Chandy reinforces our research, concluding that bosses spend only 3–4% of their day thinking about long-term strategy.

Of course, it's not simply executives' assumptions that shape their focus. A study[11] by economists John Graham, Campbell Harvey, and Shiva Rajgopal of over 400 CFOs found that almost 80% knowingly forewent economic value (positive net present value projects) to meet short-term earnings benchmarks due to peer pressure from competitors and investors' expectations. A study[12] by FCLT Global, a research body committed to encouraging long-term investment in economic growth, found that 87% of new executives and directors feel pressured to demonstrate strong financial performance within two years or less.

External pressures are intense, particularly the need to be in countless regulatory mandated meetings that shorten our attention. As *The Economist* magazine[13] points out, 'the prospect of jail is a powerful attention-grabber' in narrowing one's focus. But the biggest supposed villain of the piece, at least for executives in publicly quoted corporations, is the quarterly drumbeat of reporting that purportedly drives short termism.

Whilst there's no disputing the reality of market expectation, is there another explanation for the myopic management of many organisations? For example, how many leaders have a playbook they keep rolling out that boosts earnings by cutting marketing expenses, postpones capital investment, or reduces productive head count? Or leadership teams who ditch long-term strategies entirely in favour of maximising short-term profits and returning precious corporate capital to shareholders in the form of massive and unwise stock buybacks?

How is it that organisations that manage both short- and long-term value creation resist the pressure to capitulate to immediacy and outperform those who don't?

Corporate governance specialists Charles Nathan and Kal Goldberg[14] point out that there is questionable evidence that responsibility for the short-termism trap that many firms find themselves in should be laid at the door of investors, and particularly activist investors demanding short-term results. Their analysis suggests that it's a story created from the 'natural defensive reaction by management against claims of corporate underperformance'. Over time, this story has been told and retold to 'become an article of commonly shared faith for which convincing factual support is not necessary'.

In fact, the long view of capital markets is one of moving money to younger firms with a greater focus on long-term investment. Today, the five largest US firms by market capitalisation[15] – Apple, Microsoft, Alphabet, Amazon, and Tesla – are all relatively young, tech- and innovation-intensive companies with long-term, purpose-driven strategies. In 2020, more than a quarter of the total capitalisation of US stock markets comprised tech companies, which were trading at high price-to-earnings ratios, demonstrating the market's willingness to back the future.

In our experience, short termism is generally the result of three factors:

- A binary approach to problem-solving – the prevalence of either/or thinking.
- An unwillingness to fix deep-seated problems.
- A lack of imaginative effort to create ideas that pull the organisation forward into the future.

Both/and problem-solving, 'how do we achieve perfor-mance *and* growth?', encourages leaders to get to root causes rather than tinkering with the symptoms. In a crisis, the pres-sure towards short termism is extreme and binary thinking is comforting, which is exactly the time when we most need to balance it with long-term vision. *What will we be left with after the crisis if all we do is survive?*

THE FUTURE NOW ORGANISATION

We describe those that balance value today and tomorrow more consciously as *future now* organisations. In Figure 11.6 we

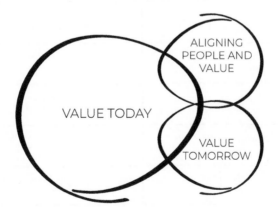

FIGURE 11.5 Future now organisations
Source: Jean Gomes

139

summarise the traits we've observed that are built from a mindset capable of holding the tension between today and tomorrow. Future now organisations run on an assumption that their existing value is always up for questioning. Whilst value today represents the largest focus of the organisation – around 70% – value tomorrow is a genuine priority in the schedule of leaders and their teams.

A future now organisation's problem-solving is guided by a long-term purpose, a North Star, that helps it to navigate uncharted territory. Leaders understand the difference between risk and uncertainty, which is often at the root of why the past present organisation doesn't see when to adapt and how to invest in the future. The future now organisation is an imagination machine, generating new ideas that can be rapidly tested in a

PAST PRESENT	FUTURE NOW
BASE LINE FALLACY The fatal assumption	ALWAYS DAY ONE The perpetual assumption
95/5 Immediacy addiction	70/30 Parsing risk & uncertainty
SHORT-TERM PLANS Survival motive	NORTH STAR Purpose motive
FEW IDEAS Cognitive inertia	ABUNDANCE Industrialise imagination
DEFENSIVE Outside in	OPEN Inside out
VALUE TODAY GROWTH ENGINE Drives the fatal assumption	VALUE TODAY AND VALUE TOMORROW GROWTH ENGINES Busts the fatal assumption
EXECUTION MINDSET Optimise	EXPERIMENTAL AND EXECUTION MINDSETS Optimise and discover

FIGURE 11.6 The past present vs future now mindset
Source: Jean Gomes

value tomorrow growth engine, complementing the value today performance engine. It remains sensitive to customers, trends, and the weak signals coming from the future, and harnesses rich qualitative information to drive adaptation. A mindset of *test and learn* allows teams to rapidly experiment, exploring new sources of value with the minimum of risk.

CREATING A SYMBIOSIS WITH THE FUTURE

In contrast to the past present organisation, value today and value tomorrow *are not* competing forces, but symbiotic ones (Figure 11.7). Leaders see value flowing between performance

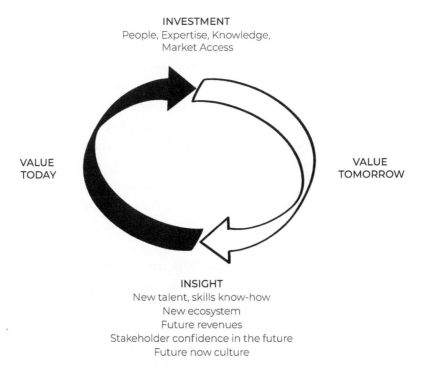

FIGURE 11.7   The symbiotic relationship between value today and
tomorrow in the future now organisation
Source: Jean Gomes

and growth engines, so they become healthily entwined. Value today feeds the future growth engine with capital, market access, and resources. Value tomorrow discovers future growth potential and feeds back vision and confidence for today's stakeholders and new ideas for how to optimise the value today performance system. Value tomorrow activities extend the organisation's capabilities and intelligence by harnessing a new ecosystem of crowds and communities, including start-ups and on-demand resources.

One of the biggest challenges in shifting to a future now focus is the dynamic allocation of resources. Most organisations struggle because an either/or battle gets played out. 'Either deliver short-term performance because we won't survive otherwise or invest in untested ideas that won't deliver revenue for years'.

Recasting an organisation's budgeting mindset is a crucial part of this shift. In the past present organisation, the budget process is one of the major blockers to innovation and future growth as it plays out as a defensive game with local teams shielding their resources. The future now organisation reframes the purpose of financial planning to be more about enabling customer outcomes, and prioritises where the greatest opportunities lie, rather than in risk and control, managing the politics of competition for scarce resources. As a result, the balance between short and long term can start to be factored into the financial community's thinking.

A clear strategic picture of quantified risks and bets, coupled with greater financial autonomy for business units, means the value trilemma starts to get managed at a much deeper level throughout the organisation. At the heart of this is a need for constant agility and flexibility. As we'll see in the next section, high-growth strategies need to be underpinned with an agile approach to funding. If growth assumptions can't be rapidly proven, money and people need to be quickly and dispassionately reallocated to something more promising. Pools of funds should be set aside for new opportunities that arise throughout the year. For example, in addition to making quarterly allocations to value tomorrow initiatives that are making the greatest progress against its strategic ambition, Google's managers can, at any time, finance new ideas.

Finance managers complement their traditional corporate skills with a venture capital approach, investing small amounts in internal start-up teams and using leading indicator metrics to manage risk and uncertainty through frequent check-ins. These feedback loops on investment performance allow leaders to make good decisions and for teams to take full responsibility for growth by linking their objectives and key results (OKRs) to financial metrics.

When David Cote, former chairman and CEO of Honeywell, took on the role, he challenged its leaders to rethink their comfort zone of short termism and lean into the paradoxes of the value trilemma. Under his tenure, Honeywell's market capitalisation grew from $20 billion to $120 billion over 16 years. He staunchly believes that to simultaneously achieve short- and long-term results, you need to banish 'intellectual laziness' and be more honest and transparent about financial controls – which to many leaders are a black box. One of Cote's principles is to invest in the future, but to keep fixed costs constant with growth. This forces the organisation to invest in the future, but not excessively. In Part 3, we'll look at how the industrial era company IMI built a value tomorrow growth engine to become a future now organisation.

BREAKING THE IMMEDIACY CYCLE

Nowhere is the tension in managing value today and tomorrow more keenly felt than in the lives of an organisation's senior leaders.

Their focus on the value trilemma directly equates to that of the organisation. A leader who has insufficient time to understand and learn how their market is changing won't be able to see the opportunities and threats shaping their future, even if their teams do. They won't be asking the right questions or spending time on creating an inspiring vision for the future. They won't be building or leveraging the network that will allow them to benefit from the abundance of external resources they could tap into. They won't be seeing the bigger picture.

Instead, they will be in a perpetual firefighting mode, feeling overwhelmed and defensive about what they're *not* doing. Either they embrace this as the only realistic option and apply the blinkers, or they feel a constant dissatisfaction that manifests itself in half-hearted attempts to innovate or transform.

The future now leader must transcend the either/or position and adopt a strategic mindset that embraces a 70/30 focus on today and tomorrow. At its simplest, this means averaging six days a month on using their minds differently, to experience, learn, reimagine, and create – mental states that seem ridiculously indulgent to the average time-poor executive. It means making some difficult choices about what you do and don't focus on.

In the case of Microsoft's founder, Bill Gates, he used to spend twice a year on *think weeks*, during which he would spend 18-hour days in a cabin in the woods reading and thinking about the future of the company. He regarded this time as an essential enabler of innovation.

Many of Microsoft's most important strategic shifts (the move to Windows, the pursuit of the internet) came immediately after a Gates think week.

You may not be able to manage to spend a couple of weeks a year thinking about the future in the woods, but baking it into everyday experience is vital to break the immediacy cycle.

Julian Birkinshaw and Jordan Cohen conducted a highly detailed study over three years of how senior managers spend their time.[16] It showed that knowledge workers spend an average of 41% of their day on discretionary work that offers little personal satisfaction and could be handled competently by others.

What's stopping them from getting this work off their plate to focus on higher-value activity? Part of it is habit, clinging to tasks that make us feel important and occupied, and part is that new work keeps piling up, preventing us from having the space to sit back and prune low-value activity. Birkinshaw and Cohen made a very simple change to these managers' schedules that saved them on average around eight hours a week – between 15% and 20% of the time. They asked participants to look at the next two weeks of their calendar and identify the activities that they could most easily get out of, either by not doing the activity, delegating it, or outsourcing it.

They were asked a series of questions to raise their awareness about the importance of the activities; for example, to consider 'how valuable is this activity to the firm?' and 'suppose you've been identified to lead a fast-track initiative and must assign some of your work to colleagues for three months. Would you drop, delegate, or keep this task?'.

They were asked to record this, most importantly to define what they were going to do with their freed-up time. This is important to reduce the emotional conflict and automatic habitual responses associated with giving up well-rehearsed patterns of activity. After two weeks, they were asked to review what had happened, particularly to question whether the purged activities found their way back into their schedule. Whilst not everyone was successful, for the majority they were able to cut screen time (email predominantly) by six hours a week and meeting time by two hours.

It's not just the length of time that we invest into the future that matters, but also the quality of thought that can be produced in these precious periods. Being able to intentionally harness convergent and divergent thinking is indispensable.

In numerous experiments, we've asked executives to block out the first 30–90 minutes of their day, at least once a week, so they can focus on high-value, long-term work without the distractions and demands that accumulate during the day. The rules are simple; they must be somewhere where they won't be interrupted, they know what work they will do and have the necessary components at hand (reports, data, tools, books, etc.), and crucially they can't do email beforehand. This last point is critical. For most of us, email is the first task of the day. It's a compulsive habit but one that defines our focus, the quality of our thinking, and the sense of control we have over our work.

What participants in these experiments find is that by harnessing their focus when it's at its clearest, they can make huge progress in a relatively short sprint. Their energy is at its highest peak in the day, and the feelings of being able to accomplish value tomorrow work gives them a sense of progress and intrinsic motivation. Think of it like this, two 90-minute sprints a week adds up to 12 hours of value tomorrow work a month that currently seems impossible for most leaders. We must just resist the lure of email a little.

HOW DOES IT *FEEL* TO BE A FUTURE NOW ORGANISATION?

How does it *feel* to be in a future now organisation? In a word, open. In a volatile market, the past present organisation oscillates between periods of fear-driven insecurity/defensiveness and relief/over-confidence having avoided threats or delivering a short-term goal. A defensive climate makes the future unsafe

DEFENSIVE	OPEN
Defends the status quo	The status quo is the platform for growth and evolution
Avoids threats to the status quo	Reframes threats as opportunities and problems to solve
Focuses on winning today	Winning today and tomorrow
We want our team to win	Our team focuses on helping other teams to win for the customer
Information is power	Collaboration makes us powerful
My value is in what I know	The real opportunity is in what I don't know
Talking to control the agenda	Listening and questioning with an open mind
Diluting energy by focusing on what we don't control	Focus 100% on what we do control
Builds self-justifying arguments to explain why we aren't embracing tough challenges	Having difficult conversations with compassion

FIGURE 11.8   Defensive vs open mindsets
Source: Jean Gomes

to discuss or work on, and encourages leaders and their teams to cling to a defensive mindset.

The future now organisation isn't immune to fear, anxieties, or insecurities. It's just that they are more open to acknowledging them and understanding what they can reveal. Leaders recognise these emotions as signs of core human needs not being met and major strategic decisions being avoided. This allows for a different type of deeper, more honest, and useful conversation to happen, and solutions are founded on a common appreciation of emotional connection.

Academics and strategic thinkers Julian Birkinshaw and Jonas Ridderstråle believe that given the acceleration of market change, it's not firms who have the best data and knowledge that win, it's those that develop the capacity for *decisive action* – 'the ability to address opportunities as they emerge, to experiment with new offerings and to make big bets when called for'. But to move in this way, you also need *emotional conviction* to avoid the drag of over-thinking or leaping wildly into the unknown. Emotional conviction is corporate emotional intelligence.

As they point out, the exponential rise in knowledge isn't possibly matched by what we can individually know. As Ridderstråle told me, 'As individuals our knowledge is growing at a gradual linear rate, but what we know at a societal level is growing at an exponential rate. So, there's a growing gap between *what I know* and *what we know*. Or to put it another way we're all becoming more stupid, relatively speaking. This means we can no longer trust individuals or small groups to make big decisions. The other assumption was that a more connected world would be a more predictable world where facts would rule. What the global economic crisis and Covid pandemic has showed us is that the more we can connect, the less we can predict. In a more complex world, where we individually know less, we are forced to believe more'.

ALWAYS DAY ONE: THE PERPETUAL ASSUMPTION

The future now organisation substitutes the unspoken baseline (and potentially lethal) assumption with an explicit alternative. The assumption that it's *always day one*. This is a powerful mindset shift that reclaims control and influence on the future. It is a core belief in the so-called unicorns – start-ups that have pivoted their way from nothing through uncertainty and achieved $1 billion valuations 10 times faster than traditional corporations. It's also a central tenant at Amazon.

Every so often, I watch the one-minute video[17] of Amazon founder, Jeff Bezos, at the 2017 all hands meeting where he answers the question from the audience, 'what does day two look like?'. As he reads out the question, there's a lot of nervous laughter and a palpable sense of the impending punchline; 'Day 2 is stasis. Followed by irrelevance. Followed by excruciating, painful decline. Followed by death'.

Silicon Valley insider Alex Kantrowitz suggests that, 'though it's tempting to read it as an order to work ceaselessly, its meaning runs deeper'.[18]

Bezos never wants his company to fall prey to the fatal assumption that what was valuable yesterday is right for its future. As he set out in his 1997 letter to shareholders,[19] 'we believe that a fundamental measure of our success will be the shareholder value we create over the long term. Because of our emphasis on the long term, we may make decisions and weigh trade-offs differently than some companies'.

Bezos wants Amazon to maintain a start-up culture, forever channelling former Intel CEO, Andy Grove's belief that 'only the paranoid survive'. Simple as it may seem, 'always day one' is a great example of a frame that allows us to see the future differently. It gives Amazon's people permission to question the assumptions they've made in the past. It allows new information in. It also changes how they feel about uncertainty and failure as they experiment.

As Amazon acknowledges, it's not for everyone, but it has created a culture where any employee can submit a new idea to be peer reviewed by experienced evaluators in the company to get funding. And importantly, decisions are seen as reversible when something new is learnt. It centres on predicting what customers want before they know they want it and resists proxies in whatever form for real customer feedback. This means allow-ing teams to embrace new trends before they are 'proven' to be relevant by someone else. It also means making 'high-velocity' decisions which may only be 70% right, instead of higher-quality decisions that take months or years to make.

70/30: KNOWING HOW TO DISTINGUISH RISK AND UNCERTAINTY

When confronted by their organisation's lack of innovation suc-cess and offered alternatives from the playbooks of exponen-tial growth organisations,[20] executives often react defensively with 'we're not Google'. This could be shorthand for 'we're not digital', 'we don't have hundreds of the world's smartest peo-ple hanging around to solve impossible problems', or 'we don't have millions to spare on moonshots'.

What it really means is, *we don't know.*

At the heart of this response is the knotty problem that executives in the past present organisation are inexperienced in distinguishing between the risk and uncertainty involved in creating value for tomorrow. A risk is something that can be assigned a probable percentage of happening. Uncertainty is where no such probability can be given. The economists John Kay and Mervyn King blame leaders in banks, investment firms, and governments for the 2008 global financial crisis because of their inability to understand the difference between risk and uncertainty. Something similar frequently happens amongst leadership teams when it comes to innovation.

When leaders spend little time on value tomorrow and they delegate what innovation efforts there are down the organi-sation with no personal involvement, they cut themselves off from the rich information and learning that would enable them to make better decisions. As the delegated work materialises, managers then tend to adopt an idealised persona of the entrepreneurs that they've absorbed from *Shark Tank* or *Dragon's Den*. Often these leaders have had *no* entrepreneurial or scaling experience, or useful reference points for their thinking – except everyone expects them to. Faced with this charade, they adopt the judger mindset which doesn't enable good assessments to be made and makes them and everyone else feel bad. Or they go with something that looks slick and convincing and roll the dice. The result, according to Stryber Analytics, is that less than 8% of ventures from corporate accelerators succeed in growing their revenues past $1 million sales within five years.

Research[21] on the mindset and behaviour of successful growth leaders found that they are '60% more likely to have a clear multiyear mandate to pursue growth initiatives, coupled with the autonomy to do so without having to show short-term results. They are 70% more likely to have multiple long-term bets rather than just a few'.

In looking at over 30 corporate incubators, we found that most – around 68% – were using a set of judging criteria based almost entirely on the company's existing rules for new projects and mergers and acquisitions. This means leaders get and give confusing signals about what they want from innovation. A past present frame prevents you from seeing what you're looking at in terms of potential, risk, and uncertainty, and asking the right questions.

DISCERNING FOUR HORIZONS OF OPPORTUNITY

In the last decade two books, *The Lean Start Up* and *Exponential Organisations*, persuaded traditional organisations to rethink their approach to new product development and adopt the start-up playbook. Together, as advisors, innovation coaches, and 'entrepreneurs in residence', we have led adoption of these tools to build growth engines in a diverse range of organisations across the tech, engineering, finance, and energy sectors.

However, exciting as these ideas are, they seldom lead to results in timeframes corporates find acceptable. Ralph Biggadike's research[22] on how long it takes new ventures to achieve the return on investment of a mature venture showed an unpalatable 10–12 years. And it requires a lot of imagination, as research by Greg Stevens and James Burley showed – it takes 3,000 ideas to find one commercial success.[23]

We wanted to find out how to increase the speed and returns that typically look unattractive to CEOs looking to transform their companies. We analysed the underlying factors that contributed to failure in early adopters and filled in the gaps. One of the biggest of those was executives confusing risk and uncertainty in decision-making regarding new opportunities.

To leaders in past present organisations, decision-making in a future now firm seems to be a mess of contradictions. In some areas, highly deliberate criteria are set for the development of new products and services. In others, what feel like total leaps of faith are being made. However, unlike the past present organisation, where one underlying set of assumptions drives decisions about tomorrow, in the future now company, multiple frames are being used to create a coherent approach to interpretating the risk and uncertainty involved in opportunities and bets.

In 2000, Mehrdad Baghai and his colleagues created the 3 Horizons model to describe a pipeline of value creation.

The model describes the profit potential of businesses at different stages of maturity. Horizon 1 (H1) activities extend and defend the existing core business. Horizon 2 (H2) is about building emerging businesses and Horizon 3 (H3) is about creating viable options for the future.

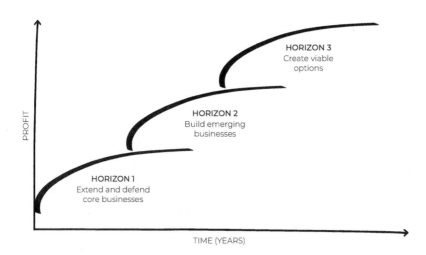

FIGURE 11.9   The 3 Horizons model – adapted from the *Alchemy of Growth*[24]

Source: Baghai, M., Coley, S., & White, D. (2000). The Alchemy of Growth. Perseus Publishing.

Over the years, the model has been updated and used in many ways to reflect the new realities of a more disruptive environment. It's a staple framework used amongst start-ups to describe how their venture will move through crawl–walk–run stages. For corporates, it's a useful way of thinking about a portfolio approach to the value trilemma.

We relabelled the x-axis as a spectrum between risk and uncertainty because the implied message in the original model is that H2 and H3 are opportunities that you will get to at some point in the future. Timing in H2/3 is everything. Invest too soon and you waste your resources before the market is ready. Act too late and it's either much more expensive to get a seat at the table, or they'd all be gone, and you're left behind with nothing. A time x-axis, we found, doesn't help in figuring out the timing challenge. It encourages, for example, executives to project their existing risk criteria onto H2/3 and therefore, they frequently end up concluding opportunities as being too early or not a strategic fit. What this interpretation also misses is that H2/3 opportunities are *not* a fit with today's core business model. This is another product of the fatal assumption thinking they should be. The way to think about H2/3 opportunities is that they are *who you might become*.

Another reason for adopting a risk-uncertainty spectrum is to recognise the non-linear nature of value tomorrow. You need to invest across all the horizons *simultaneously* not sequentially to manage a value tomorrow portfolio of bets.

In our reworking, H1, or 'the known', is about the opportunities that strengthen the organisation's existing business model, enabling it to become cheaper, faster, and better at what it already does in existing and new markets. H1 is about sustaining today's profits by prolonging yesterday's best ideas. Incremental innovation, such as the annual updates to the iPhone since 2007, can produce extraordinary returns. It can also create

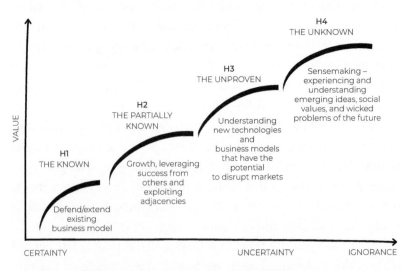

FIGURE 11.10   Four horizons of opportunity
Source: Jean Gomes, adapted from Baghai, M., Coley, S., & White, D. (2000). The Alchemy of Growth. Perseus Publishing.

an over-wariness of disrupting existing revenue streams, leaving an organisation caught out by bigger disruptive opportunities.

Because incremental innovation operates from the organisation's comfort zone, executives must be alert to the trap of diluting resources on incremental improvements that don't add up to much. Many organisations' new product development activities default into filling gaps in product ranges or providing new features that absorb engineers' curiosity but do little to grow revenues. H1 activities need to be challenged, and evidence provided, that they are solving problems that customers care enough about and are willing to pay for. H1 is therefore about *extending* the life of today's value system, *not* creating value for tomorrow. The key question is *'will this investment reduce or encourage entropy?'*.

H2 is where future growth potential really starts and it's all about making good risk assessments and setting effective measures. It's called the *partially known* because it's about harnessing *established* technologies and business models that are currently not known to us to transform the organisation's existing value creation system. The risk and reward are greater than H1, but the probabilities of failure can be understood and mitigated by bringing in the right partners and doing the due diligence to quantify the transformational effort required.

H3, often labelled the *unknown*, is, we think better termed the *unproven*. These are technologies, business models, ideas, and nascent marketplaces that exist but have yet to become viable in terms of proven success. Think of fusion power – the possibility of an endless source of clean energy which to most people still seems like science fiction. It's not unknown, it's unproven.

Each of the horizons requires a different approach to judging and metrics. In all cases, one common success factor is whether the core team of people running the project are entirely focused on it. If it's not the thing they wake up worrying about, but it is competing against their day job, then the gravity of value today will always win out. Of course, there are much heralded examples of unofficial skunk works projects where teams pursue a passion project in their own time and on their own terms, but these amount to a miniscule handful of cases.

In H3 and H4 (which we'll come to), the challenge, and the underlying assumption, are very different. Here we can't find proof that we're solving problems for customers because value creation is about creative disruption, radically changing industry norms, customer expectations and habits. Customers didn't know that an Apple iPad would solve problems and create value in their lives. Nor did Microsoft, who invented the product a full decade earlier but didn't have the imagination to figure out that it was a consumer not a corporate product.

H3/4 requires teams to *reimagine* how the world will be. Working in these horizons necessitates us to be in a space beyond what we know or can prove, which many executives quickly lose patience inhabiting – expecting answers, backed by reassuring evidence, to be fed to them. They don't get the point that they need to find a way of sensemaking that *they* own.

In a non-linear world, not placing bets on the future may be the fastest way to corporate oblivion. The World Economic Forum highlights that the number of 'frontier risks' is increasing.[25] These are challenges to our existing ways of thinking and operating as new discoveries and inventions propelling the Fourth Industrial Revolution continue. Drivers include space exploration, new gene-editing tools, artificial intelligence, and the creation of virtual worlds. Incredible as these developments are, they have the potential to produce huge unforeseen downsides. New social, health, and economic problems will emerge. We don't have to look far to see how social media is changing the world in unexpected ways. But the X-Prize founder Peter Diamandis believes that 'the world's biggest problems are the world's biggest market opportunities', and organisations need to lean into H3/4 problem-solving if they want to be around for the long term.

HORIZON 4 – WHAT IGNORANCE ARE WE (INTENTIONALLY) GENERATING?

What about the *unknown* – the fourth horizon that we added into the model? Our brains run on predictions to reduce uncertainty, so it's natural that we react to not knowing and reach out for certainty. One of the traits of the past present organisation is an intellectual and emotional intolerance to not knowing things and a subsequent lack of curiosity. 'If something can't be known, it's irrelevant' an executive told her legal and finance leaders I was facilitating. This was in response to one of her team asking if they should spend more time visualising a business model 10 years in the future. It struck me as an interesting response given that her organisation had lost nearly 40% of its market capitalisation in the previous five years because it had failed to anticipate the impact of challenger banks.

We added a fourth horizon to represent *ignorance*, the true quality of the unknown. I'm not referring to deliberate stupidity or any other negative connotation of the word, but the cultivation of intellectual humility – accepting what we don't know and strengthening our resolve to find out. Creating a future now organisation involves a constant battle to break down the hubris and arrogance that builds up with success – that 'we know better'. Expertise, track record, and incredible resources are evidence that we might indeed know better, but we also need a balancing refrain, 'where are we wrong, what don't we know, what are we missing?'. Often arrogance, which is evidently unpalatable socially, is hidden to us and to the organisation at large. The value of having a strong H4 voice constructively questioning our assumptions is that it builds long-term competitive resilience into a culture.

It requires us becoming comfortable with asking questions that provoke uncertainty. The neuroscientist Stuart Firestein provides a useful lens. Ignorance, not knowledge, he suggests, is the true engine of science. Scientists don't trade in facts, but in questions that confront ignorance.

He says, 'questions are bigger than answers. One good question can give rise to several layers of answers, can inspire decades-long searches for solutions, can generate whole new fields of inquiry, and can prompt changes in entrenched thinking. Answers on the other hand, often end the process'.[26]

How do you ask a good question to embrace the uncertainty of H4? Firestein told me that we tend to ask questions where we already have the answer or partly understand it, because 'ignorance seems embarrassing'. Instead, he suggests, we should be asking ourselves 'what ignorance are we generating?'.

Here are some questions I've found helpful to unlock the sometimes reluctant unfolding of a H4 mindset:

What does everyone know, but no one's talking about?
What new realities, ideas, anomalies, and options do we fail to acknowledge and suppress?
Who completely disagrees with our business model?
What was 'impossible' 10 or 20 years ago?
What might be possible in 10 or 20 years' time?
What mistakes do we never learn from?
What mistakes don't we allow to happen?
What do people want to work on, but never have the time or means?
How can we place a value on ignorance in our organisation – cultivating, harvesting, and turning it into value?

What happens when we make a list of everything we don't know about the coming decade, regardless of whether it seems relevant to our business or activity?

What's currently unknowable in our market or technological field?

Why might a future competitor give away for free what we currently base our business on?

What are today's university laboratories and start-ups doing to solve this problem that will deliver in 5, 10, or 20 years' time?

What would be the most surprising new skills you/we might need to learn in the coming 10 years?

What skill do you dream you have that would unlock future business models?

How will today's unborn children change our market?

A NORTH STAR

The future now organisation thinks *and* feels differently about the future. If we accept that the gravitational pull of value today is irresistible, we need to build another *attracting force* around value tomorrow to encourage us to do both. The practical means of building confidence and attention on tomorrow involves building a value tomorrow growth engine that populates the horizons with a series of bets on the future. In other words, value tomorrow starts to become more tangible, less idealised, and the province of mostly just debate.

But it's important to recognise that this system is always fragile and can easily be torn apart by the value today mindset and priorities. It needs another element to balance the system – a North Star purpose that sits hovering over the fourth horizon, providing a navigation point through uncertainty.

The topic of purpose often provokes an irritated rolling of the eyeballs amongst CEOs and leaders, who see it as the antithesis of the concrete world of decisions and hard reality. And there's no getting around it, purpose poses an existential question – *why do we exist?* The functional response, through the past present lens, is to deliver shareholder value. The future now lens combines social and commercial objectives, getting the organisation to question its future relevancy to the world. This sets a challenge from the future that unlocks new thinking, and motivation, as leaders such as Starbuck's Howard Schultz and Microsoft's Satya Nadella recognise – it also creates a culture where people's spirit is nourished.

It may be much written about, but only a fraction of the organisations who purport to have embraced the idea of purpose use it to create value in their business model. Ranjay Gulati, a Harvard Business School professor who has made a five-year study of the subject,[27] told me that most organisations he'd talked with confuse purpose with concepts such as vision, values, mission, or that it is an act of superficial virtue signalling to make them feel good.

Gulati cites the psychologist William Damon, that 'purpose is a stable and generalised intention to accomplish something that is at the same time meaningful to the self and consequential to the world beyond the self'. At the heart of this definition is the capacity to hold opposites. To do something meaningful for you *and* the world. Gulati believes 'deep purpose' is a 'unifying statement of the commercial and social problems a business intends to profitably solve for its stakeholders. This statement encompasses both goals and duties, and it succinctly communicates what a business is all about and who it's intended to benefit'.

The impact of having an actionable purpose on mindset is enormous. Simply put, it changes how people feel, think, and see.

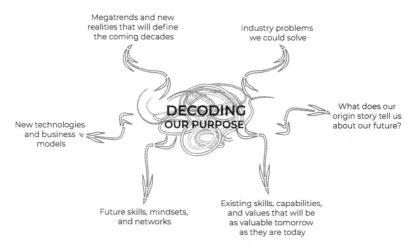

Megatrends and new realities that will define the coming decades

Industry problems we could solve

DECODING OUR PURPOSE

New technologies and business models

What does our origin story tell us about our future?

Future skills, mindsets, and networks

Existing skills, capabilities, and values that will be as valuable tomorrow as they are today

FIGURE 11.11   Decoding our purpose
Source: Jean Gomes

It creates a belief that we can embrace uncertain and complex situations and figure our way through them. It unlocks intrinsic motivation, making people feel better about their work and themselves. It attracts hard-to-reach talent, who typically want to work on things that make a real difference to the future. It gives confidence to step into uncomfortable spaces and try things that feel alien. An actionable purpose cannot be purely idealistic, it must help leaders to continually balance commercial and social goals to manage the trade-offs involved.

PURPOSE *SHOULD* CHALLENGE US

One assumption that people often make about purpose is that it's solely about being good, noble, or caring. It's much more complex, and dare I say it, important than that. It should challenge us, humble us, inspire us to take smart risks, to be open, curious, accept what we don't know, and ultimately keep us evolving.

A clearly defined purpose helps an organisation to balance today and tomorrow *and* evolve how it sees the world to match the challenges it faces with the appropriate responses. So, not just that its products and services keep pace with the world, but so does its moral identity. It evolves a worldview that knows how to do the right thing in a changing world.

Purpose as a strategic business idea reflects huge and accelerating changes in societal values. Movements such as Black Lives Matter and MeToo, enabled by social media, command global attention and have changed our culture in months rather than decades. More customers want businesses to act ethically, and not to make them feel guilty about using their products. More employees want the same thing.

INDUSTRIALISING IMAGINATION

Future now organisations have a value tomorrow growth engine fuelled by an abundance of insights, questions, and hypotheses about the future. They also need to produce a flow of ideas, stories, and scenarios *from* the future too. I'm not talking about predictions based on extrapolating from the present forward, but imagining the future like a science fiction writer would and working back to the present – and then asking, 'how would we start from here to get there?'. This is about an organisation *industrialising* imagination and experimentation. It has also gone beyond the notion that ideas alone propel innovation and can embrace counterfactual thinking, creating mental models, new worlds, of things that don't yet exist.

Entangled in the fatal assumption of the mature organisation is that we don't need counterfactual thinking to succeed. What we need is more of the same thinking. Of course, people never say that. There are always 'new' ideas being turned into products and solutions, new marketing techniques and ways of working. But are they really new? Or are they variants and extensions of what we're already doing? And people use creative problem-solving every day to find ways around barriers. But again, to what end is this being employed?

The past present organisation is bound by a paradox. Its leaders want creativity and agility, some even want radical reimaginings of the future, but they're sitting on an organisation that craves predictability, with teams that 'stay in their lanes', where being perceived to rock the boat creates fear and even revulsion (reflecting our core need to protect ourselves from harm) in managers. Overloaded with information, executives fall prey to seeking perfect data-driven understanding and risk-free options. Paralysed by analysis and sapped by churning debates, weeks and months pass by as the right process is sought to move forward. By contrast, the future now organisation accepts that somewhere between 30% and 70% accuracy is good enough to start new initiatives, fail, learn, and adapt fast and break down ignorance.

Most of what will help an organisation to create an abundance of new opportunity will feel counterintuitive and countercultural. It involves play and spending time with people who are very different and may make us feel discomfort. Withholding judgement and being open and curious are essential first steps. Disrupting this thought process is helped by new stimuli, for example seeing unfamiliar types of people and communities solving problems. One leadership team spending a weekend with an indigenous tribe, learning about how they encoded ancient wisdom through stories, got them to think about a radical departure in their purpose and strategy. They came to see that their origin story had been lost and they'd become disconnected from what had made them great in the first place. It also encouraged them to become humbler about who might be able to teach them things about the future.

ACTIVE TOLERANCE

Another quality we've observed in the future now leader is *active tolerance*, the conscious decision to understand and channel dissenters and positive deviants to constructively challenge the status quo. In the past present organisation these people are rarely hired and rapidly fired.

Arie de Geus, who made a study[28] of long-lived companies, many of which made it past 100 years and some up to 700 or more, believed that learning was the central function of longevity. Consider the conglomerate Sumitomo, whose origins are more than 400 years old. The roots of their mission statement are largely unchanged. Unlike most organisations, they also have a strong vision for the coming 100 years. De Geus's study highlighted that a learning culture ensures that these organisations remain highly sensitive to their environment and are tolerant of experimentation at the margins of the organisation.

Psychologist Todd Kashdan believes that for ideas to evolve and societies to progress, we need more principled non-compliance to challenge the status quo. 'Unfortunately, most of us fear non-conformists, perceiving them to be disloyal, reckless, destructive, or just plain weird'. In the *Art of Insubordination*,[29] he describes a series of research-based strategies to help individuals rebel constructively against the status quo. They require both the rebel and the leader to adopt the twin virtues of curiosity and humility, to accept what they don't know, and to update their beliefs considering new information.

A FUTURE NOW DIAGNOSTIC

If your organisation is in need of recalibrating its focus on the future, look at the following diagnostic which summarises the ideas and experiences we've had in helping leaders manage the value trilemma.

FUTURE NOW ENABLERS	EVIDENCE OF WHERE THIS IS HAPPENING	WHAT'S BLOCKING ADOPTION?
Test and learn is a core part of value today and tomorrow activities It allows us to imagine and test future solutions, to break down uncertainty and manage risk with confidence		
We recognise talking about how we feel unlocks trust and gets us to root causes faster		
Every failure allows us to learn who we need to become		
Safety and success come from finding the optimal balance between today and tomorrow		
Our leaders are on a steep learning curve		
Growth – we're in it together		
We've looked at ourselves and recognised what needs to change in our mindset and behaviour		
Leaders quantify 30% of their time on value tomorrow (averaging a split across of H1 70%, H2 20%, H3 10% as a community)		
We hold each other accountable to focus on value tomorrow		
Targets, rewards, and mindset encourage a continuous 70/30 focus		
We value and find the time to work on value tomorrow as a team		
We hire and promote leaders who will be able to create and manage our future business model		
Leaders are responsible for all innovation and growth teams having 100% dedicated core team members		
We spend time standing in the shoes of our customers, so we can lead a customer-first approach (experience driven – thick data)		
We maintain the problem-led test and learn approach to H1/2 growth activities		
We are building capabilities to support H2 (new partnerships, skillsets) and investing in H3 (ecosystem building, investing and education)		

FIGURE 11.12 A future now diagnostic
Source: Jean Gomes

FUTURE NOW ENABLERS	EVIDENCE OF WHERE THIS IS HAPPENING	WHAT'S BLOCKING ADOPTION?
We work with our ecosystem to generate ideas to positively disrupt markets for the future (H3)		
We define what A roles need and we always seek to hire A players		
We can embrace and support entrepreneurs into our business		
We're intentionally investing in products and services that destroy existing legacy revenue streams		
Digital is seen as a way of unlocking new business models		
We dynamically reallocate resources to new opportunities with sufficient speed or intensity		
We explore options of sharing IP to build network effects		
We fully commit resources to growth initiatives whilst holding their activities accountable to explicit leading metrics		
Our best people aspire to work on our growth projects		
Growth is driven by small flexible multi-disciplinary and autonomous teams		
We access scarce resources through a highly developed network of expert crowds and communities, thus improving agility and reducing cost		
We know what good looks like for growth roles even when it creates tension with the current organisation		
We have a mix of leading and lagging indicators that enable us to predict how successful value tomorrow growth is likely to be		
We measure and incentivise risk and growth leadership		
We separate executive focus – with a dedicated value tomorrow board		
Our acquisitions are mostly in H2/3		
Our HR, legal, and finance functions are strong, proactive advocates and enablers of growth activity		

FIGURE 11.12 (*Continued*)
Source: Jean Gomes

CHAPTER 12

THE EXPERIMENTAL MINDSET

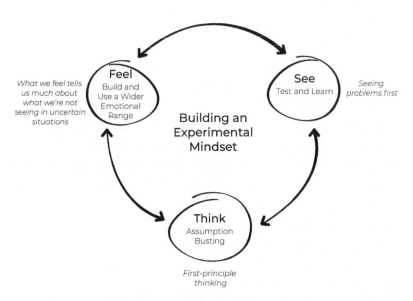

FIGURE 12.1   The experimental mindset
Source: Jean Gomes

The past present organisation is governed by a form of thought and action that aims to deliver predictable and low-risk outcomes. This *plan and act* approach is optimal when the variables are known, and uncertainty is low. It's the execution super-strength of mature organisations. The future now organisation complements plan and act with an additional approach – *test and learn* – that empowers individuals, teams, and organisations to reduce the inherent risks and costs of innovation and accelerate learning and progress through non-linear problem-solving. Test and learn propels the experimental mindset that allows us to see, think, and act like no one else.

The experiment – the randomised controlled trial – has rapidly moved out of the confines of academia and research laboratories to become part of the growth playbook of organisations. Tech pioneers first embraced experimentation because online environments made it relatively cheap and easy to run thousands of parallel tests on variants of features (known as A/B testing). Today, governments, schools, and analogue businesses have joined in, finding new ways to innovate, adapt, and grow, or to avoid policy U-turns, strategy fails, and obsolescence.[1]

Whilst the case for business experimentation, and the accompanying tools, may be straightforward to grasp, the mindset required for them to deliver value is deeply countercultural in mature institutions. One executive, having spent a day working in an experiment laboratory we set up for their company, told me: 'I've never thought like this in my life, it's counter to everything I've ever been taught or done. I can see the potential, but it feels very uncomfortable'. When emotions are at play, it's proof that the job is not just about gaining an intellectual understanding but recognising how our mindset is operating.

Plan and act has a central role in the efficiency of delivering value today. In comparing it with test and learn (see Figure 12.2), the point is to understand the differences and where each approach is needed. As new ideas are tested and validated, at some point they will need to be scaled and become part of the value today system, where plan and act methods, such as hardware manufacture, take centre stage. Understanding how they complement each

PLAN & ACT	TEST & LEARN
The optimal problem-solving approach when assumptions about problem, solution, and expected outcome have a low level of uncertainty.	The optimal problem-solving approach when assumptions about problem, solution, and expected outcome have a high degree of uncertainty.
GOALS Activity shaped by a conviction of what we're trying to achieve, how we will do it. Assumptions are baked into the goal.	**PROBLEMS** Activity shaped by a problem statement and the assumptions we will test about the problem, and the solution.
LINEAR The big assumption – that our goal, method, and outcome are right – means we maintain a linear A to Z path even if we get contra data that it's not working.	**NON-LINEAR** We test multiple assumptions about our goal, method, and outcome simultaneously to dissolve our ignorance.
PROJECTS Project mode – if we are clear about our goals, have the right expertise and good project management we will succeed.	**EXPERIMENTS** Experiments mode – if we're clear about what we're solving for, the assumptions we're making, we will learn fast.
DE-RISK & AVOID UNCERTAINTY Plan and act assumes that risk and uncertainty are reduced or avoided by adopting good process – seeks 100% certainty before moving.	**QUANTIFY RISK & EMBRACE UNCERTAINTY** Test and learn assumes that risk and uncertainty need to be quantified 30–70% good enough to move.
PUSH Drive, motivation, and approach comes top-down and from existing culture.	**PULL** Drive, motivation, and approach comes bottom-up from what is being discovered.
RATIONAL Emotions cloud our judgement.	**RATIONAL & EMOTIONAL** Emotions fuel our judgement.

FIGURE 12.2 Plan and act vs test and learn
Source: Jean Gomes

other and work together is important, so they don't become the source of a political turf war.

THE LIMITS OF PLAN AND ACT

Plan and act is the mindset shaped by the organisation's value today system. Plans form around established baseline assumptions about what has worked in the past. The knowledge of 'what works' is embedded, often tacitly, in people's expertise, processes, systems, and relationships with established suppliers and partners. Action is de-risked by strategic clarity, well-defined goals, skilled teams, and effective project management. And it works exceptionally well. . . when the assumptions being made are largely right or where there is a low level of uncertainty and surprises are small and can be accommodated with little risk to the desired outcome.

When plan and act is used to solve new or unforeseen challenges, it can still work because smart people improvise to succeed. But not always. The plan and act mindset is essentially about the certainty that we know what we're doing. It's about getting things done by going from A to B in a straight, predictable line. Once goals are agreed, the plan and act approach is intolerant of questioning 'why' and returning to first-principle thinking, even when conditions change or unchallenged assumptions begin to surface as unforeseen problems.

Generally, one of three things might happen when linearly executed projects fail due to unanticipated assumptions.

Denial – the whole project is brushed under the carpet, written off and 'forgotten'.

Blame – someone carries the can and is blamed for poor execution even though they had no prior relevant experience.

Shallow learning – very occasionally, the team does a retrospective exercise to learn from the failure. However, with a plan and act mindset, learning is problematic because the assumptions that led to the failures are either too painful to confront or hidden beneath the water like the mass of an iceberg.

In a past present organisation, there's a common belief that the plan and act approach is rational and logical. When it works, the only emotions really on show are positive and confirmatory, closing the feedback loop with a sense of 'we were right'. But this belief, based on the truth that any successful organisation has a depth of know-how and clever people, is only partially true. All decisions are to some extent shaped by emotions.

A plan and act approach in an uncertain situation throws people into the impossibility of seeking 100% certainty in situations where it's impossible to be sure. The test and learn method, however, recognises that experimentation is about starting with little or no confidence, and being comfortable that 30–70% certainty is good enough to keep moving forward.

To see past the present, we need to recast our knowledge, expertise, and beliefs as enablers of *encountering and breaking down ignorance*. This is absolutely no attack on experts. We urgently need expertise and competence; however, experts with a plan and act mindset can risk being blinkered in uncertain situations and believe they might *know* when they just believe. Experts who adopt the experimental mindset can accept and embrace *not* knowing.

The culture and worldview of the past present organisation can amplify our inherently poor ability to predict the future. Biases, complexity, and ingrained assumptions combine to encourage us to believe that what we *feel* will work is likely to be right. In a more unpredictable world, this is a dangerous strategy. The narrowed attention of the past present organisation encourages its leaders to be reductive in their thinking and strategy. A common example is the executive team's approach to digital technologies, seeing them as a tactical problem that their IT team should own, instead of it being their responsibility to figure out how they will use them to unlock future business models.

The experimental mindset comprises a way of feeling, thinking, and seeing that inspires and guides individuals, teams, and organisations to test and bust their assumptions about what's feasible, desirable, and viable in the future. It's the means to embrace ignorance boldly and find new sources of value that contradict our existing beliefs, experience, and conventions.

It's also a more optimistic and less draining approach to managing in times of protracted uncertainty. The past present organisation can be highly proficient at rising to immediate threats, by going into firefighting mode, and throwing resources and energy at short-term problems. But the narrowing of organisational attention means that learning isn't a priority, and the likelihood is that we're setting ourselves up for the next crisis. Successful business experiments generate a continual stream of new information into the organisation that enables a more natural adaption to new market realities. An experimental mindset allows leaders and their teams to adapt continuously through periods of crisis and stability with greater equanimity.

What unites the plethora of frameworks and tools (Figure 12.3) that the start-up and digital economies have created is that they help entrepreneurs to form testable hypotheses regarding their assumptions of new value propositions by running rapid low-cost, low-risk experiments to gain new knowledge.

I'm not going to describe these tools in any depth as there are many great manuals available.[2] What I do want to draw out is that when *combined* with the experimental mindset, they unlock the means to discovering, validating, and rapidly scaling new solutions and business models (Figure 12.4). Our experience of using these tools in thousands of experiments is that over time, the real asset is not the tools but the ability to create more open, adaptive mindsets.

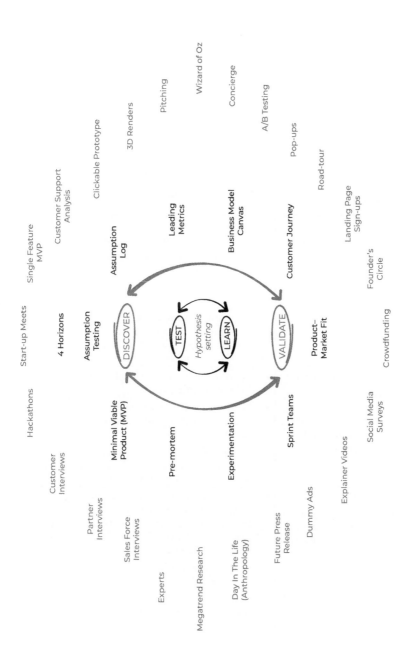

FIGURE 12.3 Test and learn methods
Source: Jean Gomes

TECHNIQUE	ASSUMPTIONS TO TEST
HYPOTHESIS A testable proposition e.g. 'we believe that customers care enough about X problem to pay Y price for Z solution'	• Cause and effect can be tested and is falsifiable (i.e. can be shown to be not true) • We will run a control experiment to compare against our experiment • Assumptions are made explicit • Quantifiable value metrics can be described and measured
MVP The smallest experiment we can run to validate our hypothesis	• We have made it small enough to run it quickly • It generates actionable data • We act on what the data tells us (i.e. we kill, pivot, or scale)
SPRINT TEAMS Small, diverse teams running two-week test and learn sprints	• Teams maintain experimental approach and don't revert to project mindset and behaviours • They know when they are in discovery versus validation mode • They have an effective and objective facilitator who sticks to the tools • There is an effective constructive troublemaker whose job it is to prevent 'group think' and let unchallenged assumptions blunt the team's experimentation power
PRODUCT–MARKET FIT Evidence that we're creating a solution to a customer problem in an attractive market	• We test MVPs at sufficient scale to create confidence of product–market fit • We have reliable market intelligence that our addressable market is sufficient to make this an attractive investment • We're using product–market fit appropriately in Horizons 1 and 2, not 3 and 4 where market disruption and creation criteria are necessary
4 HORIZONS We adjust our approach according to which horizon our hypothesis is focused on	• Our judgement criteria match the risk–uncertainty mix across the horizons. For example, we don't seek to establish clear evidence of product–market fit in Horizon 3/4 where more speculative bets need to be placed • Customers know what they will want in the future • Leaders don't feel the need to fill in the holes left by growth and innovation teams, but keep asking questions • We recognise the different emotional reactions that activities elicit across the horizons

BUSINESS MODEL CANVAS We're clear about the business model necessary to support this solution	• Our existing means to create, deliver, and capture will enable our new solution to thrive • A new business model will be required to unlock the full potential • A new business model will require skills, resources, and funding we currently don't have
CUSTOMER JOURNEY A validated map of how customers discover, learn about, evaluate, buy, receive, use, and advocate products	• Our existing understanding of the customer journey is complete and accurate • That our framework enables us to see all relevant information about the customer's experience • That this framework enables us to predict future needs to feed into new product development and innovation activities
LEADING INDICATORS Customer metrics that enable us to predict future outcomes with greater confidence	• We have established leading indicators that tell us what is likely to happen in the future vs lagging indicator that tell us what has happened in the past. For example, growth in sales pipeline, customer interactions on new product website pages, percentage of resources allocated to new products and fast growth opportunities
STAKEHOLDER INTERVIEWS Open listening to customers, sales, start-ups, partners, industry experts, hackathons, customer support analysis, social media evaluation	• We listen objectively to what our stakeholders are saying • We use that data to challenge our assumptions about the strength of value today and the challenges and opportunities to create value tomorrow • We challenge the stories we tell about our stakeholders and the stereotypes we've created about them • We recognise when we dismiss contra evidence to our beliefs based on our own standards and expectations • We seek out dissenting voices • We pay attention to how our feelings influence our judgements
PITCHING The discipline of telling a compelling evidence-based story about why your experiment is worth backing	• We know what our audience cares about • We have the evidence, narrative, and 'ask' that forms a compelling pitch • What we are presenting is worth what we're asking for • We own what we don't know • We are the right people to take this to the next stage

FIGURE 12.4 How experimental tools enable assumption busting
Source: Jean Gomes

GOALS VS PROBLEMS

Setting goals can have the deceptive effect of creating a belief that they are achievable if only we try hard enough. We also need to clarify the problems to be solved to achieve those goals – a process that is often absent in setting strategy. This is compounded in plan and act, which is shaped by a conviction that we know what we're doing. Test and learn starts from a different place; not a goal, but a problem, and the assumptions that we will test about our understanding of that problem.

As the vitality of an idea or product wanes, the past present organisation relies ever more on *pushing* its proposition into the market. With sufficient sales and marketing muscle, customers *will* buy products they don't want or need for a time. This isn't just a consumer phenomenon, I remember vividly at a tech conference a few years back, an audience of IT directors were asked to put up their hands if they'd spent more than $15 million on software in the past two years that they knew they'd never implement because they were sold a convincing story. More than half the audience's hand went up.

Test and learn creates a new force of *pull* in an organisation. Customers want the solutions we create because they solve real problems or open attractive opportunities for them. People want to work on solving problems that make the world a better place. Leaders want to invest in evidence-based opportunities, knowing what level of risk they're taking.

In *The Lean Startup*, Eric Ries[3] lays out a seemingly simple root cause of innovation failure. Ironically, most start-ups fail because of a plan and act trap – they bet all their limited funds on the belief that their idea will work. Most new product development teams in established organisations are no different, building products with little customer input in the belief that if *they* love it, so will the market. Occasionally, they are right, but the odds are low. Depending on which research studies[4] you look at, new product success rates range from 5% for new innovations to 50% for more conventional (i.e. incremental) new products.

The *product–market fit* model is a powerful way of shedding light on an organisation's customer needs blind spot. In the mid-2000s, the venture capitalist Marc Andreessen started using the phrase 'product–market fit' to describe the ideal alignment between a market with a strong demand and a new product. When product–market fit is achieved, the market literally pulls the product out of the company. Think about the queues around Apple stores when the iPhone was launched. Or the $14 billion of orders for Tesla's model 3 in the first *week* after launch.

Whilst a compelling idea, it was abstract. Dan Olsen, who had worked at Intuit as a successful product leader, took the concept and built a detailed framework called the product–market fit pyramid (see Figure 12.5), which he described in his book *The Lean Product Playbook*.[5] His framework has rapidly

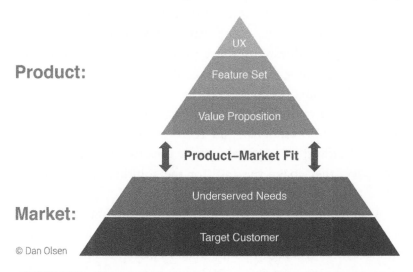

FIGURE 12.5   The product–market fit pyramid (used by permission)
Source: Olsen, D., 2015. The Lean Product Playbook. 1st ed. Wiley. (used by permission Dan Olsen)

become a staple tool amongst start-ups and corporate incubators. It's a hugely powerful lens in building the experimental mindset because it helps to reframe one of the most basic innovation errors – that teams habitually solve the wrong problems because their thinking suffers what Olsen terms 'solution pollution'. Olsen's framework makes explicit that product–market fit requires acknowledging *two* distinct spaces. The *problem space* is about deeply understanding who the customer is, their context, and under-served needs. The *solution space* is about defining the features and benefits that will meet those needs and the user experience that makes it a compelling value proposition.

As Olsen told me, 'It's so easy for product teams to slip into solution mode because that's their world. As engineers, designers, even commercial people, it's their job to build and sell things, so unsurprisingly they frame the questions too tightly, or even with their solution in mind'. By instilling the additional discipline of the problem space, teams start to extend their capacity to solve real customer problems and build things they want. Olsen makes the point that simply analysing customer pains and gains doesn't produce product–market fit. 'Customers aren't technologists and product designers; they don't know they need the next product innovation. As Henry Ford famously said, if he'd asked customers what they wanted it would have been a faster horse. What they really wanted was to go from A to B as efficiently as possible. When teams work in the problem space, they make the case for the solution space and the innovative leaps become possible'.

This highlights one of the most significant differences between the *problem-first thinking* of test and learn vs the *solution-first thinking* of plan and act. This shift is part of what helps an organisation to externalise its perception and thinking and allow the life-bringing energy that getting closer to the customer and market brings.

Looking at the behaviour of those start-ups that got it right and went on to huge success, Ries observed that they created a *test and learn cycle* that was radically different from the herd, who typically implemented their activities through a plan and act mindset – where they come up with an idea and bet everything that they were right, until they run out of money and fail.

Ries tells the story of Dropbox founder Drew Houston, who adopted a different approach. The punchline is that when Dropbox was founded in 2007, there were several similar file-sharing start-ups vying to attract funding. Most of those no longer exist, and today Dropbox has a market capitalisation of $8 billion. What Houston and his partner Arash Ferdowsi did was to run a series of small, low-cost, rapid experiments to test market demand for their idea. Whilst their rivals spent their seed capital on building what they believed would be the killer app, Dropbox showed people drawings of their landing page, created a cheap explainer video of the product as if it was real, and ran email campaigns to test appetite for certain features. Ries described this experimental approach as the minimum viable product (MVP), a way of rapidly discovering how to build a product that customers *really* wanted as fast as possible.

Each experiment gave them invaluable information about three assumptions they were making:

1. They were solving a problem that their *customers* cared about.
2. They were creating a solution that their customers believed solved the problem they cared about.
3. Customers would be prepared to pay for their solution.

The appeal of cheap, low-risk experiments to learn fast belies an important reality in established organisations – it's fundamentally *not* how they operate. Experimental organisations grew up testing *everything* – products, processes, business models, ways of working – so it's how they see the world. It's normal. In organisations like Klarna, Booking.com, and Google, teams run thousands of experiments every month. Some are automated on their digital platforms, providing a steady stream of learning; many are social experiments on processes, ways of working, and collaboration.

The evidence that experimentation gives start-ups an advantage is somewhat patchy, given that any new enterprise has multiple dependencies on success. However, in one study[6] looking at 116 Italian start-ups and the effect of rigorous experimentation, half were taught to experiment using a scientific approach, the other half were just encouraged to experiment. The randomised control trial found that 'entrepreneurs who behave like scientists perform better, pivot to a greater extent to a different idea, and do not drop out less than the control group in the early stages of the start-up. A scientific approach improves precision – it reduces the odds of pursuing projects with false negative returns'.

CURIOSITY IS LIFE. ASSUMPTION IS DEATH (MARK PARKER, CHAIRMAN, NIKE)

As we considered in Part 1, the most fundamental mindset error in organisations is that beliefs about strategies, product development, and marketing activities are founded upon facts rather than assumptions. These assumptions can become so grounded in the stories that we tell about ourselves, our customers, and competitors, that we unknowingly use them to predict causality – 'if we do this, that will happen'.

Assumptions, like our biases, are an inherent part of our predictive minds. We might quietly acknowledge them in making decisions, but often we fall short of interrogating them, seeing them more as truths than suppositions. Rita McGrath, in *Seeing Around Corners*,[7] points to the fact that seemingly sudden industry inflection points are not random or unexpected, but the final stage in a discernible process that has been building over time. Inflection points are when the level of change created by a new technology, business model, or market reality, such as disruptive legislation, result in overturning the basic assumptions that an organisation is built on. Far from being unpredictable, McGrath argues that we generally look at the wrong data, using lagging or present indicators, such as sales or customer satisfaction, to understand the future. Instead, we should be looking at *leading indicators* that help us to bust our assumptions and make better predictions about what will happen tomorrow.

Entrepreneur and academic, Steve Blank, usefully cites the five deadliest assumptions that teams repeatedly make as: 'assuming you know what the customer wants; the I know what features to build flaw; focusing on the launch date with no flexibility for direction change; emphasizing execution instead of testing, learning and iteration and writing a business plan that doesn't allow for trial and error'. Innovation consultant, Scott Anthony, adds[8] that leaders repeatedly fall prey to disruptive cycles because they believe that their biggest and most profitable customers are their best source of information; that historical data paints a picture of the future; in the face of uncertainty, that it's riskier to act than not to act; and that their shareholders won't invest in something new if it puts current returns at risk.

Unrecognised and unchallenged assumptions not only limit our field of view, but also considerably increase the complexity of problem-solving and can lead teams to simply give up and revert to what they believe they know. As with anything associated with mindset, assumption busting isn't simply a process of reasoning. Our emotions can blind us to options, opportunities, or problems staring us in the face. Our worldview can thwart us from seeing an imminent reality. And because our existing knowledge and thought processes can so dominate our perception, we simply dismiss new ideas and opportunities as irrelevant.

We've worked in the field of experimental assumption busting in three domains – developing leaders' mindsets, helping teams to innovate, and advising organisations on how to discover and develop competitive new strategies. In each domain, busting assumptions provides the means to unlock potential, energy, and growth.

For a leader, it could be the shift from the assumption that they must have all the answers, must always be right, to seeing that creating better questions will unlock both their future and that of their organisation.

This might come with the profound recognition of how often their need to be right is at odds with the uncertainty of their circumstances, and how their emotional response creates defensiveness and pushing away of others. The feeling of freedom in breaking the cycle often represents an inflection point in their development.

For innovation teams, surfacing and busting assumptions enables them to discover what was once believed impossible, impractical, or unprofitable within their organisations. The excitement and energy that comes from this process is truly remarkable.

For organisations, assumption busting is the first deep move in successful transformation. For example, a key reason for a product company's failing to transform into a services business is that it's trying to copy the processes, systems, and strategies of a services model without making a corresponding shift in the mindset and worldview amongst its leaders. Thus, executives still see problems through a product mindset and fail to bring around real change.

Elon Musk believes the source of being able to create three multi-billion-dollar organisations – PayPal, Tesla, and SpaceX – in totally different industries was assumption busting,[9] what he calls first-principle thinking. Most of us reason by analogy – 'this idea is like this idea' – he suggests, as it's less demanding cognitively. It generates copy-cat thinking which can be useful but doesn't get you to see what others can't. How many times have you heard the phrase to describe a new idea, 'it's like the Airbnb for *substitute your idea*' or 'we want to become the Amazon for *substitute your sector*'.

First-principle thinking gets you to think about boiling a subject down to its most fundamental truths and reasoning up from there. When Musk set up Tesla, the biggest obstacle as a new entrant was battery technology – both in terms of cost and capacity. He points out that critics both in and outside his organisation focused on the limitations of existing technology – for example, it costs $600 per kilowatt hour – whilst he fixated on the first principles of the problem. This involved breaking down the components of the battery to their most basic levels – metals, chemicals, the physics of how batteries work – and building them back up again. Looking at it this way, the components cost just $80 per kilowatt hour. As Musk observed, 'Clearly you just need to think of clever ways to take those materials and combine them into the shape of a battery cell and you can have batteries that are much, much cheaper than anyone realises'. In this way, he removed the underlying assumptions that prevented others seeing that there were new ways to think about the problem.

Experimentation means that teams need to debate and think together about their assumptions – beliefs about trends, customers, competitors, technologies, business models – and argue to gain new knowledge. But it's incredibly difficult to argue with objective, rational, and fact-based thinking. Not only are our assumptions mostly hidden from us, but our convictions are also more often feeling that fact. We argue to win, not necessarily to gain insight and find a better truth. Social and cognitive scientists, Hugo Mercier and Dan Sperber's research[10] suggests that mostly reasoning is in fact arguing and evolved to give us an evolutionary advantage in acquiring power, status, and additional gains over others. Part of this is the ability to lie. Firstly, to ourselves, so we can lie more convincingly to others unburdened with the dissonance of knowing that what we're saying isn't what we believe. So, there's no question, this is a difficult skill to acquire but there are ways in which you can accelerate the process. One is to build the craft we discussed in Part 1 – pulling apart our assumptions by recognising the difference between facts and stories.

It takes heightened self-awareness and a safe environment to recognise and discuss the influence of feeling and emotion on how the stories we tell might push us into a victim state. An assumption might be that *we believe our customers would value a predictive monitoring service that allows their car to send our garages an alert when a part is starting to fail. This enables us to order the part and offer customers pre-qualified appointments before the part stops working*. What customer wouldn't want that? That's where the story has already started to take hold on the team.

This 'assumption' is, in fact, an idea dressed up as a problem statement. It *might* be a brilliant idea, but it's an idea and one the team have fallen in love with. What this means is that they fail to ask, 'how might we be wrong?'. The team has already started to run experiments testing the idea with customers, but they've missed an important step in defining what actual pains and gains they are solving for the customer.

Without this insight, this seemingly unstoppable idea crashes as they can't find enough customers who are willing to provide access to their data to make the service viable in terms of investment. They find that a percentage of their customers mistrust the alerts, believing the manufacturer is attempting to simply extract more money from them. They also find that a significant number of customers don't attend the pre-agreed appointments. As they later discover, because their cars are – in the customer's eyes – still fully functioning, a competing social or work commitment will often trump the seemingly non-urgent fix.

Here are some of the assumptions they could have started to test on day one of their experimentation:

- X% of customers are concerned that an unforeseen problem with their vehicle will cause them considerable inconvenience.
- X% of our customers see the timescales for parts and fitting appointments as a significant factor in their ownership satisfaction.
- The above problems significantly and adversely influence net promoter scores.
- By providing a free predictive monitoring and service solution, we will increase sales by X%, and the number of promotors in our customer base by Y%.
- Our customers will be willing to sign up and give us access to their data.

- We can rank parts in our supply chain in terms of safety, criticality to functioning, and availability. This will allow us to prioritise customers who risk breakdown or safety issues. It will also increase the credibility that we're acting in our customers' interests.
- We believe that X% of customers will attend their appointments if we make a follow-up call to confirm 24 hours prior.

Testing these assumptions would have helped the team to recognise they had little in the way of facts about how customers saw the problem they thought they were solving for.

STAY WITH THE PROBLEM LONGER

What this points to is that teams benefit by staying longer with assumption busting in the problem space than they often imagine is necessary. The compulsion to simply validate their great idea should be replaced with a goal – to find something valuable to understand and solve first. Disrupting the compulsion is helped by circling between what we believe the problem is and then looking at it from multiple perspectives (see Figure 12.6) and from different domains: financial, technological, behavioural, regulatory, cultural, and so on. This means having the modesty to accept that we only have a partial understanding – that we *think* we know what the problem is. It also means developing our ability to defer gratification around believing we have found the solution. I can't stress how important this is, because all too often teams confuse the discovery and validation phases of test and learn. They stop learning too soon and so increase the risk of failure.

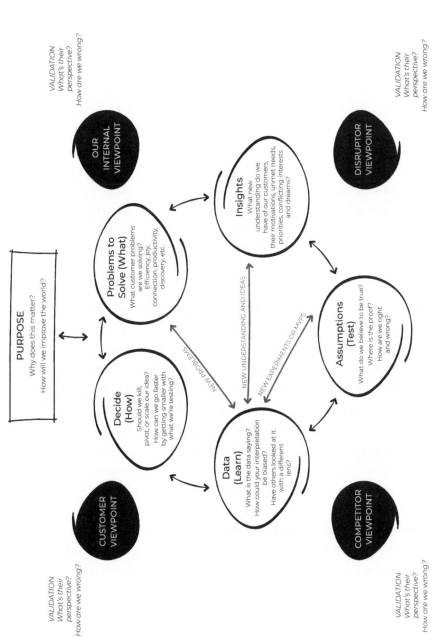

FIGURE 12.6 Staying longer with the problem
Source: Jean Gomes

HOW TO GET BETTER AT BEING WRONG

If we accept that failure is an inevitable consequence of good experimentation, how can we get more comfortable at being wrong so we can learn better? Economists Roland Bénabou and Jean Tirole have proposed a framework[11] to help us think about our tendency to use our intelligence unproductively to find counterarguments and evidence when we're wrong; otherwise known as motivated reasoning. They suggest that motivated reasoning takes three forms. *Strategic ignorance*, where we simply avoid contradictory evidence. *Reality denial*, where we argue away counterevidence. Finally, *self-signalling*, where we create our own mental model to see things the way we want to see them. As information becomes more readily available, the ability to find counterarguments increases. Motivated reasoning increases in groups where their fate is linked to holding a shared belief.

Getting more comfortable with hearing and accepting feedback requires a multi-dimensional form of self-awareness and practice. Avraham Kluger and Angelo Denisi conducted a major study[12] on the effects of feedback. Whilst negative feedback is infinitely more useful than positive feedback because it's actionable, it carries the cost of making us self-conscious. In the moment, it can lead us to choke, get defensive, or in the longer term lean towards self-doubt. The question, therefore, is how we can switch off the part of our brain that responds to negative feedback as threat, failure, and a sense of unworthiness, and instead see it as the most powerful means to improve.

One of the best ways is to increase our exposure to critics. In one exercise, we ask executives to read anonymised negative statements from their teams about their leadership, alternating between visualising the most negative person in their organisation they can imagine saying the words. At the same time, we record their heart rate. Then we ask them to take a break and do the same exercise imaging their children or people that love them giving them the same feedback in the most caring of tone. Their heart rate is generally 10–15 beats lower. Over the course of four or five flips between loved ones and critics, for most people their heart rate settles at the lower rate regardless of who they visualise.

LINEAR VS NON-LINEAR

Whilst plan and act is certain, linear, and deliberate (uncharitably, you could also add incurious and slow), test and learn is inherently non-linear. Experimentation is driven by the need to dissolve ignorance, which can best be achieved by running multiple tests in *parallel*. Plan and act wants to do things step-by-step, pushing decisions into the future. 'We will get to that in the next meeting in two weeks'. Test and learn, asks 'why can't we test that now?'.

A plan and act-driven product engineering team will toil for months or years to create the perfect product prototype behind closed doors before showing it to a customer. The test and learn team will *simultaneously* sample customer needs, showing them early ideas to garner feedback and work on possible business models. This non-linear approach keeps the team open to new information and possibilities, preventing them from closing down too soon on what they're solving for or what their solution will become.

There's a lot of plan and act at work in what organisations believe to be innovative processes. The waterfall product development and stage gate innovation approaches that prevail in many organisations bake in assumptions because of the rigid expectations their linear processes create. Design thinking, although more open to considering new possibilities, can also be prone to encouraging linear paths of thought and action.

The creator of the Swatch watch, Elmar Mock, says: 'the natural instinct for an innovator is to move in a nonlinear way, to go from concepts to know-how back to concept, to relook for new know-how, to change the concept again'.[13] Ed Lu, a former Nasa astronaut and head of Google Special Projects, told me: 'Innovation is the speed of execution. Experimentation is faster, but because it's more uncertain, it can feel slower and more frustrating'. Experimentation requires that most challenging of human abilities – delayed gratification – to allow evidence to build and lead judgements of when to kill, pivot, or scale an idea. Experiment teams often tell us how strongly compelled they feel to just go with their idea and slip back into execution mode.

As organisations build experimental muscle, they can look back at the insights they'd never have gained with just the narrow perspective of plan and act. They see the speed and opportunities that non-linear problem-solving gives them. They recognise that failure is necessary to learn and adapt, and that experimentation gives them a way of doing it safely and with low cost and less risk.

ARE WE SOLVING OR REIMAGING?

There's no doubt that test and learn can unlock incredible growth potential, but will it produce the type of thinking that will disrupt an industry or create a new one? The benefits of the scientific approach can, overused, side-line a critical ingredient in innovation – imagination. Innovation academic, Ethan Mollick,[14] suggests that *The Lean Startup*'s clarion call to 'get out of the office' and talk to customers often results in feedback for incremental improvements because they are so focused on today's problems. As Steve Jobs was fond of saying, 'It isn't the customer's job to know what they want'. Jobs believed it was Apple's responsibility to get ahead of the customer and show them what they would want in the future. As we move across the horizons to greater levels of uncertainty, the capacity to envision new permutations of need, technology, and business models requires a different approach to the analytical methods of experimentation.

In H1/2, test and learn, using the product–market fit framework, is highly effective at discovering and validating new solutions in attractive markets. As we move to H3/4, we need to shift from a focus on discernible risk to embracing greater uncertainty, and imagine how things *might* play out by creating potential scenarios, and then work backwards from the future, asking '*what would need to be true for this to happen?*'. Through this future-back method, you can start to test those 'what would need to be. . .' statements.

These are situations of high uncertainty and therefore it would require a bet on an uncertain future where the type of more tangible customer validation simply isn't available. Academic Calestous Juma[15] explains that we often resist innovation, not necessarily out of fear but because it may mean losing a part of our identity, lifestyle, or even separate us from our purpose. Innovators, he suggests, lose sight that an innovation, even if it's substantially better than existing products, will inevitably meet with resistance from those with vested interests in the status quo – either in economic, power, or identity terms.

To create breakthroughs in H3/4, teams must zoom out and look at the big picture. How might the whole system need to change for us to develop a breakthrough innovation? What will need to be invented to make our solution work that doesn't exist today? Who will we need to become? What will our customers need to become?

RATIONAL AND EMOTIONAL

An understanding of the role of mindset in experimentation is essential and often completely absent in the considerations of leaders and teams in their efforts to discover new opportunities. Being attentive to what we think and how we feel provides us with access to precious information about how we're responding to uncertainty.

The unspoken reality of experimentation in a corporate setting is that the experience fluctuates wildly between the excitement of being able to discover and grow something new, with the fear, anxiety, and doubt that our efforts will be in vain. The variables involved mean that analysis by sponsors and investors can be a minefield for effective judgement. These can include:

- A team's inexperience of experimentation and access to the target market.
- Questions over the competence of the team because of tensions and failure to act on feedback.
- An ineffective sponsor who has done little to socialise the opportunities and progress of the team with the investment team.
- A solution that appears to be expensive to build to achieve the organisation's target margin.

The points above, in fact, were the summary of board notes following a pitch by a team in a financial services company that narrowly avoided being disbanded after six months of work. They were given a further six weeks and went on to successfully validate and build a new feature in the company's mobile banking app that was attributed with significantly increasing customer satisfaction.

Experimentation in a start-up can feel euphoric if the data is validating our assumptions, or like standing at the edge of a precipice every day as investor patience runs thin, if it isn't. In a corporate, there's a complex set of factors playing out as leaders and teams phase in and out of varying degrees of excitement, doubt, safety, vulnerability, frustration, and conviction.

Good process, tools, and principles only go so far in alleviating the downsides of the emotional experience. Trust must be built in the system over time, because experimentation outcomes are inherently unforeseeable. Thinking about how to manage failure isn't as simple as saying fail fast, learn fast. Leaders need to be in the game, so they understand what's truly being learnt as much as anything to prevent them from slipping into judger mode and destroying the safety necessary for future experimentation to work.

We must accept that the process of experimentation frustrates our predicting brain's desire for certainty and generates a mass of error signals that our core needs aren't being met. When we don't fully accept the inevitability of failure, only seeking positive results as fast as possible, test and learn quickly starts to feel futile.

Part of the problem is language. The word 'failure' is loaded with meaning depending on your upbringing, life experience, and the context of your work. As neuroscientist Stuart Firestein points out, 'like so many important words, failure is much too simple for the class of things it represents. Failure comes in many flavours, and strengths and contexts, and values, and innumerable other variables'. Whilst we might say that it's OK to 'fail fast and learn fast', that's not how we experience it. In the past present organisation, failure creates a deep visceral response – it's something to avoid at all costs. In this world, whilst we can 'chalk failure down to experience', it's a black mark against us, too many and we're out. Failure is *not* seen as learning – it's taken as some indication of incompetence, inattention, error of judgement, or even character flaw. It's unsurprising then how often we hear 'this will lose me my job' when things don't go well in growth and innovation teams. It fundamentally doesn't feel safe.

Test and learn invites uncertainty, failure, and doubt. We are welcoming in all the things that most of us try to avoid, particularly in the context of a large, predictable organisation. Most experiments have a 90% fail rate, so failing quickly is a good idea. But that's a lot of failure and as we've seen, we don't like those error signals and how they make us feel.

So, what's the answer? We can't avoid these disagreeable signals, but we can comprehend and learn from them better, turning that understanding into actionable insight. It starts with recognising and accepting what we're feeling more accurately, relating it to our core needs and then asking, 'what are we feeling, *what do we need?*'.

SUSTAINABILITY

We all have a core need to feel that we can sustain ourselves in our work. Experimentation, exciting and purposeful as it can be, is also extremely demanding physically, emotionally, and mentally. Without paying attention to our needs for sleep, daytime renewal, movement, and nutrition, we rapidly drain down our system and can then equate low physical capacity with overwhelm, losing motivation or meaning.

It may seem obvious, but so often we see experimental teams reading prolonged fatigue as evidence that their enterprise is failing. Feelings of resentment – 'I'm not getting what I need' – are being interpreted wrongly and projected onto the work.

Sometimes the answer may just be to talk openly about it; to acknowledge and come to terms with being unavoidably tired doing something you care about. It might be rethinking how we work; breaking the day into sprints with effective renewal breaks like going for a walk, or other physical activity. Experimentation is, after all, a peak-performance activity, so for it to be sustainable it must embrace periodisation to allow for renewal, reflection, and assimilation of learning.

IDENTITY

In the context of corporate teams, people are taken out of the relatively secure ground of their daily roles, where they know who they are and what their work delivers. For some, without significant and continuous proof that their leaders support them and accept the possibility of failure, experimentation and the fear and uncertainty it provokes can be intolerable over time. In this state, teams will struggle to trust that experimentation works, that their leaders trust them or their team members.

One of the important ways in which to overcome this is to create a strong sense of team, with clear roles and regular checking that those roles are working for the individual and the team. Also, being upfront that roles will need to change is important as in their normal role this is setting a big red flag over one's career. Another common identity trap is that the most senior and vocal, or experienced, individuals unduly influence the team's ability to challenge assumptions and generate new ideas.

Dependent on the challenge, there might be up to nine distinct roles that team members take on. By adhering to these roles, new experimental identities can quickly be formed that prevent members from feeling isolated or worthless when outcomes don't work out as hoped for.

Some can be combined, others staffed by part-time members or special advisors. These include the sponsor, team leader, decider, facilitator, finance expert, customer expert, technology or product expert, operations/supply chain expert, MVP designer, and constructive troublemaker.

The sponsor is a senior leader who provides the team with strategic challenge and support – reviewing their progress in context with the product–market fit and team judging criteria. They help overcome internal roadblocks and provide market access. They should enable engagement and alignment with other senior leaders and be seen as a member of the extended rather than the core team. The role is not to make decisions or be part of the teamwork, but to encourage pace and commitment to the mindset, tools, and process. This is best achieved through a coaching approach using learner questions as their status can easily mean advice, assertions, or judger questions deter experimental problem-solving as the team tries to second guess what the sponsor wants.

The team leader's role is to understand the needs of the team to maintain their energy and motivation. They start meetings with check-ins, which we'll explore later, to maintain open dialogue in the face of uncertainty and setbacks. They are responsible for the collective effort of the team to deliver the outputs of the process. They ensure roles are being adopted and make the necessary changes if the team dynamic isn't working effectively. They should also maintain a close relationship with the sponsor.

The decider makes decisions for the team to keep activities moving forward when dialogue starts to churn or action stalls. They don't need to be the most senior person either, just the one best placed to make decisions that respect the process and focus on the outcomes we're aiming for. The team leader and decider are typically the same person.

The facilitator runs test and learn sprints, captures outcomes, and keeps the team on track. It's important that the decider and facilitator are not the same person. Picture the most senior person with the pen and flip chart to get a sense of what I'm talking about.

The finance expert can explain where the money gets made/spent and can ensure the financial model is credible.

The customer expert has access and regularly talks to your target customers and knows what will interest and excite them. This only forms the bridge to gaining customer insight firsthand. Their knowledge (and opinions) should never form part of the test and learn data, which is a trap we repeatedly see teams falling into.

The technology or product expert works on the solution and advises the team on how an MVP might be built.

The operations or supply chain expert is there if a solution is critically dependent on changes to an organisation's operations or supply chain. Having these perspectives grounds the team in the real problems that need to be solved for in developing their idea.

The MVP (experiment) designer builds MVPs that are small, iterative, and generate the greatest amount of learning in the fastest time possible with the least cost.

The constructive troublemaker moves the rest of the team out of their comfort zone, asking smart, strong, contrary questions or offering alternative options. This is one of the most important and difficult roles. Being *constructively* challenging means recognising how vulnerable we feel when we're attempting to play in the unknown. If the challenge feels threatening, people will stop exploring and looking critically at their thinking and assumptions, or be creative and revert to defending their expertise and position.

Conversely, if there's no real challenge to people's assumptions, and we just seek to make the team feel comfortable and safe, we won't break new ground. The constructive trouble-maker needs to find ways of helping the team to spend time with the discomfort of uncertainty and the frustration of exploring seemingly impossible thought experiments. As a consultant, I continually wrestle on the edge of this empathic challenge.

An important part of this is helping the team to be creative *and* non-attached to their ideas.

THE PERILS OF SELF-EXPRESSION

One of the most appealing aspects of working in an innovation team is the prospect of being able to meet our need for creative self-expression by generating and exploring new ideas. In the corporate world, this is generally regarded as a rare luxury. The past present culture sees creative sessions as generally producing indulgent, often impractical and irrational suggestions which mostly get rejected to the wastebin.

When you have that first 'ah-ha!' moment, the dawning of a new idea, it's largely a feeling or a fuzzy image, difficult to articulate verbally. That's because the creative, imaginative networks in your brain don't deal in verbal reasoning. The idea is like a new-born baby, and it needs to be nurtured long enough to stand on its feet before it can be tested with tough love to see if it's viable.

Organisations need to create the space for new ideas to emerge and mature. One way of building this muscle is to get leaders to do the opposite of what they would normally do when confronted with new ideas, which is to critique them with a wafer-thin coating of appreciation before dismissing them. Instead, we get them to say, 'here's 10 things I like about this idea' and 'here's how I would make it 10 times better'. The rule is that they must build on the original idea, not change it. It's interesting just how hard most managers find this, highlighting their default mode of judgement. For ideas to stand any chance of living, we need to cultivate open-minded consideration, which is never a given in the past present culture.

When it comes to the techniques organisations typically use, brain storming is a terrible idea. What starts out as hope that we'll have fun generating creative new options, rapidly descends into people feeling threatened as my old idea battles your old idea. Brainstorming was introduced to the world by Alex Osborn, an advertising executive, in the 1950s. He claimed that collective idea generation improved creative output by nearly 50% compared to individuals working on their own. In fact, studies[16] show that the opposite is the case. Some will disengage and let others do the work. This might be due to social anxiety, creative preference (introverts don't tend to enjoy brainstorms), or a lack of motivation. Over time, the most creative people feel self-conscious pouring out a stream of ideas and there's the risk that they start to match the performance of their less-creative peers. A group can also only hear one idea at a time, so brainstorming is counterintuitively less productive than individuals working alone. A more effective method is to move back and forth between individual problem and idea generation and group exploration, development, and selection.

YOU ARE NOT YOUR IDEAS

One of the ways to increase creativity and the number of ideas available to test, is to build a mindset of non-attachment. In other words, that you are not your ideas. One of the most creative people I've ever met is Steve Tidball, a former advertising executive and co-founder of Vollebak,[17] a start-up that designs clothing from the future. Achieving creative freedom to experiment was the ultimate goal. From a standing start, the company won numerous awards, from *Time*, *Wired Magazine*, and *Fast Company*. Remarkable products include the world's first graphene jacket (the single-carbon-atom-thick wonder material that won the Nobel prize in 2010[18]), the world's first solar-charged jacket, and 100-year sweatpants designed to withstand the most extreme of conditions. Spend time with Tidball and your mind races with possibilities. The most interesting thing for me is not the ideas, which are amazing, but his mindset.

Tidball believes that 'any idea is a product of the architecture of your mind. If you're not fundamentally truthful about who you are, what made you and where you come from, I don't truly believe your ideas can be successful. I believe there's an absolute correlation between self-knowledge and world class ideas'.

Together with his twin brother Nick, they've seen the development of their mindset as inseparable from the creative process that drives the company forward. 'With greater self-knowledge, we've let go of who we thought we should be and accepted more fully who we are – the ideas have just continued to get better'. An early experience in advertising started his journey to a non-attachment to ideas. 'I discovered that one of the best creative directors in the agency had a routine of secretly giving away one of his best ideas every week to a junior creative. In one of the most ego driven of industries; this was mind-blowing to me'.

So how did Tidball build the ability to separate ego and ideas? There were several influences. 'One was having children. You must be more connected to your children than your ideas if you want to be a good parent. This means coming to terms with responsibility and letting go of a previous version of yourself and life. I saw the consequences of not embracing this simple truth. I have an immensely creative friend who despite being a parent was seldom actively engaged in their child's upbringing. He is still unable to partner with others on creative work without believing every idea is his. Though he's a brilliant creative thinker, his inability to detach his ego from his ideas has alienated him from many wonderful people and left him in a perpetual state of anxiety and distrust of others'.

Another significant factor is what Tidball refers to as creating a wider emotional register. 'Most of us live within a tight emotional range, attempting to avoid feeling too much, either positive or negatively'. The Tidball brothers are both competitive athletes, regularly running ultramarathons. 'What confronting the absolute limits of human performance does is to connect me with far deeper emotions than I'd ever experienced before. You go from feeling invincible to you're about to die. This has given me a much wider emotional scale. Today, when someone doesn't like my "little" idea it barely matters to me. The purpose of parenting and this bigger emotional scale don't necessarily always separate me from my ideas completely, but the attachment and others' comments have far less power over me'.

Tidball doesn't think building an emotional register is limited only to those who engage in extreme physical activity. 'It starts by confronting any limit to what you're currently experiencing in your life. For example, if you only occasionally go for a short walk, walking for four hours will do it. If you never intently listen to anyone without forming a response or thinking about something else, just doing that for 10 minutes will push into experiencing emotions in a way you've never felt before'.

Part of this is acknowledging and letting go of the embarrassment faster. 'I think there's a deep sense of embarrassment, which may be rooted in our Victorian values – that I'm ashamed about my body. In an Ultramarathon, where you have to defecate in public, you have to let go of worrying what the world thinks of you. Being more aware of embarrassment and metabolising it faster by accepting and not trying to justify has been incredibly helpful'.

Today, Tidball looks back at his former career as an ideas battle. 'You walked into a room and presented an idea and you face a war that their idea is better than yours. At the start of your career, you experience that others nearly always have better ideas than you. And unconsciously you hold onto that sense that others' ideas are better than yours – a very powerful and unhelpful architecture. But we've got to remember ideas are easy. It's committing to them that's hard. You take an enormous amount of pressure from the process when you accept that. Now, I see all "nos" as a means of finding a "yes". Not in the sense of selling but as useful information to find the answer'.

How does he know when an idea is good? 'A predictable indicator of an idea's potential is that it makes you laugh when you hear it for the first time. That's because there's a surprise element that makes you grin with a satisfying sense of rightness. The other thing is that you want to tell your friends about it. The kernel of a good idea is that it's funny and social. We imagine it as having legs and arms on it, it's like a primitive creature that can be evolved. We made a prototype for a garbage watch[19] made from electronic waste. I immediately knew I could bolt ideas onto that all day long – it could take more ideas, more partners, more launches – it could build'.

'When you get to 20 years of experience of playing with ideas, you develop an instinct because you're drawing on a vast framework of reference points. You can feel if an idea will fit, lead, or lag the zeitgeist. We play a game, "can you imagine that on the front cover of a magazine?". Don't design the product, design the headline. At Vollebak, we don't have a problem–solution mentality anymore. We operate far more like artists or chefs. "What has no one done and what would be interesting?". There's no review panel, no one to say no, until it goes to the world'.

THE POWER OF THE CHECK-IN

How can we operationalise gaining better insight from our feelings and emotions? Increasingly, organisations are embracing the check-in, a team practice grounded in the simplest of questions: *'how are you feeling?'*. A check-in is simply starting a meeting by taking it in turns to ask the question 'how are you feeling?'. Each respondent takes a breath and tunes into how they are *actually* feeling, rather than answering with an automatic response like 'fine', 'good', or the increasingly popular, 'busy'.

So, why is this valuable? As we've seen in Part 1 of this book, turning inwards to acknowledge how we're physically, emotionally, and mentally feeling creates an immediate state change in our brains. These include the activation of the hippocampus (learning), the insular cortex (resilience), and mirror neurons[20] (empathy), making you more open and attentive to others.

In other words, a simple question can make you more receptive, better at understanding and retaining new things, and more empathic. As we're so easily overloaded with email and back-to-back meetings, this simple technique can switch us from being tied up in our own heads to becoming truly engaged with others.

A second benefit is that by regularly tuning in to how we're feeling, we can start to better understand that our emotions have a profound influence on our performance. The more complex a decision is, the more likely emotional bias will affect the judgement. If we're feeling bruised after an argument with a friend, for instance, we're more likely to be closed to new ideas in a meeting later in the day.

Knowing and naming our emotions helps to relabel them so we can allow our executive functions – the thinking brain – to use them more productively. Negative emotions aren't all bad. They help us focus on threat, alert us to risk, and highlight things we're not paying attention to.

Check-ins also help us to avoid assumptions that lead to conflict. Imagine you're the leader of a team. You're looking forward to a session with them to discuss some new ideas. You could be in the room with them, but on this occasion you're all on a video call. You're keen to start, so after a couple of superficial conversations, you dive in to generating ideas. You notice one member of your team is very quiet and frowning. You don't say anything, but you're feeling a little frustrated as you want this to be a positive session with everyone contributing. Eventually that frustration mounts up and you feel compelled to pick on the person – 'I'm really interested in your ideas Mo – what are you thinking?'.

Mo doesn't say anything for some time, and then replies, 'I haven't got anything right now – sorry'. You find yourself getting quite irritated. That's your first and last reflection.

In fact, you are triggered. Your fight or flight response has been aroused and from now on, what's driving the show is not what you want from the meeting, but to defend your sense of value in front of the team. You don't see this, but it's quite apparent to everyone else.

So, you ask a pointed, judger question: 'Is the process not clear Mo?'. Even though you're attempting to be level, your emotions are totally on show through the tone of your question. What you're actually saying is: 'Mo, why aren't you engaging? Mo, what's wrong with you?'.

This immediately puts the whole team on high alert, triggering their threat responses too. The conditions for creativity and divergent thinking have evaporated. You know it and it triggers you even more. Oh dear. But now you have to press on for another 45 minutes. . .

Let's rewind. Instead, you start the meeting with a check-in. Everyone is great. But when it comes to Mo, they clearly look shut down. They say, 'I'm not good, but I'd rather not talk about it right now'. You've already established a couple of simple rules with the team about the check-in process; we all answer the question to the extent that people feel comfortable in answering, no one has to bare their inner soul! And if they are in a particularly bad way, opting out is fine. The only extra step in that situation is the leader asks: 'Is there anything you need from me or the team?'. That opens permission for the person to say, for example, 'I'd just like to listen in this meeting', or 'I might need to step out for five minutes to take a call'.

You find out later, when they are ready to talk, that Mo's daughter had a bad accident, falling off a wall she shouldn't have been playing on at school that morning, and is terribly worried for her, a little embarrassed, and also very distracted. What the check-in did was prevent you from making an incorrect assumption about why Mo was closed off. In the earlier scenario, you told yourself a story based on limited facts that Mo didn't think the session was worthwhile and by implication you're wasting their time. That false story was what triggered you and pushed your team into a defensive state.

As more organisations embrace the potential of experimentation to discover, validate, and scale value faster than ever before, they also have to embrace the mindset that enables creative, brave, and non-linear thought.

CHAPTER 13

THE OPEN MINDSET

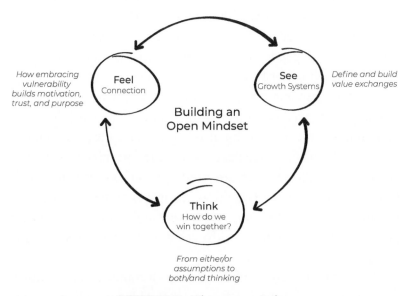

FIGURE 13.1   The open mindset
Source: Jean Gomes

My long-time collaborator, Annemie Ress, believes the idea of a new normal is unhelpful and unrealistic given the realities of our world; 'there's just new' she says. 'We need to build a mindset that stays alert to, and is acceptant of, changes and wicked problems beyond our immediate comprehension'.

Our interconnected and interdependent economies, disruptive technologies, and societal norms changing at lightning speed, can either encourage us to cling to old certainties and close down, *or* to become a new, more open form of human being. Another counterintuitive and countercultural idea sits at the heart of the open mindset that enables us to progress together in an age of uncertainty. That is to embrace our vulnerability as things change in order to become stronger together.

An open mindset helps us to see how our feelings, assumptions, and frames help or hinder the reasoning and emotional flexibility necessary to adapt together. Human progress is founded on our capacity to work with others and hold some degree of shared understanding of the world. Progress and co-operation, whether it's in a marriage or between teams in an organisation, depends on our ability to change our and others' minds through better listening and argument.

As work becomes more chaotic, our ability to remain composed and engaged depends not only on the resources the more human mindset can rally, but also in growing a deeper and more positive relationship to the exposure we feel as things constantly change. This allows us to see how our mindset interacts with others, promoting the conditions to feel safe and open to listen and argue together more effectively and reduce the growing polarisation that many workforces and communities are suffering from.

Building an open mindset starts with training our attention on our unconsciousness reflexes to shield our vulnerabilities which close us and others down. By accepting more often where we feel exposed, weak, or under-resourced, we release some of the unseen grip these feelings have on us. By recognising these feelings in ourselves, it leads us to see more of the potential in an individual, team, or system, and consider how new value exchanges can be built.

OPEN MINDSETS

An open mindset isn't just an acceptant or acquiescent one. It seeks to let in and interpret more information. It doesn't operate in isolation either. It recognises that our mindsets are always interacting and shaping one another's energy, assumptions, frames, and emotions, deeply influencing what we know and do. As our collective endeavours take us into more unexplored territory, seeing how our mindsets work *together* is an essential means of unlocking greater insight, trust, and shared purpose.

In any interaction between individuals, there are inner and outer exchanges taking place. Outwardly, the context they share, their knowledge, skill, status, and past experiences in the relationship set the stage for *extrinsic* value exchanges. Inwardly, however, their mindset and sense of value dominates their experience. How their values, frames, assumptions, emotions, and feelings combine *intrinsically* determines the value they bring to the table.

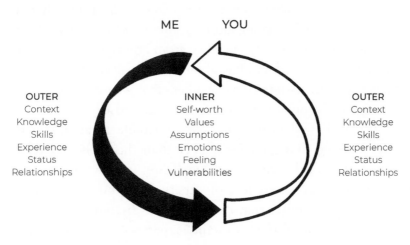

FIGURE 13.2   Meeting of open mindsets
Source: Jean Gomes

We all know that we can feel as if we're a totally different person, depending on whose presence we're in. If we can create a safe environment, understanding how these value exchanges are operating and being open to being more vulnerable means we gain greater control and the possibility of deepening our connections.

We can acknowledge outer vulnerabilities; that our skills, knowledge, or relationships are lacking in some respect given what we face. And we can also appreciate inner vulnerabilities; how our sense of value feels under threat as a result; how our values – what we stand for – might feel unaligned with others; that our emotions are telling us a core human need isn't being met in this relationship.

Deepening shared awareness of feelings of vulnerability enables individuals and teams to act upon them rather than letting them create a hidden undertow. In this climate, it becomes OK to not have the answers, not to know how to talk to someone who isn't like you, or recognise negative emotions that you have about someone such as guilt, envy, or fear.

When these vulnerabilities are acknowledged and shared, we can switch to becoming more curious. Our focus moves from unconsciously protecting ourselves from others, to growing our awareness and understanding about them. It allows us to deeply challenge those assumptions of others that we might hold, and see beyond the outer realm of status or expertise.

What these factors combine to enable is an *inclusive way of being* that goes far deeper than the tools and techniques of typical diversity and inclusion training. It's rooted in growing our awareness of others and who we are with them. It is a mindset that confronts our discomfort of being with people with different qualities, perspectives, values, and experiences.

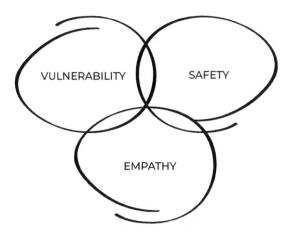

FIGURE 13.3   Building the inclusive instinct
Source: Jean Gomes

At Warner Music, we've been part of helping to create an *inclusive instinct* in its culture. This is where leaders recognise that their vulnerability, combined with greater empathy for people who are different from them and fostering conditions for psychological safety, come together to create progressive and transformative cultures. 'When vulnerability, safety and empathy combine, it's simply remarkable how quickly diverse teams can gel and lose all of the wariness that these conversations typically create', explains Scott Allender, who heads up the company's global leadership development.

OPEN TEAMS

An organisation's basic operating unit of value creation is the team. Whilst teams represent the greatest opportunity to improve an organisation's performance and future growth, remarkably *how* they operate is left mostly to chance. In virtually every organisation we've worked with, we see the same pattern of team dysfunction rising.

The increasing demand for individual work, almost entirely conducted on screens, means people turn up to meetings poorly prepared, distracted, and often resentful. Even when there is an agenda and chairperson, there's seldom thought given to the questions participants need to work on, the outcomes they need to produce as a result, and crucially the mindset necessary for the meeting to be successful. Invariably, agendas are unrealistically ambitious, adding to the feelings of overwhelm and that we're not in control. In this climate, the chief victim is the quality and speed of decision-making.

It may be a truism, but it's worth reiterating that the most important source of value creation is judgement. The consultant firm Bain & Co. suggests that there's a 95% correlation with financial performance.[1] In another survey[2] by McKinsey, only 20% of respondents think their organisations excel at decision-making. For 'an average Fortune 500 company, this could translate into more than 530,000 days of lost working time and roughly $250 million of wasted labour costs per year'.

In the teams we observe, decision-making is continuously disrupted not only by uncertainty and rapidly changing priorities, but because they are bewildered by their ever-changing composition. The idea of 'forming, storming, norming and performing' into a great team seems like a relic from the past for many, as team members relentlessly swap in and out, changing the dynamic, understanding, and needs of the team. Group norms that so powerfully shape every team go unnoticed in the maelstrom. We've yet to come across any organisation that has a successful blueprint for how teams get built, managed, and evolved as things change.

At best, they rely on conventional team-building practices designed for closed units of performance. At worst, they simply leave people to work it out for themselves. In these circumstances, it's difficult to build the trust that's so essential for teams to succeed. As management thinker Patrick Lencioni so succinctly puts it, when there's an absence of trust, people conceal weakness, errors, and disagreements, so they fear conflict which erodes commitment and accountability and causes an inattention to results.[3]

Less than 20% of people today sit in one team at work. They move in and out of many depending on dotted line, functional, and other responsibilities. The rising demand for collaboration is driven as leaders recognise how silos and competing microcultures disaggregate their business model and hinder agility and growth. As a result, collaboration has increased by 50% in organisations,[4] but much of the work often falls to a small number of specialist individuals who risk continuous burnout and neglecting their core responsibilities.

However, get collaboration right and the benefits are significant. In a study[5] of 1,100 companies, researchers found that though many professed to have open, collaborative cultures, only a small percentage delivered on the claims. Those that did were five times as likely to be high-performing organisations. In a study[6] conducted at Stanford, when researchers primed participants to behave collaboratively, they stayed on task 64% longer than independent workers, demonstrated higher engagement levels, better performance, and less fatigue. The influence of the priming continued for several weeks.

A combination of team disruption and lack of a playbook for how *teaming* works at a mindset level means the experience of working within a team, which should be motivating and enhancing, is increasingly less often the case.

Think about an innovation sprint team that's formed to find a new solution to a pressing customer problem. Seven members are chosen for the cognitive and cultural diversity they bring. Team members are resourced with 50% capacity to the team for three months. But a lack of shared identity and purpose, dominant egos, not listening to each other, fear of challenge, and lack of enjoyment in working together is resulting in emotional outbursts, blame, churn, and burnout.

Or consider two functional teams needing to set aside their priorities and ways of thinking to collaborate for 30% of the week to drive a major shift in the business model. A lack of mutual empathy and feeling valued has created a pitched battle, with both sides describing how their aims and inputs are more important and misunderstood than the outputs they could create together.

Or envisage a group of 15 operational change teams who are trying to provide services at scale to the organisation and need to adopt a *team of teams* approach to shift cultural change and adoption. A lack of a transparent vision beyond individual teams' interests, insufficient guiding principles for coordinating efforts and agile working, and a disconnect from the end customer has resulted in a failed initiative, politics between the group and the rest of the organisation, and a defensive insular mindset mounting within teams.

In these circumstances, it's more common to encounter *groups* of individuals working on inputs, rather than being true teams with a shared purpose, strong identity, clarity of mission, and aligned focus on outcomes. So, how do we enable people to do their best work in every team setting? One way is by helping them to become more aware of how their mindsets influence the team.

BUILDING SHARED AWARENESS

I created the mindset quadrants (Figure 13.4) as a simple tool to help teams at Sony, eBay, Save the Children, and others to quickly diagnose the impact of mindset on their focus, decision-making,

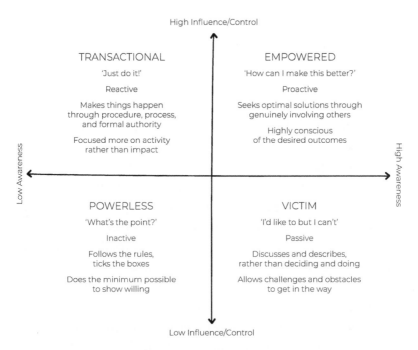

High Influence/Control

TRANSACTIONAL

'Just do it!'

Reactive

Makes things happen
through procedure, process,
and formal authority

Focused more on activity
rather than impact

EMPOWERED

'How can I make this better?'

Proactive

Seeks optimal solutions through
genuinely involving others

Highly conscious
of the desired outcomes

Low Awareness

High Awareness

POWERLESS

'What's the point?'

Inactive

Follows the rules,
ticks the boxes

Does the minimum possible
to show willing

VICTIM

'I'd like to but I can't'

Passive

Discusses and describes,
rather than deciding and doing

Allows challenges and obstacles
to get in the way

Low Influence/Control

FIGURE 13.4 Mindset quadrants
Source: Jean Gomes

and motivation. Whilst this first take on mindset focused mostly on awareness, belief, and accountability, there was an implied message about emotion, but at this point I hadn't explicitly pulled on that thread. Today, we still find it's a good way of quickly getting a team to think about its mindset without having to dive deeply into thinking, feeling, and seeing.

It considers two dimensions – awareness and control. *Empowered* describes an individual or team being highly aware of what's happening in any given situation, and where they are exerting maximum control or influence towards achieving their goals. This is the optimal state to perform. A prevailing question, 'how can we make this situation better?', sits in people's minds. At its best, a sense of freedom and responsibility creates a win–win mentality.

The *victim* state describes the mindset where individuals or teams focus on analysing and debating problems, but exercise little or no influence or control over outcomes. An everyday example is a meeting where 99% of the time is taken discussing and describing an issue but nothing on creating solutions, determining ownership, and getting granular about outcomes and actions. This mindset erodes confidence and trades away accountability, but research[7] shows that around 30% of an organisation's workforce spend much of their time here.

Transactional represents a mindset where individuals and teams act with little or no regard for others or the consequences on bigger goals than theirs. It may be the result of individuals whose personality type means they just have little regard for others, but it's more often to do with their situation, for example, being a beleaguered or very siloed team that can't see the wood for the trees. The other cause of the transactional mindset is that in spending too long being in the victim state, individuals and teams will eventually have to do something. When it's too late to think, action can be short-sighted and counterproductive.

Powerlessness – a state of low control and awareness – is the definition of passivity, waiting for the environment to dictate what happens to you. Surprisingly higher numbers of people in organisations than you might think hold a mindset that says and feels 'everything is OK' even when it's clearly not.

Powerlessness can also be a response to having tried to make change over a long period of time and repeatedly not being listened to – the result is a deep sense of futility.

HOW TO USE THE MINDSET QUADRANTS

When mindset is holding a team back, getting the conversation going about what's standing in the way can be very difficult.

A good starting point is to use the check-in to enable a team to begin being more comfortable with what it's feeling. The next step could be to use the mindset quadrants to help the team think about its challenges by looking inward. Start by walking them through the mindset quadrant model, explaining the four states.

Then create a grid (Figure 13.5) on a whiteboard, or online document for virtual meetings, and start to plot the challenges facing the team against the mindset quadrants. For example, a sales team that's failing to support the growth of a new innovative product. The underlying reason could be because they fear it will cannibalise their immediate orders for existing products but they're not being honest about what they feel, so they tell a story to rationalise it away – 'customers are not ready or it's too expensive'. These are not facts, but emotionally driven narratives to prevent them from testing their assumptions. The mindset is victim, and the behaviour is inaction, masked by creating defensive arguments. Leaders might adopt an equally defensive reaction to the victim mindset of the team and becoming judgemental. This results in a parent–child stalemate. The organisational issue is that the bonus schemes for teams and leaders encourage this status quo.

	EMPOWERED	VICTIM	TRANSACTIONAL	POWERLESS
MINDSET				
BEHAVIOUR				
LEADERSHIP				
SYSTEM				

FIGURE 13.5 How is mindset influencing performance?
Source: Jean Gomes

This analysis will help to create more understanding of what's really going on, build more trust, and ultimately help the team to develop a mindset that is more capable of seeing and doing more.

BUILDING OPEN CULTURE

In the small number of organisations where we've seen a consistently positive and productive experience of working in teams, regardless of their fluid composition, the underlying reason is that a collective mindset had been cultivated across the organisation. People feel purposeful and safe, even in situations of considerable ambiguity, knowing that together they'll work it out. Strong shared meaning, values, and strategic clarity all play their part, but it's people's mindset that is the foundation on which this is built.

Rapidly forming shared mindsets begins with increasing our *vulnerability with others* to create greater understanding and trust. In our work on building open teams, we recognise that distracted, often defensive and time-poor people have little capacity to recognise what they're bringing into a situation. Impatient leaders compound the problem by neglecting or paying lip service to the influence that their and their team's mindset is having. They just want to get on with it, frustrated by any discussion about what people feel.

Amy Edmondson's nuanced work[8] on psychological safety highlights that effective teaming, in all its forms, is about people being able to be themselves and express concerns, ask difficult questions, and talk about their mistakes without being 'humiliated, ignored, or blamed'. 'Psychological safety is not immunity from consequences, nor is it a state of high regard. People know they might fail, they might receive performance feedback that says they're not meeting expectations, and they might lose their jobs due to changes in the industry environment, or even to a lack of competence in their role', she explains. It's not that people don't feel fears, but they are not hindered by them. 'They feel willing and able to take the inherent interpersonal risks of candour. They fear holding back their full participation more than they fear sharing a potentially sensitive, threatening, or wrong idea'.

Google sought to discover what makes a team great and found that Edmondson's work held the key.[9] They interviewed 200 people, looking at over 250 attributes in 180 teams. They had assumed that *who* was on the team would be the most important variable in terms of skills and traits. What they found was that *how* team members interacted, how they structured their work and viewed their contributions were the most important factors of their best-performing teams.

By far the most significant factor they found was the influence of psychological safety, which underpinned four other factors (see Figure 13.6). As Google's Julia Rozovksy explains, 'Individuals on teams with higher psychological safety are less likely to leave Google, they're more likely to harness the power

| 1. PSYCHOLOGICAL SAFETY: Can we take risks on this team without feeling insecure or embarrassed? | 2. DEPENDABILITY: Can we count on each other to do high-quality work on time? | 3. STRUCTURE & CLARITY: Are goals, roles, and execution plans on our team clear? | 4. MEANING OF WORK: Are we working on something that is personally important for each of us? | 5. IMPACT OF WORK: Do we fundamentally believe that the work we're doing matters? |

FIGURE 13.6 Five key dynamics that set successful teams apart from other teams at Google

Source: Conceptualised from: Rework.withgoogle.com. 2015. re:Work - The five keys to a successful Google team. [online] Available at: <https://rework.withgoogle.com/blog/five-keys-to-a-successful-google-team/>
Rework.withgoogle.com. 2022. re:Work - Guide: Understand team effectiveness. [online] Available at: <https://rework.withgoogle.com/guides/understanding-team-effectiveness/steps/help-teams-determine-their-needs/

of diverse ideas from their teammates, they bring in more revenue, and they're rated as effective twice as often by executives'. Google encourages its managers to use self-assessment tools[10] to raise self-awareness amongst their teams. For example, it asks them to acknowledge the fear of asking for or giving constructive feedback; a hesitance around expressing divergent ideas or asking 'silly' questions; and if all team members feel they can fail openly, or will they feel rejected?

Feeling safe in the face of difficult conversations or uncertainty is essentially about managing a paradox. Our fear, anxiety, or embarrassment won't simply go away because we know others trust us, but the ability to be vulnerable with others makes it more possible to hold the tension between those feelings and the action we need to take. Here, it's worth making an important distinction between *feeling* and *being* vulnerable. One is a reaction; the other is an intent.

Intentionally being vulnerable unlocks conversations of immense worth. For the individual, it enables them to acknowledge feelings of weakness, shame, grief, or fear, and not confuse them with their sense of worth. Sharing these feelings reduces our sense of being isolated from others. Being able to trace the feelings back as error signals to unmet core human needs allows the individual and the team to avoid unproductive symptomatic conversations and get to root causes. When individuals focus on their core needs, they get to more authentic statements. In these moments, we often hear sentiments such as 'I don't feel valued by you in this situation', 'I don't feel this will work', or 'I don't feel this matters'.

The psychologist Timothy R. Clark, who's made a 25-year study[11] of psychological safety both as a leader and a researcher, believes its development follows a sequence that matches human needs. Firstly, when we join a group or organisation, we want to be included, then we want to learn, next to contribute and finally to be able to challenge the status quo without fear of being side-lined, humiliated, or penalised.

Achieving all these levels of safety poses a profound set of questions to leaders. Do we truly believe and act on the idea that everyone is equal? Do we let everyone have the chance to learn and grow? Do we really empower people to contribute in a way that brings out their best? Are we open and receptive to everyone challenging our beliefs and the status quo?

Why is this important beyond buy-in or making individuals feel OK? When core human needs are suppressed or denied by a culture, trust starts to wane because we can't talk openly about something we need. Safety allows the honest conversations that enable information to flow, which allows better understanding of risk, uncertainty, and where accountabilities lie. Ultimately, being vulnerable creates a deep sense that we're in this together.

Those conversations will often be awkward, imperfect, and sometimes painful to begin with, but over time, they become natural and a source of immense value to employees and the organisation. We have found that giving time to explore two questions – *what are we bringing in?* and *what are we here together to do?* – starts a powerful, collective mindset-building process that generates safety.

In a deeper version of the check-in, we get people to share and listen to what they and others are bringing to the space – their expectations, goals, expertise, anxieties, beliefs in what is happening, assumptions, and feelings. This increases human connection, allowing the group to see more of what's going on inside and between themselves. How is what we're bringing to the party helping, or hindering, us in winning together? What are we not seeing?

The leader's contribution in making this conversation productive is disproportionately influential. The ability to find the balance between setting high expectations and acknowledging the potential for missteps, gaps in knowledge or ability, is crucial. So is stepping in when a team member's safety is being violated. Edmondson suggests the leader needs to reframe from having all the answers and giving the orders to setting the direction and facilitating input to improve the clarity and value of plans. Being a *not knower* isn't about lacking confidence, but having the *determined humility* to allow others to not know too and become resolute in finding answers.

In unsafe environments, competent people don't fail. Of course they do, but it's not obvious; as either they scrabble around to fix mistakes before they can be seen, or they hide them. Either way, they and their teams don't learn as well as they could. This means role-modelling being wrong and admitting mistakes.

Much is made of leaders seeking feedback to demonstrate openness and invite further engagement, but in our research fewer than 15% of leaders openly share the negative feedback they receive from their teams and stakeholders. Although a much greater percentage act on the feedback, the lack of an explicit feedback loop highlights a significant missed opportunity to use vulnerability to their advantage. In a study[12] conducted amongst over 100 managers and their teams, the leaders who shared negative feedback given to them in their performance reviews experienced significant gains in the reported psychological safety of their team. Being able to bring an objective piece of information to light for their teams seemed to allow a freer conversation. Conversely, if a manager asked for feedback from their teams, they didn't get the same value. Either they got feedback that didn't seem specific or relevant much of the time, or the leader became defensive hearing the information for the first time.

In exploring the question *what are we here to do?*, we get individuals or teams to examine what's clear, ambiguous, or not being talking about. We ask, *why us?* What can we do together that we can't do alone? It may seem self-evident, but consistently when we ask, it's not.

RECOGNISING THE DEFENSIVE MINDSET AT WORK

Below are some of the most well-known psychological defensive mechanisms[13] that operate within us. When they run unchecked, particularly amongst leaders, they have deep influence on closing down an organisation's culture.

Using the chart in Figure 13.7 as a stimulus for either individual reflection or team discussion can help to track patterns in defensive responses that can unlock the open mindset.

OPEN ORGANISATIONS

Organisations responding to the realities of a non-linear world are evolving a new mental model that replaces the hierarchical and inward-looking pyramid of command and control with a more open, organic community of shared interests that extends beyond the traditional borders that used to delineate it.

The cultural values of industrial-era organisations – compliance, stability, efficiency, and predictability – were driven by the collective assumption that the top of the organisation provided the ideas and answers. Traditional hierarchies simply cannot keep pace with the speed of market change. Successful innovation, by its very nature, is the result of embracing uncertainty, speed, and empowering risk-taking throughout the organisation.

DEFENSIVE MECHANISMS	DESCRIPTION	REFLECTION
DENIAL	The refusal to acknowledge or accept reality – often associated with a situation that feels overwhelming, chaotic, or unfathomable. The core is the denial of the feelings that the reality of this situation provokes in us	Where are we not listening? Where are we not looking? What facts are we avoiding? How do these things make us feel?
REPRESSION	Keeping ugly or irrational beliefs at an unconscious level where they cannot be examined but manifest in anxiety and fear	What are the irrational stories told in our organisation? What are automatic responses to challenges that hold no water? What are they allowing us to avoid?
PROJECTION	Attributing one's unacceptable thoughts, feelings, and motives to others	How much energy do we spend criticising our competitors and other stakeholders, vs investing it in creating value for our customer? What are we projecting onto others that we fear about ourselves?
DISPLACEMENT	Satisfying an impulse, such as anger, on a substitute person or object	Where are we redirecting our focus from where it should be to a less challenging circumstance?
RATIONALISATION	Unconsciously creating an argument to justify an action that reflects badly on you	What are the self-justifying arguments we make that enable us to preserve the status quo? Where are we not doing the right thing? What story do we tell to avoid confronting this?
REACTION FORMATION	Beyond denial, a psychological defence in adopting a stance or behaviour that is the opposite of what we feel or think – somehow our normal feelings seem to be unacceptable to us	What beliefs or behaviours do we espouse or exhibit that are diametrically opposed to what we really believe to be true?
REGRESSION	Faced with stress, reverting to an earlier stage of development – a time when we felt safe	Where do we become childish in our reactions to stress rather than acknowledging our frustration or anxiety?
INTELLECTUALISING	Using intelligence to make convincing arguments to avoid confronting reality	Where are we solving the wrong problems and having the wrong arguments?
ISOLATION OF AFFECT	Emotional responses are detached from ideas or experiences	Where have we become numb – lost the capacity to feel what's happening to us?

FIGURE 13.7 Recognising defensive mechanisms

Sources: Various including: Vaillant, G., 1992. Ego mechanisms of defense. Washington, DC: American Psychiatric; Psychology Today. 2022. Defense Mechanisms. [online] Available at: <https://www.psychologytoday.com/gb/basics/defense-mechanisms#10-major-defense-mechanisms> [Accessed 15 September 2021]; Psychologistworld.com. 2022. 31 Psychological Defense Mechanisms Explained. [online] Available at: <https://www.psychologistworld.com/freud/defence-mechanisms-list> [Accessed 29 September 2021].

Open organisations encourage values such as transparency, learning, creativity, community, and co-creation. Underpinning those values is an open mindset that enables organisations to harness the power of crowds and communities. Rooting team life in psychological safety reduces the 'othering' of stakeholders, seeing and understanding them as humans rather than target audiences and customer bases to exploit, or suppliers to extract value from as quickly and cheaply as possible.

A deeply embedded cultural norm in hierarchies is the withholding of information and knowledge. As one HR director at a global electronics company once confided in me, his strategy for employee communication was 'tell them little, tell them late'. Sharing knowledge and being transparent with precious information feels alien to those shaped by a 'knowledge is power' culture. Building open mindsets around knowledge means leaders need to proactively seek out where knowledge sharing isn't happening and understand the motivations and emotions at work.

One way of flipping this mindset is by encouraging people's first responses to requests for information, knowledge, and help to be 'yes' instead of the reflexive 'no'. Together with Annemie Ress, we worked with hundreds of leaders at BBVA, a global financial group, to help build an open mindset, receptive to its digital transformation. One simple technique we employed was asking managers to experiment with saying 'yes' to every request they received. It didn't automatically mean always giving people what they wanted. Instead, we asked these managers to say the word 'yes' and then think, 'how can I help?'. This reframing changed their assumptions and feelings immediately. 'No' is the language of anti-risk, of defending the status quo. 'Yes' opens new possibilities and answers.

After a few weeks of running these experiments, managers reconvened, excitedly telling us how powerful their experiences had been. New relationships between teams had formed, information was being shared more freely, and the emotional climate associated with 'no' had changed. Counterintuitively, they found that it was enjoyable, productive, and not overwhelming to say 'yes'. When an open mindset spreads, information flows more freely, allowing new feedback loops between customers, partners, and across the organisation to form. These become sources of value exchanges, for example, allowing customers to co-create products, marketing, and training.

IS THERE A SWITCH MARKED 'OPEN' IN YOUR ORGANISATION?

What could catalyse openness to take hold in your organisation? The answer might involve finding a way to undermine a highly visible way in which your culture currently stays closed. Many leaders avoid discussions around culture change because they deem it to be too difficult and take too long to impact on their goals. Instead, they focus on strategy and behaviours to drive change. This neglects two crucial realities. The first is that culture is determined more by what leaders value, not what they say. If they say one thing, but focus their time and attention on something else, what do their people do? They follow their lead because that's where safety lies. This blind spot continues to explain why so many organisations underperform. The second is that culture is shaped by the collective mindset of an organisation as much as it is by its strategy and history. In this respect culture can, as we have observed, change very quickly when mindsets shift, particularly when the senior team makes the first move.

Culture is the operating system of a business model. It develops over time as a means of operationalising how people create, capture, and deliver value. Its origin story is typically buried deep in the unique mix of circumstances, qualities, and endeavours of its founders. And it can also be the biggest liability to an organisation's future if its DNA isn't fully comprehended.

Chris Hirst, today the Global CEO of Havas Creative, led a remarkable culture shift at the advertising agency Grey London in the late 2000s by adopting an open mindset. Grey is one of the world's most famous advertising agencies. Since its inception in 1917 in New York, the company has grown into a global company, renowned for its strategic thought and diversified capabilities. By the end of 2007, things didn't look so great at Grey London. Growth had stalled, reflecting a reputation 'as grey as its name'.

Together with David Patton, who joined from Sony Electronics, they decided to eliminate every aspect of the traditional agency model that limited creative collaboration for its people and clients. They simply called it 'open'. It started one weekend, in their prestigious Hatton Garden offices, by ripping down partitions and walls. The real breakthrough, however, came when they decided to kill 'sign off', and in the process discovered the organisation's tipping point for culture change.

Sign-off is the age-old and jealously guarded power of the creative directors in advertising agencies to decide what ideas and work will be presented to clients. Enshrined in this one tradition is an ecosystem of beliefs and behaviours, politics and drama. Killing it broke the shackles on collaboration. With the creative director's veto gone, everyone – regardless of discipline or position – was freer to join in the creative process. Previously, most employees weren't invited in, or the inhibited 'non-creative' team members felt that if their involvement wasn't so great, it proved an insurmountable barrier for them to contribute.

Killing sign-off showed that the leadership was serious about everyone, including clients, being joint partners in the creative process. It was an extraordinarily bold move given that it challenged the very foundations of how agencies had always been run. For one thing, within a year, 80% of the senior creative leadership at Grey had decided to leave because of their loss of power. But that didn't matter. The rapid influx of new creative talent more than willing to work openly within multidisciplinary teams was transformative.

In the 1960s, sociologist Morton Grodzins coined the phrase *tipping point* to describe the moment at which previously rare behaviour became rapidly more common. Studies of dramatic social change show that typically it's not broad-sweeping activity that creates transformation, but a relatively small number of highly specific acts that catalyse wider change. These catalysts create the tipping point by destabilising the status quo, making system-wide change possible.

In deleting sign off, Grey's leadership had identified the flip switch of change and begun a seemingly irreversible positive feedback loop. Hirst suggests that 'in very small agencies, sign-off was an irrelevancy because everyone knows what's happening. As companies get larger, there's an inevitable creep of processes to ensure consistency and "quality". The problem is that it creates a culture of compliance and gatekeepers who focus on control rather than outcomes. Neither generate an open collaborative environment'.

'Looking back, the big lesson from the decision to abolish sign-off was that if you want to create a disruptive business model from a conventional one, you must be prepared to disorder it and be ready for the disruption you'll generate. I guess, deep down, most leadership groups aren't acceptant of that'.

This happened just as the advertising market collapsed, with the worse economic crash in memory. However, Grey London grew steadily during a period of market chaos, increasing client satisfaction and employee engagement figures from bottom to top quartile between 2007 and 2012. They won the accounts of companies like Allianz, Lucozade, News International, and Sony that would previously have been unimaginable. They produced some of the decade's most memorable campaigns, rewriting the rulebook on the synthesis of old and new media. They grew their revenues by an average of 14% a year and nearly tripled their profit margin. Headcount grew by 70% and they netted the most awards since the business was established in the 1960s.

OPEN MINDSETS CREATE ABUNDANCE

In building connections outside the organisation, the open mindset evolves the value exchanges with suppliers, collaborators, and partners to shift thinking from scarcity to abundance. A scarcity mindset abounds when leaders seek to maximise returns with existing resources. Decisions become either/or, zero-sum thinking. 'It can be done, or it can't'. An abundance mindset sees beyond the organisation's boundaries and the potential for leveraging external thinking and resources to achieve more.

For example, instead of building everything in-house, Apple's incredible growth was based on harnessing hundreds of partners to build a global ecosystem that turned it into one of the world's most valuable companies. Partnering involves pooled mindsets where shared purpose, rewards, and human connection go beyond typical supplier relationships. Each side must grow beyond the exchange of money, products, and services.

When I think of the future of open organisations, I often reflect on the astonishing achievements of NASA in the 1960s. The evening of 20 July 1969 was during the school holidays, so staying up late to watch the Apollo 11 lunar module touching down on the evocatively named Sea of Tranquillity was fine with my otherwise strict parents. The memories of that evening were imprinted on my young mind. Only *eight* years earlier – a couple of years longer that it takes to design and manufacture the average car – President John F. Kennedy had pledged to land a man on the moon when NASA's sum space experience was one 15-minute sub-orbital flight.

In 1962, at Rice University, he gave a speech outlining a detailed vision of what this would entail. 'We shall send to the moon, 240,000 miles away from the control station in Houston, a giant rocket more than 300 feet tall, the length of this football field, made of new metal alloys, some of which have not yet been invented, capable of withstanding heat and stresses several times more than have ever been experienced, fitted together with a precision better than the finest watch, carrying all the equipment needed for propulsion, guidance, control, communications, food and survival, on an untried mission, to an unknown celestial body, and then return it safely to earth, re-entering the atmosphere at speeds of over 25,000 miles per hour, causing heat about half that of the temperature of the Sun. . . and do all this, and do it right, and do it first before this decade is out. . .'.

Historian Arthur Schlesinger summed up the feeling it inspired across much of the world: 'It gave many an infinite sense of potential; if we can land on the moon, we can do anything'. For NASA's leadership, there was no precedent and no route plan, they had to make it up as they went along. What's worth remembering about the Apollo project was that whilst the technological challenges were daunting, NASA viewed managing the incredible depth and range of talent necessary as infinitely more complicated and demanding. As *Science Magazine* put it in 1968: 'In terms of numbers of dollars or of men, NASA has not been our largest national undertaking, but in terms of complexity, rate of growth and technological sophistication, it has been unique. It may turn out that the programme's most valued spin-off of all will be human rather than technological – better human knowledge of how to plan, co-ordinate and monitor the multitudinous and varied activities of the organisations requires to accomplish great social undertaking'.

From the start of the project, NASA had to scale incredibly fast, hiring some 400,000 people and coordinating the outsourced efforts of over 20,000 industrial firms and universities. Look at the 1960s pictures of Mission Control and you'll be struck by the youthful faces of the teams, most of whom were fresh out of college. The average age at NASA on the night of Apollo 11's splashdown was 28.

Howard 'Bill' Tindall, a key architect of the management techniques during the Apollo programme, explains: 'A thing that was extraordinary, and this was throughout the whole manned-space flight program, was how things were delegated down. I mean, NASA responsibilities were delegated to the people and they, who didn't know how to do these things, were expected to go find out how to do it. And that is what they did'.

Indeed, NASA was presciently creating the 'hacker's ethic' so much at the heart of Silicon Valley's culture. Chris Kraft, instrumental in establishing the agency's Mission Control operation and one of its best-loved managers, said that 'there was a tremendous feeling of openness among our organisations. We grew up telling each other we were making mistakes when we made them. And that is how we learned. It was extremely important for us to say the mistakes we made as we made them because that helped us to grow. And that feeling was very much a part of our organisation'.

Imagine what organisations today, armed with infinitely more capable technologies and resources, could achieve in solving humankind's greatest challenges – including climate change and social inequality – if they recaptured the open ethos of NASA in the 1960s.

PART 3

MINDSETS
IN MOTION

CHAPTER 14

BUILDING A FUTURE NOW ORGANISATION

By 2018, IMI, an industrial-era organisation with a proud 160-year heritage, was looking to generate extraordinary growth. Annemie Ress and I proposed that by embracing the future now and experimental mindsets, its leaders could unlock a new type of customer engagement and accelerate the development of differentiated products and new revenue *five to ten times faster than industry norms.* As these mindsets have started to take root, a remarkable transformation has begun.

IMI is a global engineering company, with over 10,000 employees, operating in 50 countries, that designs and manufacturers some of the most complex fluid and motion-control technologies on the planet, ranging from applications in nuclear power plants and submarines, scaling hydrogen production,

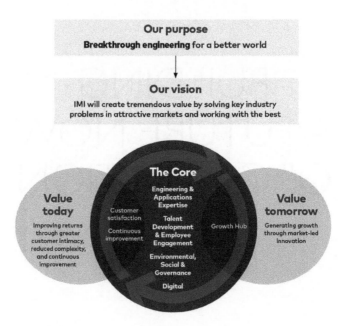

FIGURE 14.1   Excerpt from IMI's 2021 annual report
Source: IMI plc, 2021 Annual Report:
https://www.imiplc.com/investors/results-and-presentations/year/2021

to artificial intelligence-driven factory automation and highly sophisticated commercial heating systems.

The integrity of its value today capabilities was ably demonstrated during the Covid pandemic when, as one of only two manufacturers in the world who produced the incredibly precise valve controls necessary for life-saving ventilators, IMI stepped up production tenfold in a matter of weeks, helping to save thousands of lives.

Although it had a long track record of disrupting and leading in its markets for generations, entropy had set in. In part, this reflected a rapid deterioration in some of its core markets – such as conventional power. But more significantly, the balance between performance and growth had been lost as the organisation had become more introverted, engrossed in honing its execution processes. In the previous five years, new product development had met only half of its forecasted revenues. For the past decade, growth had been slim, and margins were in decline.

Roy Twite had seen the transformational impact of our work on mindset amongst Halma's 45 CEOs (another engineering group), where he sat as a non-executive director. At the time, he headed up one of IMI's three divisions, IMI Critical Engineering, and he invited us to run an experiment to test our approach.

We started in London with a workshop for 60 of his most senior leaders and high performers. Over three days, we immersed them in the future now and experimental playbook and mindsets, and co-designed experiments to see if they could find customer problems in high-growth markets and start to develop solutions that could grow faster than they had in the past. They had three months before pitching back as start-ups vying for investment.

Almost immediately, despite the general openness of the group, they hit a barrier when we asked them to start talking to customers there and then. There was mild panic at the thought of talking to customers about abstract questions and problems. Like other mature companies, customer interactions were a highly controlled and procedural affair, limited to a small community of sales, product, and service specialists. Having ruled out the option for them of indirect methods like online questionnaires or talking to their own salespeople, to their credit, they overcame their anxiety and started to pick up the phone and email customers.

Within hours they were breaking down their own resistance and discovering a wealth of new information that had always been within their reach. In three months, they talked to hundreds of customers and started on the journey to building a new level of market connectivity that had been absent for many years.

Today, Roy Twite is IMI's CEO and the pilot has matured, across its three divisions, into growth accelerators that are transforming the company's future. Over 700 people have been involved in sprint teams. IMI Critical, who led first, now have four start-ups that generated £21 million in bookings in 2021, on average taking 18 months to achieve their first £1 million of sales. The impact of the growth mindset shift has also energised its core business, seeing its margins and growth increasing, and its rate of patent creation has doubled. Investors are now highly engaged in IMI's growth story as all three divisions have promising exponential growth pipelines. IMI's margin increased from 14% in 2017 to 20% in 2021, and it confidently expected its new ventures in the Growth Hub to generate at least £40 million in 2022.

One of the most notable achievements is a bold move to capture part of the hydrogen economy. Jackie Hu, who now heads IMI Critical, says 'our previous level of ambition would have been to try to move into this sector by adapting our existing technologies such as valves for fuelling stations. Not only would this lead to relatively low growth and margins, but it would also take many years to establish any competitive advantage'.

Instead, Hu challenged a team to leapfrog competitors and build a transformative new hydrogen electrolyser-based system that would appeal to an underserved part of the market. In *less than a year*, the team had secured new IP and orders for £1 million in 2022, in a market set to be worth trillions over the coming decades.

Let's set this in context. In incubators, the success rate of start-ups realising the first wave of potential (getting to $1 million of sales) is less than 10%. Y Combinator, one of the world's leading incubators, operates on a 93% failure rate, but has invested in, and nurtured, Reddit, Dropbox, Airbnb, and others, and makes a profitable return. Corporate incubators typically have a success rate of 8% of ventures getting to $1 million of sales.[1] If the success rate is low, then the idea that revenue mysteriously appears within a year to 18 months is also a myth. Our experience is that most corporates find it takes three to five years for their new enterprises to achieve their first $1 million of sales. In a survey of 10,000 entrepreneurs, Elaine Pofeldt, a Forbes writer, found only two had managed the $1 million inside a year feat.

THE GROWTH HUB

Since 2018, each of IMI's three divisions – IMI Precision, IMI Critical, and IMI Hydronic Engineering – have built their own *value tomorrow* growth engines, collectively called Growth Hub, with dedicated leaders and managers. Annemie Ress and I work as entrepreneurs in residence, mentoring the system and helping the mindset become embedded into the culture. Activities move through four phases using rapid test and learn methods to track megatrends, discover customer problems in attractive markets, establish product–market fit, and then scale if a detailed set of growth and risk/uncertainty criteria are met. A major culture-change programme to foster growth mindsets has meant that *test and learn* thinking is percolating into value today. In addition, the company is building a web of global relationships into the start-up and digital ecosystems, providing access to otherwise difficult-to-access talent, knowledge, and resources.

A portfolio of Horizon 1, 2, and 3 opportunities has been developed, supported by a community of external industry experts, sprint coaches, and start-ups to complement internal teams. A Growth Advisory Board of seasoned growth leaders from a diverse range of industries help Twite and his senior team learn about new growth ideas and technologies, and advises on how to evolve the Growth Hub.

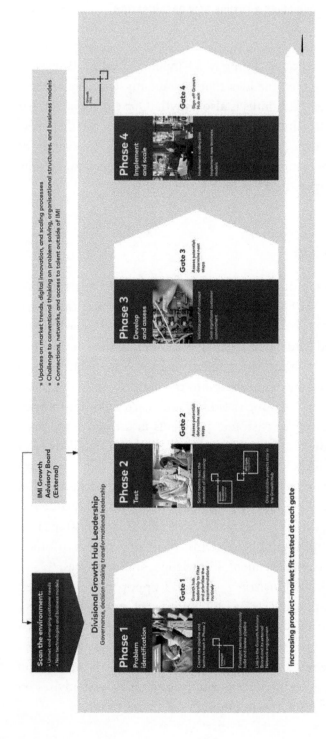

FIGURE 14.2 Summary of IMI's market led innovation model
Source: IMI plc, 2021 Annual Report:
https://www.imiplc.com/investors/results-and-presentations/year/2021

EXTERNALISING IMI

For Twite, the heart of IMI's problem lay in the reality that mature industrial companies often have an incredibly narrow and pre-determined view of the customer. 'Everyone fools themselves that their new product meets a need. What's really happening is we selectively hunt for information to validate our beliefs and it just keeps us defending the status quo. And, let's be honest, it's very hard to establish a customer problem, validate it, come up with a solution and then check that the solution really does create the value. Once you accept this and you put your brightest people on these challenges, they start to solve the hard problems'.

'What the last few years has taught us is what incredible energy we've gained from getting closer to customers. Now, the mantra of customer problems is taking hold in our culture, we're becoming more creative in how to get customers involved at every stage'. Another major milestone came when Twite set the company's purpose to be *Breakthrough Engineering for a Better World*. 'It unlocked a huge amount of emotional energy and a determination to find bigger problems, for example, asking, how could IMI become a leader supporting the decarbonising of the world? We stopped thinking "where was our credibility?", and started to believe we could do it, if we wanted to. This new belief in the future just didn't energise us, but also our investors, partners, and customers too'.

ASSUMPTION BUSTING

For an industry that is steeped in quality, precision, and minimising risk, what was about to happen was an anathema. A team of IMI engineers were showing a prospective customer they'd never

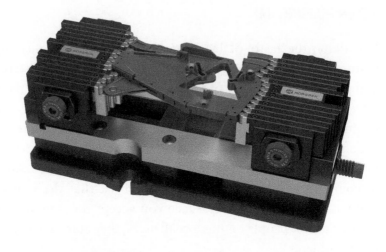

FIGURE 14.3   IMI's Adaptix soft jaw
Source: http://www.igentics.com/, I., 2022. Adaptix™ Soft Jaw - Norgren.
[online] Norgrenworkholding.com. Available at: <https://www.norgrenwork-
holding.com/en> [Accessed 15 September 2022].

met, in a market they'd never worked in, an untested prototype.
And it failed. . . spectacularly, breaking itself and the part it
was supposed to be holding. The product is called Adaptix
(Figure 14.3), one of IMI Precision Engineering's most hotly
anticipated Growth Hub projects. It aims to change the way millions of machine shops around the world work. Picture one of
those metal pin art frames in which you can create a 3D impres-
sion of your hand or face, and you'll get a sense of the product –
which uses an ingenious set of pins to adapt around any part being
machined in seconds, eliminating the need for custom-made soft
jaws to be swapped in and out as new parts are machined. What
so surprised the team was that far from dismissing the product, the
manager of the machine shop loved it, appreciated being involved
early in the development process, and started recommending it to
his friends in the industry that afternoon.

The deeply held assumption by IMI's engineers that a new product had to be 100% ready before it could be tested with customers just got busted.

In one of the first pitches, Twite recalls the impact of having an assumption turned sideways. The insight, following dozens of conversations with power plant managers, was that 92% of power plants had unplanned outages – for which they would incur huge fines and numerous other operational headaches. The prevailing belief in IMI was very different – that outages were planned every three to four years, which limited the opportunities to provide replacement valves. 'My jaw dropped', says Twite. Busting this assumption led to the development of a customer-centric 3D-printing solution called Retrofit 3D that's contributing millions to IMI's growing pipeline.

Caroline Zyla, an engineer who heads IMI Precision's Growth Hub, was previously responsible for managing new product development and a self-avowed disciple of the company's process-led thinking. 'Being honest, I thought the growth ideas and tools were great if you were a software company. I couldn't see them working in the realities of manufacturing highly complex industrial products. My world, up to this point centred on engineering specification and execution; the word "customer" wasn't something we ever talked about much'.

Everything in Zyla's world up to that point was governed by a *plan, do, check, act* process – the iterative design and management method used for the control and continual improvement of processes and products, derived from the father of quality control, William Deming. 'The test and learn work I'm now doing is the most fun I've had in 18 years with the company'.

So what convinced her? 'One of the first growth teams I facilitated using the tools and mindset, resulted in us killing a project that IMI would have undoubtedly pushed forward with in the past. At the outset, it seemed obvious to the team that they should back the idea, but when they looked at the value from the customer's perspective, it wasn't there. In a couple of hours, they'd saved thousands of engineering hours, and potentially millions in building something there wasn't a market for. It was an ah-ha! moment for me because even those people in the meeting, who in the past would have doggedly wanted to keep going, just let go because they could see the value wasn't there'.

Another ah-ha! moment was our recommendation to build a prototype for the Adaptix idea very early on to test with customers. 'I was adamant this was a bad idea', says Zyla, 'and that our advisors (she's referring to me) were wrong. It was too risky to show customers at that stage'. However, she took a leap of faith and commissioned the prototype. The team started to show customers, getting a surge of positive feedback and interest. 'I realised how constrained we made ourselves in getting market insight. At this stage, getting understanding was not about the quality of our engineering, it's the quality of our thinking that we need to show earlier on'.

For Jackie Hu, one of the biggest assumptions that surfaced early on was the poor quality of customer insight that informed product development and the realisation of how much of it was third, fourth, or fifth hand. 'The agent tells the salesperson, they tell their manager, their manager tells their manager and so on. Each add their biases and stories and eventually, it's sugar-coated for senior management. How close can that be to the truth and how easy is it to challenge our assumptions because there are so many layers?'.

This got Hu to recognise that his organisation didn't have effective feedback loops, 'we were making decisions on perhaps a 10% version of reality', he says. 'Now we know who we're talking to, we're getting closer to the truth, perhaps 70%, so decisions are faster and better'.

'For all the excitement and expectation of experimentation', Hu says, 'the hardest part of creating pull through assumption busting is that you still must face up to ugly truths. Despite our best efforts we will fail; sometimes customer don't like us; we're too slow or unresponsive and that's hard. It's much easier for the salespeople to say the product is too expensive than bring back more difficult news. But this isn't just about better products, it's about improving the whole business model and culture every day'.

Phil Clifton, who heads the IMI Hydronic division, made the cultural shift underpinning the Growth Hub his priority. 'The ideas and ways of working were deeply counter-cultural for our industry, and I wanted to ensure we created safety and familiarity'. Kieran Griffin, who leads the development of IMI Hydronics' Growth Hub, sees the diversity of team members being one of the most essential elements of effective assumption busting. 'If a team becomes too engineering, or commercial led, they quickly develop a comfort zone, playing to their strengths. Inevitably a blind spot opens which is painful to expose if you don't have productive arguments'. One way IMI has achieved this is to make extensive use of its graduate population who bring fresh thinking, naïve questions, and energy into the process. 'They ask many of the best questions and have a determination to learn and do not get defensive about their failures. We've seen a direct correlation between success and the diversity of Growth Hub teams', says Griffin.

Clifton invested in IMI's first Growth Hub team comprised of entirely external start-up members. 'It's an experiment in opening the boundaries of our organisation and seeing if it's possible to grow into new areas with talent that wouldn't normally be attracted to our industry. Although it's still in the pre-scaling phase, the results are promising and we're gaining invaluable lessons for the future'.

BALANCING RISK, AMBITION, AND REALITY

One of the recurring traps organisations find themselves falling into with innovation and growth programmes is the inability to find the right balance of accountability, ambition, and support for teams. Jackie Hu is a believer that without skin in the game, teams and leaders in a corporate setting will generally default to playing it safe and not taking the risks necessary. 'It's hard because we're asking them to be like start-up entrepreneurs, but they didn't join a corporate to take that level of risk and they don't get the same upside if it succeeds. This means we needed to evolve to a new hybrid type of intrapreneur model. Within the Growth Hub, this matches the nature of the work across the four stages. In the scaling phase where entrepreneurial behaviours are most critical, we're hiring people who do want the risk/return and they have dedicated boards to ensure sufficient challenge'.

For the rest of the system, the key is effective sponsorship from the executive leadership group. Caroline Zyla believes that creating safety is vital when you're balancing ambitious targets which set expectations in budgets, with a paradoxical message that it's OK to fail. 'That's an awkward balancing act. The key is a highly engaged senior sponsor who really understands the risk profile and can represent it to the senior team. This creates a strong sense of safety and prevents surprises building up at pitches'.

For Beth Ferreira, who leads IMI Precision Engineering and joined the company soon after the Growth Hub had started, diversity is key to the organisation's future. Ferreira had a successful track record in industrial firms who were struggling to grow because operational focus had taken over. Before moving into general management, her early career was in commercial roles across the world, so the customer perspective is an important part of her identity.

What attracted her to IMI was the bolder ambition for growth than the firms she'd worked with in the past. 'I could see a line of sight from the purpose of Breakthrough Engineering for a Better World, Twite's vision, the huge market opportunities for growth, and the appetite to go after growth in Horizon 2 and 3'. The other thing that felt different to Ferreira was that there was a safe space to test and learn at scale. 'This wasn't a little sandbox over in the corner, it was a strategic commitment to transform the company into a new type of industrial player', she says. 'In addition, there were open-minded people on our team who were prepared to adapt if things went wrong and not slip back into old ways'.

Ferreira acknowledges that her strength of pragmatism over-used could inhibit the type of thinking necessary to test and learn, however, she says: 'One of the things I love most is the diversity of people we're hiring to challenge our thinking. There's a natural tendency for us working in corporates to limit our ambitions with our unconscious biases from past experiences. This can lead to thinking, I can't change the market structure, the IT solutions we use, or our go to market channels. This shrinks the realm of the possible and becomes a self-fulling prophecy'. A significant step in avoiding this has come from hiring a diverse range of specialists, some of whom have never had manufacturing or engineering experience. 'Embedding different thinking into our businesses for challenge and constructive trouble-making, has definitely opened our collective mindset'.

MANGING THE VALUE TRILEMMA

What has IMI learnt about the value trilemma challenge? Hu believes the biggest lesson has been to avoid the Growth Hub from becoming centralised or cordoned off. 'To not have a battle between today and tomorrow, we're making it the responsibility of the whole organisation to take care of performance and growth. This puts accountability closest to the customer, so we can create faster feedback loops, and the culture change extends to the margins of the company'.

Griffin sees the need to maintain a high degree of focus on product–market fit. 'It's easy for the value today mindset to kick in and think that it's a "one and done" task. What we've learnt is that we must keep challenging our assumptions continuously. One of the biggest areas is to not assume that we're building a product that needs the same underlying business model as our current offerings'.

Each of the Growth Hub leaders and coaches have gone beyond just being trained in the mindset models and playbook tools, but been part of growth teams to gain first-hand experience of the challenges facing the people they support. Zyla says, 'this was essential as it helped me to understand the complexity facing teams, and how do you balance the advantages of the organisation without becoming limited by them?'.

Clifton recognised the very different challenges that value today and tomorrow present to his team and established separate value today and tomorrow boards. 'This ensures we get sufficient time on growth topics, but also that we give ourselves the chance to get into the big picture thinking state necessary to work on them'. A major input has been the Horizon Z team, which looks at the megatrends shaping the Hydronic market. 'Horizon Z's mandate gives the team the freedom to play, creating scenarios beyond Horizon 3. And, by regularly rotating team members, we're seeing more creative problem solving happening in value today activities', observes Clifton.

THE REAL MEANING OF GROWTH MINDSET

David Powell-Wiffen, who leads the Growth Hub in IMI Critical Engineering, believes that building a growth mindset means holding a tension between assumption busting, a focus on outcomes, and resilience. 'My whole engineering career has been about attempting to perfect products, processes, and systems. This creates a culture that obsesses over the certainty of inputs. But in situations where you don't know what input will get you a desired outcome, you have to get comfortable with a *70% is good enough* approach. It took time to really trust that it could work. What we found was that an outcome focus forces you to confront the assumptions you'd otherwise ignore. Today, I'm much more relaxed with uncertainty, not knowing, and learning by doing.'

Powell-Wiffen is now acutely aware that his mindset sets the limits of what's possible. 'Now, I recognise that every setback, every failure means being constantly alert to slipping into a victim mindset and not letting yourself imagine things are being done to you – you must believe you have control and agency, even when it feels like you don't. Now, when I feel like this and I'm having a rough day, I take the test and learn approach and ask myself, what's the smallest step forward I can make? That gets your mojo back'.

'One of the biggest lessons happened at the start of Covid. We'd planned to launch a cross-divisional growth programme with a dozen teams across the world in person. With a week to go, we had switched the initiative to online, to the concern of several senior managers who were worried we'd lose the benefits of learning in person. But it was a success and helped IMI to accelerate virtual ways of working during the pandemic'.

Powell-Wiffen's latest experience of this is a project called IMI-X, which recruits start-ups and runs short experiments to test out new opportunities and the potential to collaborate further. 'In the past, we would have spent months trying to make this flawless because it was completely new to us. Now, having come up with the idea, we launched it successfully in a couple of weeks attracting an incredible start-up in the AI and machine learning space who are keen to work with us'.

LEARNING TO LIVE AND THRIVE WITH FAILURE

Duncan McBurnie, who heads Business Development for IMI Precision Engineering, looks back over the past three years and agrees that the shift to customer focus has been profound. 'Our early growth initiatives were solutions looking for a market. Today, at all levels in the business, the problem first approach is taking hold. Setting ambitious financial goals that assume exponential growth has made us become very serious about sticking to the concepts of product–market fit and experimenting with different business models and channels to market to scale successfully. In the past, if we hit problems in the launch phase of a product, there was more of a tendency to accept that it was a failed product – which often was right as we had failed to test enough with customers in the development phase. Now, however, teams are given more time and space to iterate on finding the successful channel to market. This newfound corporate patience is especially necessary when we are moving into new markets but is only there because of the confidence gained through the test and learn phase with customers that yields belief in product–market fit'.

McBurnie believes IMI's risk appetite and attitude to failure has taken a similar quantum shift: 'When we started Growth Hub, we knew the theory that most start-ups fail and yet there was an initial aversion to kill a project as it felt like a sign that we were doing something wrong. It took time for it to sink in that we were tying up precious resources in projects that looked exciting but couldn't prove customer pull. Getting failure right starts with knowing that 80–90% of projects will fail over time. If you have a good spread of projects across the four stages of the Growth Hub, then you can accept that and strategically failure starts to become intellectually OK. At the other extreme to a fear of failure is *fear of success* which we have seen afflict some teams where the potential of huge success has seemed daunting, resulting in teams setting low and short-term goals rather than shooting for the ambitious goal. Here I love the energy and experience that some of the people we have hired bring which has helped our teams have the confidence to shoot for the moon'.

'Killing projects is an intense experience for everyone involved', says Powell-Wiffen. 'Teams have put in their all. Expectations quickly start to grow that we have something exciting amongst senior managers. The key, we've learnt, is to keep testing product–market fit and communicate with everyone so there's no gap in expectation building. The other point, which may seem strange, is to do it as quickly as possible. It forces the team to be really honest about their data and push themselves to find better insights if it's possible'.

Being honest and decisive also generates some of the best pivots teams have made, leading to new, bigger opportunities. One team, who believed there was a market for a predictive maintenance system for industrial plants to avoid the costs of repair and downtime from cracks and leaks, found clients were not prepared to share real-time data. As the project was close to being killed, they found that *a* customer was happy to provide historical information and IMI Insyt was born, which achieves the same outcome but in a different way. Again, from a standing start, the product made its first £1 million of sales within 12 months.

BREAKING THE RULES

Sukhjit Purewal is the Finance Director of IMI Precision Engineering and not someone the organisation expects to break the rules. 'The first wave of Growth Hub projects was entirely Horizon 1 focused', he recalls. 'We were trying to keep in our comfort zone'. That extended to what people were asking for in their pitches. 'Please back my beautiful idea with £2 million and give me two years was what I think my team were basically saying. It was still plan and act but with a sprinkling of customer validation'. Now, teams ask for the smallest amount possible in terms of time and resources to gain the next evidential step in product–market fit.

Purewal recognises that 'I had to unlearn almost everything I'd learnt as a finance business partner to support the growth process. The strict accounting and reconciliation mindset aims to deliver stability and certainty. Now, I had to expand my repertoire to risk and speculative ventures, and it was uncomfortable'. What made the difference were frank conversations with his boss, Beth Ferreira, to align on the nature and levels of risk they were taking and the non-linear path that would ensue. 'Safety plays a major part – I feel that we're in this together'.

'It may sound odd for a finance person to say this, but my biggest lesson is that breaking and remaking rules with serious intent is necessary if you're going to build something like the Growth Hub. In time it will develop its own parallel set of procedures, some of which will be alien to our value today engine, and it took me time to understand that. But you can't wait to figure them out, you just need to do it to learn. We're constantly running micro-experiments to test things like incentives that allow us to move quickly because we're not setting precedents; we're finding out how to make future good policy'.

IMI implemented Meta's Workplace to support collaboration and culture change. 'For someone who wasn't particularly keen on social media, I am now somewhat addicted. There's so much happening every day, it's proved to be an amazing way of keeping up', comments Roy Twite.

Throughout IMI, the check-in has had a powerful impact. Twite's team start and end meetings with check-ins, finding it opens thinking and identifies issues that might otherwise go unspoken. As Kieran Griffin observes, 'the check-in has brought problems out into the open faster and with more honesty and greater willingness to solve them. Its effect has been incredible'.

CONCLUSION

In the coming decades, the automation of work and life will continue to demand that we ask what our purpose is. Unforeseen consequences of technological progress, combined with the vast challenges of climate change and the global competition for scarce resources, point to an even greater need for the most precious of human qualities to be nurtured and amplified as sources of value creation and wellbeing. This entails that our education and adult development place as much regard on cognitive skills such as critical thinking as on a wider palette of intellectual virtues such as moral reasoning, empathy, and creativity. Without such a broadening of our understanding of intelligence, we will continue to confuse the accrual of more knowledge with the means to grow healthier and wiser as a species.

Antonio Damasio, the neuroscientist, suggests that whilst our rationality enables us to generate options, it's our emotions that drive us to action. Our capacity to counteract polarising feelings and narratives comes from improving our metacognitive and empathic capacities. Creative problem-solving is intensified when we enlist divergent thinking. Emotional granularity allows us to interpret situations and relationships with greater insight and increases our sense of agency. The moral dilemmas that we face can't be outsourced to machines, so our growing dependence on co-bots and other forms of augmented intelligence demand that we increase our focus on moral reasoning. In a progressively more complex and non-linear future, the expansion of our mindset offers both greater freedom and capacity. Whilst the science of mindset is intriguing, the means to build it remains a relatively simple craft skill which we all have access to; we just need to prioritise it.

Scientist Lucy Hone believes that there are three qualities of resilient people. First, is the acceptance that life continuously throws adversity at us, and resilient people accept that 'shit happens', that suffering is part of human existence. They are not victims locked into 'why me?' patterns of thinking. Second, they have a high degree of self-awareness, paying attention to what they can and cannot influence, putting themselves into maximum control of their lives and 'tuning into the good'. Third, resilient people ask, 'is what I'm doing helping or harming me or others?'. In other words, their mindset is key.

Speaking with the longevity investor and visionary Sergey Young, he believes that within a few decades our life spans will routinely extend to 100–150 years and beyond, given the advances in health, medicine, and gene therapy. In fact, his personal mission is to live to 200. Who knows how possible this is, but in his research, 60% of Americans he polled don't want to extend their lives regardless of it being healthy and productive into old age. The most revealing point isn't about living longer, but why many people don't want the lives they currently have.

As we face our future, building mindsets that allow us to understand our circumstances more fully, see our options, the problems we need to solve, and how our relationships are working, give us the opportunity to live more fully and create a better world.

ACKNOWLEDGEMENTS

In writing this book, I've had the help and inspiration of many people to whom I would like to express sincere thanks. Although I've been working on *Non-Linear* for more than a decade, it really started to unfold in my mind through conversations with Lisa Feldman Barrett about her theory that our emotions are constructed not hardwired. I'm indebted to pioneering scientists who've talked to me, including Anil Seth, Mark Solms, Steve Fleming, Beau Lotto, Marcus du Sautoy, Tim Lomas, Todd Kashdan, Stuart Firestein, Robert Burton, Neil Greenberg, Kyung Hee Kim, and the science writer Annie Murphy Paul. Also, the economist John Kay, futurists Kevin Kelly and Monika Bielskyte, the productivity specialist Oliver Burkeman, and business thinkers Chris Hirst, Jonas Ridderstråle, Gerard Puccio, Alex Kantrowitz, Rita McGrath, Elvin Turner, Azeem Azhar, Ranjay Gulati, Martin Reeves, Sergey Young, Simon Roberts, and Will Page. Further, Ben Osborn, who led the world's first roll-out of the Covid vaccine through non-linear thinking at Pfizer.

As clients, thanks go to Maria Osherova, Scott Allender, Jessica Meiklejon-Zinic, and Max Lousada at Warner Music; Jean-Pascal Tricoire and Olivier Blum at Schneider Electric; Roy Twite,

Jackie Hu, Beth Ferreira, Phil Clifton, David Powell Wiffen, Duncan McBurnie, Caroline Zlya, Kieran Griffin, and Sukhjit Purewal at IMI; Kate Goodger at Laing O'Rourke; Simon Timson at Manchester City Football Club; Isobel Langton at The Exeter; Leon Smith and Dan Lewindon at the Lawn Tennis Association; Sally Bolton at The All England Lawn Tennis Club; Simone Macleod-Nairn at Macquarie Group; Jennifer Ward and Andrew Williams at Halma; Chris Brownridge and his leadership team at BMW UK; Barbara Mastoroudes at Alexander McQueen; Ali Fox Robinson at Pfizer; Jeremy Darroch, Stephen van Rooyen, Debbie Klein, Anna Cook, JD Buckley, Philip Edgar-Jones, James Stevens, and Angela Brennan at Sky; Joe Garner and Rachel Dale at Nationwide Building Society.

To our team, I'm hugely appreciative to you for the powerful conversations that have crystallised new ideas and practices and for testing them with many thousands of people; Emma Sinclair, Arjun Sahdev, Michael Weaver, James Glover, Jo Mears, Daisy Tallis, Phil Kerby, Michelle Beagley, David Andrews, Talia Grantham, Emily Clements, Oscar Hutton, and Bhav Radia. To Annemie Ress, my long-time business associate who forever challenges the status quo and inspires the 'new', much gratitude. My thanks must also go to Tony Schwartz who, at the Energy Project, changed my life by giving me a fundamental appreciation of the power of renewal together with endless intellectual insights and challenges.

To my family – Sally-Ann, Lauren, and Saffron – my deepest thanks go to you for your support, eternal love and belief in me.

Thank you.

REFERENCES

INTRODUCTION

1. Rittel, H., & Webber, M. (1973). Dilemmas in a general theory of planning. *Policy Sciences*, 4(2), 155–169.
2. Larson, E. (2022). *Myth of Artificial Intelligence*. The Belknap Press of Harvard University Press.
3. Kay, J., & King, M. (2021). *Radical Uncertainty*. The Bridge Street Press.

CHAPTER 1

1. Sisk, V. F., Burgoyne, A. P., Sun, J., Butler, J. L., & Macnamara, B. N. (2018). To what extent and under which circumstances are growth mind-sets important to academic achievement? Two meta-analyses. *Psychological Science*, 29(4), 549–571. https://doi .org/10.1177/0956797617739704
2. Li, Y., & Bates, T. C. (2019). You can't change your basic ability, but you work at things, and that's how we get hard things done: Testing the role of growth mindset on response to setbacks, educational attainment, and cognitive ability. *Journal of Experimental Psychology: General*, 148(9), 1640–1655. https://doi.org/ 10.1037/xge0000669

3. https://www.tes.com/news/growth-mindset-where-did-it-go-wrong
4. Young, J. (2019). New study shows where 'growth mindset' training works (and where it doesn't). *EdSurge News*. Available at: https://www.edsurge.com/news/2019-08-07-new-study-shows-where-growth-mindset-training-works-and-where-it-doesn-t [accessed 10 September 2019].

CHAPTER 2

1. Seth, A. (2021). *Being You: A New Science of Consciousness*, 1st ed. Penguin Publishing Group.
2. Chalmers, D. J. (1996). *The Conscious Mind: In Search of a Fundamental Theory*. Oxford University Press.
3. van Maanen, L., van der Mijn, R., van Beurden, M., Roijendijk, L., Kingma, B., Miletić, S., & van Rijn, H. (2019). Core body temperature speeds up temporal processing and choice behavior under deadlines. *Scientific Reports*, 9(1), 10053.
4. Friston, K. (2010). The free-energy principle: A unified brain theory? *Nature Reviews Neuroscience*, 11, 127–138. https://doi .org/10.1038/nrn2787
5. Biswal, B., Yetkin, F. Z., Haughton, V. M., & Hyde, J. S. (1995). Functional connectivity in the motor cortex of resting human brain using echo-planar MRI. *Magnetic Resonance in Medicine*, 34, 537–541. https://doi.org/10.1002/mrm.1910340409

CHAPTER 3

1. Russell, J. (1980). A circumplex model of affect. *Journal of Personality and Social Psychology*, 39, 1161–1178. https://doi.org/ 10.1037/h0077714
2. Danziger, S., Levav, J., & Avnaim-Pesso, L. (2011). Extraneous factors in judicial decisions. *Proceedings of the National Academy of Sciences of the United States of America*, 108(17), 6889–6892. https://doi.org/10.1073/pnas.1018033108

REFERENCES

3. Schwartz, T., & Gomes, J. (2010). *The Way We're Working isn't Working*, 1st ed. The Free Press.

4. Damasio, H., Grabowski, T., Frank, R., Galaburda, A. M., & Damasio, A. R. (1994). The return of Phineas Gage: Clues about the brain from the skull of a famous patient. *Science (New York, N.Y.)*, 264(5162), 1102–1105. https://doi.org/10.1126/science.8178168

5. Nast, C. (2021). Listening to your heart might be the key to conquering anxiety, *WIRED UK*. Available at: https://www.wired.co.uk/article/sarah-garfinkel-interoception [accessed 14 August 2021].

6. Burton, R. (2009). *On Being Certain*. St. Martin's Griffin.

7. Dunn, B. D., Galton, H. C., Morgan, R., *et al.* (2010). Listening to your heart: How interoception shapes emotion experience and intuitive decision making. *Psychological Science*, 21(12), 1835–1844. https://doi.org/10.1177/0956797610389191

8. Sokol-Hessner, P., Hartley, C. A., Hamilton, J. R., & Phelps, E. A. (2015). Interoceptive ability predicts aversion to losses. *Cognition and Emotion*, 29(4), 695–701. https://doi.org/10.1080/02699931.2014.925426

9. Critchley, H. D., Wiens, S., Rotshtein, P., Ohman, A., & Dolan, R. J. (2004). Neural systems supporting interoceptive awareness. *Nature Neuroscience*, 7(2), 189–195. https://doi.org/10.1038/nn1176

10. Kandasamy, N., Garfinkel, S., Page, L., *et al.* (2016). Interoceptive ability predicts survival on a London trading floor. *Scientific Reports*, 6, 32986. https://doi.org/10.1038/srep32986

11. Sugawara, A., Terasawa, Y., Katsunuma, R., *et al.* (2020). Effects of interoceptive training on decision making, anxiety, and somatic symptoms. *BioPsychoSocial Medicine*, 14, 7. https://doi.org/10.1186/s13030-020-00179-7

12. Paulus, M. P., Flagan, T., Simmons, A. N., *et al.* (2012). Subjecting elite athletes to inspiratory breathing load reveals behavioral and neural signatures of optimal performers in extreme environments. *PloS ONE*, 7(1), e29394. https://doi.org/10.1371/journal.pone.0029394

13. Haase, L., Stewart, J. L., Youssef, B., *et al.* (2016). When the brain does not adequately feel the body: Links between low resilience and interoception. *Biological Psychology, 113*, 37–45.
14. Garfinkel, S. N., Seth, A. K., Barrett, A. B., Suzuki, K., & Crtichley, H. D. (2015). Knowing your own heart: Distinguishing interoceptive accuracy from interoceptive awareness. *Biological Psychology, 104*, 65–74.
15. Medeiros, J. (2020). Listening to your heart might be the key to conquering anxiety, *WIRED UK*. Available at: https://www.wired.co.uk/article/sarah-garfinkel-interoception [accessed 11 January 2021].
16. Quadt, L., Garfinkel, S., Mulcahy, J., *et al.* (2021). Interoceptive training to target anxiety in autistic adults (ADIE): A single-center, superiority randomized controlled trial. *EClinicalMedicine, 39*, 101042. https://doi.org/10.1016/j.eclinm.2021.101042
17. Grynberg, D., & Pollatos, O. (2015). Perceiving one's body shapes empathy. *Physiology & Behavior, 140*, 54–60. https://doi.org/10.1016/j.physbeh.2014.12.026
18. Galvez-Pol, A., Antoine, S., Li, C., & Kilner, J. M. (2022). People can identify the likely owner of heartbeats by looking at individuals' faces. *Cortex, 151*, 176–187.

CHAPTER 4

1. Barrett, L. (2017). *How Emotions are Made*, 1st ed. Macmillan.
2. Siegel, E. H., Sands, M. K., Van den Noortgate, W., *et al.* (2018). Emotion fingerprints or emotion populations? A meta-analytic investigation of autonomic features of emotion categories. *Psychological Bulletin, 144*(4), 343–393. https://doi.org/10.1037/bul0000128
3. Brackett, M. (2019). *Permission to Feel*, 1st ed. Quercus.
4. Fredrickson, B. L. (2004). The broaden-and-build theory of positive emotions. *Philosophical Transactions of the Royal Society of London, Series B: Biological Sciences, 359*(1449), 1367–1378. https://doi.org/10.1098/rstb.2004.1512

5. Koven, N. S. (2011). Specificity of meta-emotion effects on moral decision-making. *Emotion*, *11*(5), 1255–1261. https://doi.org/10.1037/a0025616

6. Shaver, J. A., Veilleux, J. C., & Ham, L. S. (2013). Meta-emotions as predictors of drinking to cope: A comparison of competing models. *Psychology of Addictive Behaviors*, *27*(4), 1019–1026. https://doi.org/10.1037/a0033999

7. Norman, E., & Furnes, B. (2016). The concept of "metaemotion": What is there to learn from research on metacognition? *Emotion Review: Journal of the International Society for Research on Emotion*, *8*(2), 187–193. https://doi.org/10.1177/1754073914552913

CHAPTER 5

1. Recommended thinking books include *The Six Secrets of Intelligence* by Craig Adams (2019, Icon), *Thinking Better: The Art of the Shortcut* by Marcus Du Sautoy (2021, Fourth Estate), *Rationality What It Is, Why It Seems Scarce, Why It Matters* by Steven Pinker (2021, Allen Lane) – although this does come with a highly, to my mind, polarised argument for logic being the cure-all for mankind's irrationality, and *Thank You for Arguing: What Aristotle, Lincoln and Homer Simpson Can Teach Us About the Art of Persuasion* by Jay Heinricks (2020, Crown Publishing). The latter is more about argument than logic, but teaches us much about how to think.

2. Crum, A. J., Corbin, W. R., Brownell, K. D., & Salovey, P. (2011). Mind over milkshakes: Mindsets, not just nutrients, determine ghrelin response. *Health Psychology*, *30*(4), 424–429. https://doi.org/10.1037/a0023467

3. Kashdan, T., & Kane, J. (2011). Post-traumatic distress and the presence of post-traumatic growth and meaning in life: Experiential avoidance as a moderator. *Personality and Individual Differences*, *50*, 84–89. https://doi.org/10.1016/j.paid.2010.08.028

4. Levy, B. R., Ryall, A. L., Pilver, C. E., Sheridan, P. L., Wei, J. Y., & Hausdorff, J. M. (2008). Influence of African American

elders' age stereotypes on their cardiovascular response to stress. *Anxiety Stress Coping, 21*(1), 85–93. https://doi.org/10.1080/10615800701727793

5. Benammar, K. (2012). *Reframing: The Art of Thinking Differently.* Uitgeverij Boom/SUN.

6. Harari, Y. (2014). *Sapiens: A Brief History of Humankind,* 1st ed. Harvill Secker.

7. Adams, M. (2016). *Change your Questions, Change your Life.* Barrett Koehler.

8. Toyota Motor Corporation (2003). The "thinking" production system. Available at: https://web.archive.org/web/20201121032113/https://media.toyota.co.uk/wp-content/files_mf/132386273essenceTPS.pdf [accessed 21 March 2022].

9. McGrath, R. (2022). Assumptions we need to question now. Available at: https://thoughtsparks.substack.com/p/assumptions-we-need-to-question-now?token=eyJ1c2VyX2lkIjozNDE1NTQ2OCwicG9zdF9pZCI6NTA0MTA0NTcsIl8iOiJPVEhIRyIsImlhdCI6MTY1MTk0NjgyMiwiZXhwIjoxNjUxOTUwNDIyLCJpc3MiOiJwdWItMjgxMzYYzIiwic3ViIjoicG9zdC1yZWFjdGlvbiJ9._Z02S7hfjZL2RFMXJv4YCAApMnV8yp8d7QxgES0sbxc&s=r [accessed 2 April 2022].

CHAPTER 6

1. Gregory, R. (2013). Hollow mask brain illusion. Available at: https://www.youtube.com/watch?v=6YIPtJlCbIA [accessed 7 January 2022].

2. Manassi, M., & Whitney, D. (2022). Illusion of visual stability through active perceptual serial dependence. *Science Advances, 8*(2).

3. Manassi, M. (2021). An illusion of stability. Available at: https://www.youtube.com/watch?v=cLqVwvdOzuk [accessed 7 January 2022].

4. Manassi, M., & Whitney, D. (2022). Everything we see is a mash-up of the brain's last 15 seconds of visual information.

REFERENCES

Available at: https://theconversation.com/everything-we-see-is-a-mash-up-of-the-brains-last-15-seconds-of-visual-information-175577 [accessed 7 January 2022].

5. Manassi, M., Ghirardo, C., Canas-Bajo, T., *et al.* (2021). Serial dependence in the perceptual judgments of radiologists. *Cognitive Research*, 6, 65. https://doi.org/10.1186/s41235-021-00331-z

6. Antinori, A., Carter, O., & Smillie, L. (2017). Seeing it both ways: Openness to experience and binocular rivalry suppression. *Journal of Research in Personality*, 68, 15–22.

7. Anderson, E., Siegel, E., & Barrett, L. (2011). What you feel influences what you see: The role of affective feelings in resolving binocular rivalry. *Journal of Experimental Social Psychology*, 47(4), 856–860.

8. Sugovic, M., Turk, P., & Witt, J. (2016). Perceived distance and obesity: It's what you weigh, not what you think. *Acta Psychologica*, 165, 1–8. https://doi.org/10.1016/j.actpsy.2016.01.012

9. Jolij, J., & Meurs, M. (2011). Music alters visual perception. *PLoS ONE*, 6(4), e18861. https://doi.org/10.1371/journal.pone.0018861

10. Gomes, J., & Allender, S. (2022). The evolving leader: The power of not thinking with Simon Roberts on Apple Podcasts. Available at: https://podcasts.apple.com/gb/podcast/the-evolving-leader/id1529641273?i=1000555009616 [interview 13 October 2021].

11. Smith, W., Lewis, M., & Tushman, M. (2016). "Both/and" leadership. *Harvard Business Review.* Available at: https://hbr.org/2016/05/both-and-leadership?autocomplete=true [accessed 4 February 2017].

12. Robinson, K. (2006). Do schools kill creativity? Available at: https://www.ted.com/talks/sir_ken_robinson_do_schools_kill_creativity [accessed 7 August 2007].

13. Cookson, C. (2018). King's College aims to uncover what makes a good business brain. Available at: https://www.ft.com/content/75849cd2-c190-11e8-95b1-d36dfef1b89a [accessed 2 March 2022].

CHAPTER 7

1. Dunlosky, J., & Metcalfe, J. (2009). *Metacognition*. Sage.
2. Fleming, S. M., Weil, R. S., Nagy, Z., Dolan, R. J., & Rees, G. (2010). Relating introspective accuracy to individual differences in brain structure. *Science, 329*(5998), 1541–1543. https://doi.org/10.1126/science.1191883. Erratum in *Science, 336*(6082), 670.
3. Lapate, R. C., Samaha, J., Rokers, B., *et al.* (2020). Perceptual metacognition of human faces is causally supported by function of the lateral prefrontal cortex. *Communications Biology, 3*, 360. https://doi.org/10.1038/s42003-020-1049-3
4. Qiu, L., Su, J., Ni, Y., *et al.* (2018). The neural system of metacognition accompanying decision-making in the prefrontal cortex. *PLoS Biology, 16*(4), e2004037. https://doi.org/10.1371/journal.pbio.2004037
5. Dunning, D. (2011). Chapter five - The Dunning–Kruger effect: On being ignorant of one's own ignorance. *Advances in Experimental Social Psychology, 44*, 247–296.
6. Atir, S., Rosenzweig, E., & Dunning, D. (2015). When knowledge knows no bounds: Self-perceived expertise predicts claims of impossible knowledge. *Psychological Science, 26*(8), 1295–1303. https://doi.org/10.1177/0956797615588195
7. Sala, F. (2003). Executive blind spots: Discrepancies between self- and other-ratings. *Consulting Psychology Journal: Practice and Research, 55*, 222–229. https://doi.org/10.1037/1061-4087.55.4.222
8. Rollwage, M., Dolan, R., & Fleming, S. (2018). Metacognitive failure as a feature of those holding radical beliefs. *Current Biology, 28*(24), 4014–4021.e8.
9. Baird, B., Mrazek, M. D., Phillips, D. T., & Schooler, J. W. (2014). Domain-specific enhancement of metacognitive ability following meditation training. *Journal of Experimental Psychology: General, 143*(5), 1972–1979. https://doi.org/10.1037/a0036882.

10. Bernier, M., Thienot, E., Codron, R., & Fournier, J. (2009). Mindfulness and acceptance approaches in sport performance. *Journal of Clinical Sport Psychology, 4.* https://doi.org/10.1123/jcsp.3.4.320

11. Griffin, T. D., Mielicki, M. K., & Wiley, J. (2019). Improving students' metacomprehension accuracy. In J. Dunlosky & K. A. Rawson (Eds.), *The Cambridge Handbook of Cognition and Education* (pp. 619–646). Cambridge University Press.

12. Kuepper-Tetzel, C. (2022). How to improve your metacognition and why it matters. Available at: https://www.learningscientists.org/blog/2017/3/30-1 [accessed 16 May 2022].

13. Anderson, M. C., & Thiede, K. W. (2008). Why do delayed summaries improve metacomprehension accuracy? *Acta Psychologica, 128,* 110–118.

CHAPTER 8

1. Travis, F., Valosek, L., Konrad, A., *et al.* (2018). Effect of meditation on psychological distress and brain functioning: A randomized controlled study. *Brain and Cognition, 125,* 100–105.

2. Gizewski, E. R., Steiger, R., Waibel, M., *et al.* (2021). Short-term meditation training influences brain energy metabolism: A pilot study on ^{31}P MR spectroscopy. *Brain and Behavior, 11,* e01914. https://doi.org/10.1002/brb3.1914

3. Buric, I., Farias, M., Jong, J., Mee, C., & Brazil, I. A. (2017). What is the molecular signature of mind–body interventions? A systematic review of gene expression changes induced by meditation and related practices. *Frontiers in Immunology, 8,* 670. https://doi.org/10.3389/fimmu.2017.00670

4. Polcari, J. J., Cali, R. J., Nephew, B. C., *et al.* (2022). Effects of the mindfulness-based blood pressure reduction (MB-BP) program on depression and neural structural connectivity. *Journal of Affective Disorders, 311,* 31–39. https://doi.org/10.1016/j.jad.2022.05.059

5. Kral, T. R. A., Davis, K., Korponay, C., *et al.* (2022). Absence of structural brain changes from mindfulness-based stress reduction: Two combined randomized controlled trials. *Science Advances*, *8*(20), eabk3316. https://doi.org/10.1126/sciadv.abk3316

CHAPTER 9

1. Jeon, Y. K., & Ha, C. H. (2017). The effect of exercise intensity on brain derived neurotrophic factor and memory in adolescents. *Environmental Health and Preventive Medicine*, *22*, 27. https://doi.org/10.1186/s12199-017-0643-6
2. Leckie, R. L., Oberlin, L. E., Voss, M. W., *et al.* (2014). BDNF mediates improvements in executive function following a 1-year exercise intervention. *Frontiers in Human Neuroscience*, *8*, 985. https://doi.org/10.3389/fnhum.2014.00985
3. Ackerman, A., & Puglisi, B. (2019). *The Emotion Thesaurus*. Jadd Publishing.

CHAPTER 10

1. Outside Consulting (2021). Research conducted amongst managers in a global financial services company in 2021.
2. 1 – (|nbeatsreal – nbeatsreported|)/[(nbeatsreal + nbeatsreported)/2].
3. Murray, B. (2002). Writing to heal. Available at: https://www.apa.org/monitor/jun02/writing [accessed 3 July 2018].
4. Sohal, M., Singh, P., Dhillon, B. S., & Gill, H. S. (2022). Efficacy of journaling in the management of mental illness: A systematic review and meta-analysis. *Family Medicine and Community Health*, *10*(1), e001154. https://doi.org/10.1136/fmch-2021-001154
5. Garfinkel, S., Seth, A., Barrett, A., Suzuki, K., & Critchley, H. (2015). Knowing your own heart: Distinguishing interoceptive accuracy from interoceptive awareness. *Biological Psychology*, *104*, 65–74.

CHAPTER 11

1. https://www.adizes.com – reproduced by permission from the Adizes Institute Worldwide.
2. Adizes, I. (1999). *Managing Corporate Lifecycles*. Prentice Hall.
3. https://hbr.org/sponsored/2017/07/digital-transformation-is-racing-ahead-and-no-industry-is-immune-2
4. Siebel, T., & Rice, C. (2019). *Digital Transformation*. Rosetta Books.
5. Reeves, M., & Fuller, J. (2021). *The Imagination Machine*, 1st ed. Harvard Business Review Press.
6. Madsbjerg, C. (2017). *Sensemaking*. Hachette Books.
7. https://www.mckinsey.com/business-functions/organization/our-insights/what-makes-an-organization-healthy
8. Keller, S., & Schaninger, B. (n.d.). *Beyond Performance 2.0*, 2nd ed.
9. Barton, D., Manyika, A., Koller, T., Palter, R., Godsall, J., & Zoffer, J. (2017). Where companies with a long-term view outperform their peers. Available at: https://www.mckinsey.com/featured-insights/long-term-capitalism/where-companies-with-a-long-term-view-outperform-their-peers# [accessed 27 June 2021].
10. Olesiński, B., Rozkrut, M., & Torój, A. (2016). Measuring the consequences of short-termism in business – the econometric evidence for a sample of European companies. *Collegium of Economic Analysis Annals*, 2016(41), 63–78.
11. Graham, J., Harvey, C., & Rajgopal, S. (2005). The economic implications of corporate financial reporting. *Journal of Accounting and Economics*, 40(1–3), 3–73.
12. FCLT Global (2016). Rising to the challenge of short-termism. Available at: https://www.fcltglobal.org/docs/default-source/default-document-library/ fclt-global-rising-to-the-challenge.pdf [accessed 7 August 2020].
13. The Economist (2011). What do bosses do all day? Available at: https://www.economist.com/business/2011/05/05/what-do-bosses-do-all-day [accessed 14 July 2020].

14. Nathan, C., & Goldberg, K. (2019). The short-termism thesis: Dogma vs. reality. Available at: https://corpgov.law.harvard.edu/2019/03/18/the-short-termism-thesis-dogma-vs-reality/ [accessed 5 July 2020].

15. https://companiesmarketcap.com/usa/largest-companies-in-the-usa-by-market-cap/

16. Birkinshaw, J., & Cohen, J. (2022). Make time for the work that matters. *Harvard Business Review.* Available at: https://hbr.org/2013/09/make-time-for-the-work-that-matters [accessed 3 May 2022].

17. YouTube.com (2022). Jeff Bezos on why it's always day 1 at Amazon. Available at: https://www.youtube.com/watch?v=fTwXS2H_iJo [accessed 20 June 2017].

18. Kantrowitz, A. (2020). *Always Day One.* Penguin Books.

19. Media.corporate-ir.net (1997). Amazon.com letter to shareholders. Available at: https://media.corporate-ir.net/media_files/irol/97/97664/reports/Shareholderletter97.pdf [accessed 7 August 2020].

20. There's some incredibly useful sources of tools and ideas for building value tomorrow growth engines – recommendations include *Exponential Organisations* (2014) by Salim Ismail, Michael S. Malone, and Yuri van Geest, who decoded the capability of so-called exponential organisations which are capable of scaling 10× faster than traditional organisations. *Sprint* (2016) by Jake Knapp, John Zeratsky, and Braden Kowitz provides a blueprint for running short experiment sprints to test ideas in a week developed in Google Ventures. More in the Experimental Mindset section.

21. Cvetanovski, B., Hazan, E., Perrey, J., & Spillecke, D. (2019). Are you a growth leader? The seven beliefs and behaviors that growth leaders share. Available at: https://www.mckinsey.com/business-functions/marketing-and-sales/our-insights/are-you-a-growth-leader-the-seven-beliefs-and-behaviors-that-growth-leaders-share [accessed 17 May 2021].

22. Biggadike, R. (2022). The risky business of diversification. *Harvard Business Review.* Available at: https://hbr.org/1979/05/the-risky-business-of-diversification [accessed 15 May 2022].

23. Stevens, G. A., & Burley, J. (1997). 3,000 raw ideas = 1 commercial success!, *Research-Technology Management*, 40(3), 16–27, https://doi.org/10.1080/08956308.1997.11671126

24. Baghai, M., Coley, S., & White, D. (2000). *The Alchemy of Growth*. Perseus Publishing.

25. Parrado, E., Woods, N., & Kuritzky, M. (2021). What are frontier risks and how can we prepare for them? Available at: https://www.weforum.org/agenda/2021/06/what-are-frontier-risks-and-how-can-we-prepare-for-them [accessed 12 March 2022].

26. Firestein, S. (2013). *Ignorance – How it Drives Science*, 1st ed. Oxford University Press.

27. Gulati, R., & Fink, L. (2022). *Deep Purpose*, 1st ed. Penguin Business.

28. Geus, A. (1997). *The Living Company*. Harvard Business School Press.

29. Kashdan, T. (2022). *The Art of Insubordination*. Avery.

CHAPTER 12

1. https://assets.publishing.service.gov.uk/government/uploads/system/uploads/attachment_data/file/753468/RiseExperimental-Government_Cross-GovTrialAdvicePanelUpdateReport.pdf

2. Great experimental guides include: Bland, D., Osterwalder, A., Smith, A., & Papadakos, T. (2019). *Testing Business Ideas*. Wiley. Blank, S., & Dorf, B. (2020). *The Startup Owner's Manual*. Wiley. Knapp, J., & Zeratsky, J. (2016). *Sprint: How to Solve Big Problems and Test New Ideas in Just Five Days*. Simon & Schuster. Osterwalder, A., & Pigneur, Y. (2010). *Business Model Generation*. Wiley. Thomke, S. (2020). *Experimentation Works*. Harvard Business Review Press. Turner, E. (2020). *Be Less Zombie*, 1st ed. Wiley.

3. Ries, E. (2011). *The Lean Startup: How Today's Entrepreneurs Use Continuous Innovation to Create Radically Successful Businesses*. Crown Publishing.

4. There's considerable debate on the level of new product failure rates, largely because there's a big difference between true innovation, incremental product development, and sectors where brand and marketing is more influential than product features (food, clothing, etc.). Schneider, J., & Hall, J. (2011). Why most product launches fail. *Harvard Business Review*. Available at: https://hbr.org/2011/04/why-most-product-launches-fail [accessed 7 February 2022]. Castellion, G., & Markham, S. (2013). Myths about new product failure rates. Available at: https://newproductsuccess.org/new-product-failure-rates-2013-jpim-30-pp-976-979/ [accessed 19 March 2022].

5. Olsen, D. (2015). *The Lean Product Playbook – How to Innovate with Minimum Viable Products and Rapid Customer Feedback*. Wiley.

6. Gambardella, A., Camuffo, A., Cordova, A., & Spina, C. (2018). A scientific approach to entrepreneurial decision making: Evidence from a randomized control trial. Bocconi University Management Research Paper No. 6.

7. McGrath, R. (2019). *Seeing Around Corners*. Houghton Mifflin Harcourt.

8. Michelman, P., & Anthony, S. (2020). The lies leaders tell themselves about disruption. *MIT Sloan Management Review*. Available at: https://sloanreview.mit.edu/audio/the-lies-leaders-tell-themselves-about-disruption/ [accessed 10 September 2021].

9. Rose, K. (2012). Foundation 20 // Elon Musk. Available at: https://www.youtube.com/watch?v=L-s_3b5fRd8 [accessed 5 April 2021].

10. Mercier, H., & Sperber, D. (2011). Why do humans reason? Arguments for an argumentative theory. *Behavioral and Brain* Sciences, 34(2), 57–74. https://doi.org/10.1017/S0140525X10000968

11. Bénabou, R. (2015). The economics of motivated beliefs. Available at: https://www.princeton.edu/~rbenabou/papers/REP_4_BW_nolinks_corrected%201a.pdf [accessed 8 March 2022].

12. Kluger, A. N., & DeNisi, A. (1996). The effects of feedback interventions on performance: A historical review, a meta-analysis, and a preliminary feedback intervention theory. *Psychological Bulletin*, 119(2), 254–284.

13. Bidwell, M. (2016). Reviving the Swiss watch industry: The remarkable story of Swatch with Elmar Mock. Available at: https://www.youtube.com/watch?v=e79t2Ru1EHM&t=1s [accessed 16 April 2022].

14. Felin, T., Gambardella, A., Stern, S., & Zenger, T. (2020). Lean startup and the business model: Experimentation revisited. *Long Range Planning*, 53(4). https://doi.org/10.1016/j.lrp.2019.06.002

15. Juma, C. (2016). *Innovation and its Enemies*. Oxford University Press.

16. Mullen, B., Johnson, C., & Salas, E. (1991). Productivity loss in brainstorming groups: A meta-analytic integration. *Basic and Applied Social Psychology*, 12(1), 3–23.

17. https://www.vollebak.com

18. https://www.graphene-info.com/graphene-introduction

19. https://www.vollebak.com/product/garbage-watch/

20. Wicker, B., Keysers, C., Plailly, J., Royet, J. P., Gallese, V., & Rizzolatti, G. (2003). Both of us disgusted in My insula: The common neural basis of seeing and feeling disgust. *Neuron*, 40(3), 655–664. https://doi.org/10.1016/S0896-6273(03)00679-2

CHAPTER 13

1. Blenko, M., & Mankins, M. (2010). The decision-driven organization. *Harvard Business Review*. Available at: https://hbr.org/2010/06/the-decision-driven-organization [accessed 9 October 2021].

2. Aminov, I., De Smet, A., & Jost, G. (2019). Decision making in the age of urgency. Available at: https://www.mckinsey.com/business-functions/people-and-organizational-performance/our-insights/decision-making-in-the-age-of-urgency

3. Lencioni, P. (2002). *The Five Dysfunctions of a Team*. Wiley.

4. Cross, R., Rebele, R., & Grant, A. (2016). Collaborative overload. *Harvard Business Review*. Available at: https://hbr.org/2016/01/collaborative-overload [accessed 20 November 2021].

5. Gaskell, A. (2017). New study finds that collaboration drives workplace performance. Available at: https://www.forbes.com/sites/adigaskell/2017/06/22/new-study-finds-that-collaboration-drives-workplace-performance/?sh=58398e153d02 [accessed 7 August 2021].

6. Carr, P. B., & Walton, G. M. (2014). Cues of working together fuel intrinsic motivation. *Journal of Experimental Social Psychology, 53*, 169–184.

7. Nielson, G., Pasternack, B., & Van Nuys, K. (2005). The passive-aggressive organization. *Harvard Business Review*. Available at: https://hbr.org/2005/10/the-passive-aggressive-organization [accessed 23 February 2020].

8. Edmondson, A. (2019). *The Fearless Organisation – Creating Psychological Safety in the Workplace for Learning, Innovation, and Growth*. Wiley.

9. Rework.withgoogle.com (2015). re:Work – The five keys to a successful Google team. Available at: https://rework.withgoogle.com/blog/five-keys-to-a-successful-google-team/ [accessed 16 March 2022].

10. Rework.withgoogle.com (2022). re:Work – Guide: Understand team effectiveness. Available at: https://rework.withgoogle.com/guides/understanding-team-effectiveness/steps/help-teams-determine-their-needs/ [accessed 16 March 2022].

11. Clark, T. (2020). *The 4 Stages of Psychological Safety*. Berrett-Koehler.

12. Coutifaris, C., & Grant, A. M. (2021). Taking your team behind the curtain: The effects of leader feedback-sharing and feedback-seeking on team psychological safety. *Organization Science, 33*(4), 1251–1699.

13. Ziegler, D. J. (2016). Defence mechanisms in rational emotive cognitive behaviour therapy personality theory. *Journal of Rational-Emotive and Cognitive-Behaviour Therapy*, *34*(2), 135–148. https://doi.org/10.1007/s10942-016-0234-2

CHAPTER 14

1. Stryber Analystics.

ABOUT
THE AUTHOR

Jean Gomes is a *New York Times* bestselling author and trusted advisor to CEOs. He works alongside leaders to help them solve their biggest challenges, including exponential growth, creating a wellbeing culture, and rethinking how organisations function in an uncertain environment. His consultancy, Outside, works to be a driving force of human evolution by harnessing the emerging science of mindset and self-awareness. He is also co-host of the podcast, *The Evolving Leader*, which explores progressive ideas about the future of leadership.

INDEX

Page numbers followed by *f* refer to figures.